NEW YORK STATE TODAY:
POLITICS, GOVERNMENT, PUBLIC POLICY

D1295181

Fred Bartle
Gerald Benjamin
Karen S. Burstein
Barbara L. Carvalho
Alan S. Chartock
Peter W. Colby
Dennis R. DeLong
Alan Emory
Diane M. Fischer
Theresa Funiciello
Keith M. Henderson
Alan Hevesi
Edward Howe
Robert P. Kerker
Edward I. Koch
Sarah F. Liebschutz
Stan Lundine
Michael E. Lynch
Karen Markoe
Lee M. Miringoff
Paul D. Moore
Donald Reeb
Edward V. Regan
Sam Roberts
Alice Sardell
Howard A. Scarrow
Sanford F. Schram
Charlene S. Seifert
Paul A. Smith
Robert J. Spitzer
Leonard P. Stavisky
Henry Steck
Jeffrey Stonecash
John K. White
Sen-Yuan Wu
Glenn Yago

NEW YORK STATE TODAY:

POLITICS, GOVERNMENT, PUBLIC POLICY

edited by

PETER W. COLBY
JOHN K. WHITE

Second Edition

State University of New York Press

Published by
State University of New York Press, Albany

© 1989 State University of New York

All rights reserved

Printed in the United States of America

No part of this book may be used or reproduced
in any manner whatsoever without written permission
except in the case of brief quotations embodied in
critical articles and reviews.

For information, address State University of New York
Press, State University Plaza, Albany, N.Y., 12246

Library of Congress Cataloging-in-Publication Data

New York State today: politics, government, public policy/edited by
Peter W. Colby, John K. White.—2nd ed.
p. cm.
Includes index.
ISBN 0-88706-979-7. ISBN 0-88706-980-0 (pbk.)
1. New York (State)—Politics and government—1951- 2. New York (State)—Economic policy. I. Colby, Peter W. II. White, John Kenneth, 1952- .
JK3416.N48 1989
974.7′043—dc19 88-19983
CIP

10 9 8 7 6 5 4 3 2 1

Contents

List of Figures

List of Tables

Preface

New York State Today provides a fresh, up-to-date introduction to the politics, government, and public policies of the Empire State. We anticipate that its principal use will be in freshman-sophomore state and local government courses across our state. It will also be of value to all New Yorkers wishing to gain a better understanding of the causes and consequences of the political events affecting their lives.

The contributing writers to this volume have backgrounds in academia, politics, journalism, and government—a variety of perspectives that provides readers with a variety of insights as to how New York is governed. As editors, we acknowledge our debt to all of them. We would also like to thank the many individuals whose earlier studies of New York State set a high standard we have tried to live up to. These books form a substantial body of literature for those who wish to pursue further study. Some of the most outstanding are listed in the bibliography at the end of this volume.

We have incurred several obligations in assembling this volume, but particularly to Peggy Gifford at SUNY Press, who encouraged the editors to sustain their interest in New York State politics; and to our families: Joanna, Jennifer, and Jacquelyn Colby, and Margaret and Janet White.

PETER W. COLBY
JOHN K. WHITE

Introduction

The workings of government are well known, but not often well understood. We know that the laws that protect us and regulate our behavior are written and enforced by government. Most of us also know that many of the services we use daily—such as the roads, parks, water supply, sewage disposal, and education system—are produced by government agencies. And we are all very much aware of the taxes we pay to support these and other services.

Likewise, we are familiar with the many elections that take place, and about one-half of us vote in most elections. Most of us know at least some of the officials we elect to public office in New York State; many of us could name the current governor, for example, and a few may know their representatives in the State Senate and Assembly.

But what relationships are there between the delivery of services and who gets elected to carry out the job? How does all this fit together? And how does what goes on in the state capitol in Albany relate to what happens in the national capitol in Washington, D.C., or in local city halls around the state?

Before we begin to learn about the particulars of New York State government, we need a way to organize our thinking. One good way to do this is to use a model. The model depicted below in Figure 1 provides us with definitions of the basic concepts that we will study, categories for classifying the many facts we will learn, and explanations of how the various aspects of our subject matter are tied to one another.

Working backwards, *public policy* is the product of government action, *government* is the institution that produces the action, and *politics* is the process by which individuals and groups try to shape the decisions of government. More specifically, politics is citizens, interest groups, and political parties that try to elect certain candidates to office or to influence the decisions of those who serve in public office (whether elected or appointed). Government includes not only the governor and the legislature but also the courts and the bureaucracy—the three branches and the people in them who plan, decide, and implement public policy decisions. The purposes of public policies are as wide-ranging as the aspirations of citizens: from safer roads to cheaper utility costs, from a public university system to a cleaner environment, from lower taxes to a stronger economy. Government collects revenues and disburses them in ways intended to bring us closer to stated policy goals.

Government is different from other institutions because its decisions are binding on all citizens. We *must* pay our taxes, obey traffic laws, attend school until age sixteen, and so forth. Because of the compelling na-

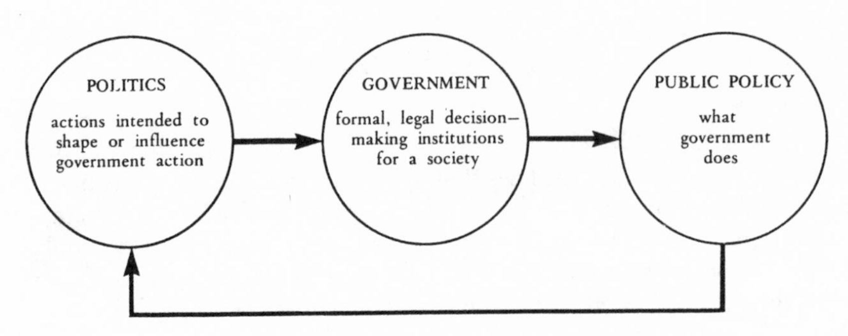

Figure 1. A Model of the Political System

ture of public policy decisions, we place great emphasis on the ability of the people to control government; we fear the possibility that government will enact policies with which we disagree but still must follow. On the other hand, most of us recognize the importance of many of the tasks performed by government, and want a government strong enough to do them well. The purpose of the political process is twofold: to produce a government capable of effective action, and to enable citizens to control their government. Doing either well is no mean feat; doing both well has been something of an impossible dream for most of the political systems of the world.

In this book we are concerned with the New York State polity; thus, we will center our attention on the politics, government, and public policies of the Empire State. However, state government does not exist in a vacuum. New York is one of fifty states, and home to approximately 6,000 of the 80,000 local governments in our country. As part of the federal system, New York is bound by the Constitution of the United States and the actions of the president, Congress, and federal courts under the Constitution's authority. Today, many public policies involve all three levels of government—federal, state, local—with the higher levels generally setting standards, issuing directives, and providing financing, and with the lower levels actually doing the work.

Of course, New York is not totally subservient to the government of Washington. All governments are bound by the limitations of the Constitution. That document reserves considerable power to state governments. Moreover, the Constitution cannot be changed without the concurrence of three-quarters of the states.

Local governments are different. They are solely the creations of state government, and they may be abolished or have their powers modified at any time without their consent. In principle, then, local governments are wholly dependent on state governments, but states operate in concert with the federal government. In fact, the differences are not so striking. New York State must be intensely and actively involved in pursuing its policy and financial priorities in Washington, just as local governments are organized to lobby in Albany (and Washington!) for their particular interests. Therefore, we will frequently touch on New York's relations with Washington and local governments as we tell our story.

Following our politics/government/public policy model, Part I deals with the subject of politics, concentrating on New York's political culture, parties, voting, and elections. After an introductory essay by the editors, Paul Smith offers an overview of the people of our state and their attitudes toward politics and government; Howard Scarrow describes the laws governing our state elections and their intended and unintended consequences; Jeff Stonecash describes the evolution of the current "standard operating procedure" of state and local relations that shapes so much of the way New York State does business today; and Peter Colby offers an insight into the prevailing political culture of New York City.

The political culture of New York State is a varied one. Karen Markoe traces the historical development of the Democratic and Republican parties. Robert Spitzer, in a crucial addendum to her discussion, reminds us that there are a number of other political parties that have been very important in the political life of our state. Although the United States as a whole may be characterized as having a two-party system, no discussion of New York State politics is complete without careful consideration of the Conservative, Liberal, and Right to Life parties. Alan Emory explains how U.S. Senator Alfonse D'Amato has used the tools of incumbency to build a political machine in Washington, D.C.

Lee Miringoff and Barbara Carvalho furnish a closeup of Mario Cuomo's reelection in 1986, helping us to further our understanding of the interaction of political culture, voting trends, campaign strategies, and political parties—in short, what a major election in this state is all about. John K. White takes a look at a new political agenda to which elected officials are responding, and its shaping of recent election outcomes. Finally, New York Mayor Ed Koch, a Democrat, and New York State Comptroller Ned Regan, a Republican, give their insider views on the condition of the political parties and their impact on elections in New York in the late 1980s.

Part II delves into the workings of government. The editors discuss the current government of New York State; Fred Bartle offers a fascinating look at the four constitutions that have served as the basic legal authority for our state governance; Gerald Benjamin considers the changing nature of the governorship; Lieutenant Governor Stan Lundine looks at the nature of the office he currently holds, and offers suggestions for strengthening the post; and Alan Hevesi, a scholar and practicing politician, explains how the state legislature really works.

Much of the business of New York State is done by the bureaucracy. Michael Lynch and Dennis DeLong describe the vast "fourth branch" of our state government. *New York Times* reporter Sam Roberts describes a day in the life of Manhattan Supreme Court Justice Harold J. Rothwax. Keith Henderson introduces the several public authorities, which perhaps play a larger role here than in any other state. Robert P. Kerker presents a cogent discussion of how all the elements of government come together in the budget-making process, noting the powerful role exercised by the Division of the Budget. Finally, Paul Moore explains the complex mechanisms whereby the state delivers services to local governments.

In Part III we turn to the real purposes of all the political maneuvering and governmental activity described in the first two sections of the book. Although the size and scope of this volume preclude an in-depth study of each of the many public policies pursued by the state, a selection of some of the more interesting is presented. The editors examine the state's current public policy. Alan Chartock begins the discussion of interest groups: the substantive role they play and their lobbying strategies which shape public policy making in the Empire State. Leonard Stavisky examines the crucial and expensive area of education, and Sarah Liebschutz examines state economic development policies. Alice Sardell takes a look at health care policy, an issue of paramount importance in the late 1980s given the scourge of Acquired Immune Deficiency Syndrome (AIDS). Theresa Funiciello and Sanford Schram study the welfare system and the question of whether current standards and practices are preventing it from achieving its declared goals. Karen Burstein explains the state civil service system. Edward Howe and Donald Reeb make clear the importance of the much-criticized property tax. Henry Steck gives attention to a public policy of much concern to many readers of this book: higher education. Lastly, a Rockefeller Institute of Government study speculates on the future of New York State in the year 2000. A selected bibliography at the end of the volume will guide readers in search of more information about the politics, government, and public policies of New York State.

This book is written at an introductory level so that persons with little or no background in political science or New York politics can understand the material without difficulty. Hence, for those who wish to become experts in state affairs, this work can only be the beginning. But it is our hope that through our collective efforts some readers will be attracted to the study and the practice of New York State government. In any case, all those who conscientiously and carefully work their way through this volume should be considerably better equipped to understand the daily politics, governmental activities, and public policy debates in New York State.

PART I
Politics

The Politics of New York State Today

by

Peter W. Colby and John K. White

EDITORS' NOTE: *The introductory essay describes the history and current electoral dimensions of the dominant division in New York State politics between the upstate Republicans and downstate Democrats.*

New York was first explored and settled by the Dutch in the early 1600s, and came under English rule in 1664. After 150 years as a colony, it declared its independence in 1776. One year later the state had its first constitution and first elected governor. After the Revolutionary War, New York became one of the thirteen original United States of America. It was the most populous state in the union from 1820 to 1970, and throughout two centuries of statehood has played a leading role in the nation's affairs. The rivalry between downstate (New York City) Democrats and upstate (the rest of New York State) Republicans that dominates our state politics in the 1980s had its beginning in the first European settlements! A good way to start to understand the New York politics of today, then, is to learn a little history.

Upstate and Downstate: Origins of Conflict[1]

The early Dutch in what is now New York State were in commerce, especially fur trading. Later patroon ships were used to bring in permanent settlers who began farming. The center of power in the colony called New Netherlands was New Amsterdam, where merchants and traders shipped goods to Europe and the Dutch settlements and outposts in the Hudson Valley. In short order more and more English immigrants settled around New Amsterdam, and the origins of the upstate versus downstate conflict can be found in the early protests by the largely English farmers on Long Island and in what is now Westchester County against the terms of trade set by the Dutch West India Company. Long after Peter Stuyvesant handed over the colony to the Duke of York, the division between urban commercial interests and rural agricultural interests persisted.

The American Revolution further split the city from upstate. From September 1776 until the end of the war, the British held New York City. Meanwhile, upstate was engulfed in fighting; a third of the Revolutionary War battles were fought there. As the Americans won battle after battle in the East, thousands of Tories fled to safety behind British lines in New York City, turning it into a stronghold of Loyalists to the British Crown. After the war, the military battles became political ones as upstaters, led by Governor George Clinton, favored harsh actions against the Tories, and wavered on ratification of the Constitution. Downstaters took opposite stances.

The state's central location in the new nation and the early development of New York City as a port made the state the focal point for commerce, transportation, and immigration. By the 1800s, the city had become the nation's economic and cultural capital. Upstate changed, too, from a rural backwater to a region that included growing cities and industry along the Hudson River north to Albany, and through the Mohawk Valley to Buffalo. The Erie Canal and railroads linked these cities with the rest of the state and nation, further enhancing economic growth. The presence of the now populous upstate cities, which might have been expected to mitigate the differences between New York City and upstate, did nothing to diminish the well-established rivalry.

The upstate-downstate rivalry became the predominant political fissure in the state, with the Democrats the protectors of New York City and the Republicans in control of upstate. Two related events in the 1890s were crucial in institutionalizing the rivalry. New York City, which at the time consisted of what is now Manhattan and part of the Bronx, consolidated with Brooklyn, Queens, and Staten Island, and annexed the rest of the Bronx. This doubled the population and established borders that remain to this day. Upstate fears of the city's political and economic ascendancy were greatly increased, and in reaction to the consolidation, the 1894 State Constitutional Convention enacted two provisions concerning legislative apportionment: First, all counties except Hamilton and Fulton (which shared a district) must have at least one member in the Assembly; second, no two counties divided by a river (a provision aimed at Manhattan, Brooklyn) could hold one-half of the seats in the State Senate. The result was a legislature controlled by upstate interests, regardless of the relative populations of the city and the rest of the state. Democratic Governor Al Smith dubbed the arrangement "Constitutionally Republican," since it was virtually impossible for downstate-based Democrats to elect a majority in either the State Assembly or State Senate.

In the late nineteenth century and early twentieth century, regulation of liquor sales was a highly emotional issue. Prohibition was generally favored by upstate and opposed by New York City. City residents saw the issue as one on which old-fashioned "hayseeds"[2] sought to impose their straight-laced morality on them. Upstaters viewed the sale of liquor as a symbol of moral decadence. The split reflected religious, ethnic, and lifestyle differences between upstate and downstate.

The image of rural upstate clearly is outdated (only one-sixth of the state's population lives in the forty-four rural counties with fewer than 200,000 residents each). Nonetheless, social and cultural differences remain. The city is home to the vast majority of the state's Blacks, Hispanics, and Jews, reinforcing differences between upstaters and city dwellers. However, as time has gone by, ethnic differences have given way to bread and butter issues: legislative apportionment, taxes, and disbursement of state revenues. Some of these disputes are geographic, such as spending for roads upstate versus dollars for mass transit downstate.

Other issues arise in demographics. Thus, state assumption of the medicaid costs of local government is looked upon by many as a bailout of New York City, which has a disproportionate share of the state's poor.

Elections as Regional Conflict

Although there has been a general consensus that upstate-downstate divisions are fundamental to understanding the political history of New York State, the precise dividing line between the two regions and their continued relevance to contemporary political disputes is a source of controversy. Some argue that the marker lies between New York City and the rest of the state (thus, Long Island becomes part of "upstate"). Others say that the state can be divided into three regions: New York City, its surrounding suburbs, and the rest of the state. Still others maintain that the old conflicts are becoming more muted in an era of television and personality-based politics.

The 1982 gubernatorial election suggests enduring regional conflict. Democrat Mario Cuomo defeated Republican Lewis Lehrman in New York City by 575,000 votes. But Lehrman carried the rest of the state by 400,000 votes. County returns showed a similar pattern: Cuomo won all five city boroughs, but lost fifty-two of the fifty-seven upstate counties.

The 1986 election produced an entirely different result. After his narrow win four years before, Mario Cuomo consolidated his personal popularity into something approaching a political fortress. His hapless Republican opponent, Andrew O'Rourke, won just five of the state's sixty-two counties.[3] Cuomo's sweep extended into traditional Republican strongholds; he managed to win Franklin Roosevelt's home county, Dutchess, something the former president could not accomplish in his first election as governor in 1928. Cuomo even struck at the heart of the Republican machine in Nassau County, defeating O'Rourke by a margin of nearly two to one there. In New York City, Cuomo's margin surpassed 630,000; outside the city, it was even greater: more than 800,000. Cuomo's ticketmate, Attorney General Robert Abrams, also defeated a little-known GOP opponent by nearly 600,000 votes in New York City, and in the rest of the state by 729,000 votes.

Although regional differences were muted in the gubernatorial and attorney general's races in 1986, they were evident in several other political contests held that year. Republican State Comptroller Ned Regan lost to his Democratic rival in New York City by 248,000 votes, while carrying the rest of the state by 799,000 votes. Another Republican, U.S. Senator Alfonse D'Amato, lost the Big Apple by 267,000, while winning nearly everywhere else in the state by a 574,000 plurality. Still, in comparison with other Republican candidates in years gone by, the Regan and

D'Amato losses in New York City were comparatively small—thus muting the traditional upstate-downstate rivalry.

Congressional and state legislative contests in 1986 retained their traditional upstate-downstate character. Of the state's twenty Democratic congressmen, twelve were from New York City. Similarly, of the twenty-five Democratic state senators, nineteen were from the city. In the State Assembly, fifty-six of the ninety-one Democrats, including Speaker Mel Miller, hailed from New York City. On the other side of the fence, all fourteen Republican congressmen were upstaters, as were thirty-one of thirty-six Republican state senators, and fifty-three of fifty-six Republican assemblymen.

Many election analysts argue that the growth and maturation of the suburbs surrounding New York City are dividing the state into three rather than two distinct regions.[4] Today, one-fourth of the New York electorate is located in the city's suburbs. The 1982 election of Cuomo points to the suburbs' importance. If the results are analyzed in terms of city, suburbs, and upstate, the suburbs (Nassau, Suffolk, Rockland, and Westchester counties) emerge as the real battleground of the election: Cuomo won 68 percent of the city vote; Lehrman 58 percent of the upstate vote; and the suburban counties split almost evenly. But in 1986 there were no battlegrounds to speak of as the Republicans lost on all three political playing fields: Cuomo won 70 percent of the votes cast in New York City, 59 percent of the upstate votes, and 57 percent of the suburban votes.

Still, dividing the state into three regions provides some useful insights into New York politics. Table 1 shows the steady decline of the New York

Table 1

PERCENTAGE OF STATEWIDE VOTE FOR PRESIDENT, NEW YORK CITY, SUBURBS, AND UPSTATE, 1952–1984.

YEAR	NEW YORK CITY	SUBURBS	UPSTATE
1952	48	14	38
1956	45	17	39
1960	42	18	39
1964	42	20	38
1968	38	22	39
1972	36	23	40
1976	33	24	43
1980	31	24	45
1984	33	24	43

Note: Percentages do not total 100 because of rounding.

City vote at the expense of the suburbs and the rest of upstate. In 1952, nearly one-half of the total votes cast in that year's presidential election came from New York City; by 1984, less than one-third.

Tables 2 and 3 indicate that New York City is still of considerable importance to Democratic candidates, especially in primary elections.[5] More than one-half of the state's registered Democrats reside there, and generally 60 percent of the statewide Democratic primary vote comes from there.[6] Only 14 percent of enrolled Republicans live in New York City, and they contribute the same meager percentage to Republican intra-party contests. Thus, primary elections reinforce the tendency of Republicans to be the party of upstate and the Democrats the party of downstate.

Table 4 indicates how voting within each of the three regions deviates from the overall pattern for the state. The appeal of particular candidates and issues (and the presence or absence of third-party contenders) is different from election to election, but it is clear that the common perception of the Democratic city, Republican suburbs, and Republican upstate remains basically accurate.

The Political Parties[7]

Political parties have a unique and important role in our federal system. For nearly four decades political scientists have passionately argued the parties' case. In 1942, E.E. Schattschneider wrote: "The political parties created democracy. . . . Modern democracy is unthinkable save in terms of parties."[8] Eight years later the Committee on Political Parties of

Table 2

PERCENTAGE OF STATEWIDE DEMOCRATIC VOTE FOR PRESIDENT, NEW YORK CITY, SUBURBS, AND UPSTATE, 1952–1984

YEAR	NEW YORK CITY	SUBURBS	UPSTATE
1952	59.8	9.6	30.7
1956	59.8	12.2	29.1
1960	50.5	15.0	34.4
1964	44.5	17.4	38.2
1968	46.9	18.1	35.0
1972	45.5	19.5	35.0
1976	42.0	21.6	36.4
1980	38.6	19.2	42.3
1984	42.6	19.9	37.5

Note: Percentages do not total 100 because of rounding.

Table 3

PERCENTAGE OF STATEWIDE REPUBLICAN VOTE FOR PRESIDENT, NEW YORK CITY, SUBURBS, AND UPSTATE, 1952–1984

YEAR	NEW YORK CITY	SUBURBS	UPSTATE
1952	37.8	17.4	44.8
1956	35.7	19.5	44.8
1960	33.2	21.7	45.0
1964	35.7	25.3	38.9
1968	29.5	26.3	44.2
1972	30.1	25.8	44.1
1976	22.8	27.1	50.1
1980	24.9	29.3	45.8
1984	23.0	27.6	49.3

Note: Percentages do not total 100 because of rounding.

the American Political Science Association called political parties the "indispensable instruments of government."[9] In 1980, the Committee for Party Renewal, a bipartisan association of political scientists and party activists, declared: "Without parties there can be no organized and coherent politics. Parties are indispensable to the realization of democracy."[10]

The vigorous defense of parties constitutes a recognition of the important functions they have exercised historically. All New Yorkers, upstaters and downstaters, look for means of communicating their needs

Table 4

PERCENTAGE DEVIATION OF TWO-PARTY TOTAL VOTE FOR PRESIDENT, NEW YORK CITY, SUBURBS, AND UPSTATE, 1952–1984

YEAR	NEW YORK CITY	SUBURBS	UPSTATE
1952	+10.4 D	+13.8 R	+9.0 R
1956	+12.3 D	+10.4 R	+9.6 R
1960	+10.2 D	+9.2 R	+6.7 R
1964	+4.4 D	+8.6 R	+0.5 R
1968	+11.2 D	+9.2 R	+5.8 R
1972	+10.3 D	+6.6 R	+5.9 R
1976	+14.6 D	+4.5 R	+7.9 R
1980	+10.9 D	+10.3 R	+1.8 R
1984	+15.0 D	+8.0 R	+6.8 R

Note: For example, in 1984, Republican Ronald Reagan received 52.9 percent of the two-party vote in New York State as a whole, but only 37.9 percent of the New York City vote. Thus, the city deviated from the statewide pattern by 15 percent in favor of Democratic candidate Walter Mondale.

and desires to state officials. Political parties are the primary arrangement for accomplishing this task. They organize citizens to elect candidates to office and shape the decisions that officeholders subsequently make. In this way, parties simplify choices by offering candidates and platforms that voters can support or reject. U.S. Senator Ernest Hollings (D-S.C.) says that a political party exists "not just to win elections but to move a country. Its purpose is not to placate a cacophony of voices, but to attract diverse groups to a common purpose. It is built not on television, but on a national vision."[11]

Political parties comprise three more or less distinct components: the party-in-the-electorate, the party organization, and the party-in-government. The party-in-the-electorate may be defined in several ways: as anyone who is a self-declared party member; as anyone who votes in a party primary; or as anyone who supports a particular party's candidates in a general election. By any definition, it is quite easy to become one of the party-in-the-electorate—anyone can "join" or "resign" at any time. The party organization is what most people commonly think of as the political party, because it consists of party officers and others who actively preserve and promote the party machinery. Finally, the party-in-government includes the party members who were elected to office as well as the public officials appointed by the elected leaders.

Although New York has five official political parties (defined by state law as any political organization that received 50,000 or more votes for its candidate at the most recent election for Governor), the Republicans and Democrats win nearly all the elections. However, the political balance between the two major parties is changing. For years the "conventional wisdom" held that the state was securely Democratic. After all, it had produced such illustrious Democrats as Alfred E. Smith, Franklin D. Roosevelt, and Herbert Lehman. Mario Cuomo is the latest extension of a long and distinguished Democratic lineage. And a quick scan of the political landscape appears to confirm the Democrats' hold: They enjoy a 1,217,303 voter registration advantage;[12] they maintain healthy leads in most demographic groups (Table 5), with the exceptions of Protestants and conservatives; and they control all of the state offices except that of comptroller. But a changing political environment is making the "conventional wisdom" more frequently prone to error.

- In the past five presidential elections, Democrats have won New York State only twice: Hubert Humphrey in 1968, and Jimmy Carter in 1976.
- In 1980, conservative Republicans Ronald Reagan and Alfonse D'Amato scored upset victories, prompting veteran *New York Times* political reporter Frank Lynn to conclude that the wins "rang

Table 5

NEW YORK STATE ELECTORATE BY PARTY AFFILIATION, 1987 (in percentages)

DEMOGRAPHIC GROUP	DEMOCRAT	REPUBLICAN	INDEPENDENT	OTHER
Religion				
Protestant	38	43	14	6
Catholic	44	31	18	6
Jewish	70	13	10	7
Race				
White	41	35	17	6
Black	83	2	8	7
Education				
Less than high school	55	28	9	8
High school	44	33	14	8
Some College	46	31	19	4
College graduate	42	31	21	5
Sex				
Male	45	31	19	6
Female	50	30	14	7
Ideology				
Liberal	62	20	9	8
Moderate	49	30	17	4
Conservative	33	42	18	8
Age				
30 or under	53	24	14	8
31–44	50	21	24	6
45–60	41	40	13	6
Over 60	43	40	11	6

Source: Marist Institute for Public Opinion, survey, 4–6 January 1988. Text of question: "Are you currently registered to vote as a Democrat, a Republican, an Independent, a Conservative, or a Liberal?" Percentages do not total 100 because of rounding.

down the final curtain on the Dewey-Rockefeller-Javits era of liberal Republicanism in New York."[13]

- The same two conservative Republicans were easily reelected in 1984 and 1986, respectively. Ronald Reagan defeated Walter Mondale in the Empire State by 54 percent to 46 percent. Alfonse D'Amato overwhelmed Democrat Mark Green by 57 percent to 41 percent.

These three examples point to changes in the party coalitions and their "pitches" to the voters. Joseph Margiotta, a former Nassau County Republican chairman, explains that the electorate "has moved to the right.

> When Nelson Rockefeller was governor, the economy was such that you could move forward with new progressive programs costing vast sums. A shrinking economy and inflation mean that the day in which you could enjoy the luxury of these programs is gone. People are worried about their pocketbooks. Property taxes are strangling many citizens. There has to be a cutback of government spending.[14]

Although most voters often select only between Democratic and Republican candidates, New Yorkers have additional choices. The Liberal party was founded in the 1940s in New York City largely as a reaction to machine control of the Democratic party. The Conservative party began in the early 1960s in opposition to the Republican party leadership of Governor Nelson Rockefeller and Senator Jacob Javits. Each party views its role as a "check" on the Democratic and Republican parties. As Dick Behn once wrote:

> Essentially, the minor parties think they're more virtuous than the major ones. The Liberals think they're more Democratic than the Democrats and the Conservatives originally thought they were the only true Republicans left in New York. The Liberals reached the pinnacle of their influence in the Democratic Party in 1948 when their line carried the state for Harry Truman in the face of apathy by the state's Democrats. The Conservatives' founders thought Nelson Rockefeller and company had abandoned the basic principles of the GOP in favor of me-too liberalism.[15]

The Conservative and Liberal parties rarely have elected candidates on their own, but each has used the ability to make or withhold cross-endorsement of major party candidates to influence nominations, general election outcomes, and even public policy decisions.

Finally, there is the Right to Life party. Although it is legally a full-fledged political party in New York, Right to Lifers are actually an interest group in disguise: they exist to promulgate one public policy position, opposition to abortion, rather than to win elections. Although the impact of the party on public policy decisions is debatable, it has generated a great deal of publicity for its cause.

Many citizens would like to see political parties function according to a "responsible party model." Political scientist Austin Ranney explains the concept.

> In a modern community, . . . the only way to achieve government that is both efficient and democratic is to establish responsible party government: put a major party in control of the government for a fixed period of time; let the people judge how well or how badly the party has used its

> power; and, according to the people's judgment as expressed at the polls, let the party continue in power or be replaced by the opposition party. In short, efficient and democratic government can be achieved only by establishing collective *party* responsibility rather than a series of isolated, disconnected individual responsibilities of particular officeholders to their local constituencies.[16]

For the responsible party to function, each party must stake out distinctive positions on major issues that are supported by all its candidates for office. The winning party then takes office and carries out its policies. The losers "watchdog" the party in power and develop alternative policies for the next election. Voters thus have a chance to express their opinion of the performance of the winners as weighed against their opinion of the opposition party. The model works best when two parties are closely competitive, so that each must adopt policies representative of the wishes of the citizens and put them into effect once in power—or risk losing the next election.

The responsible party model envisioned by Ranney and others is not even remotely functioning in New York State. Not only is the model not working, the political parties are not working. The former Democratic boss of Tammany Hall, George Washington Plunkitt, once predicted what would happen if the parties collapsed: "First, this great and glorious country was built up by political parties; second, parties can't hold together if their workers don't get offices when they win; third, if the parties go to pieces, the government they built up must go to pieces too; fourth, then there'll be hell to pay."[17] In recent years the decline of parties has been precipitated by the politics of personality; candidate-oriented campaign organizations; growing ranks of unaffiliated voters; New Yorkers' independence at the ballot box, as evidenced by the record number of split-ticket votes in 1986; and loss of public esteem for all political parties as a consequence of the scandals that have beset the Democratic party both in New York City and the legislature.

Still, political parties in New York have an important role to play. They provide vehicles for professional politicians and activist amateurs to participate in electoral politics. Although candidate-centered political organizations and various civic organizations exist for those interested in public affairs, parties remain the major means of organizing political activity.

Moreover, party labels provide voters with means of identifying candidates as Democrats, Republicans, or members of some third party. Although the party designation does not mean that a candidate supports every aspect of the party's platform, the label does convey some general information about the policy preferences of the prospective officeholder.

In New York, for example, Democrats are more likely to support labor union views, while Republicans tend to advance the interest of business.

In addition, Democrats and Republicans offer candidates for nearly all political offices at the state and local level. Without political parties to assist in the recruitment of individuals to run for office, many races would never be contested. Thus, while many complain about the quality of candidates, at least the parties ensure that New York votes have some choice in elections.

Furthermore, party affiliation provides a rough guide for political leaders as to who their friends and enemies are. Political analyst William J. Keefe states, "While party members may be marching to different drums, most of them are playing the same tune."[18] Alliances that transcend party lines and rivalries within party ranks are common, but Republicans generally work together, as do Democrats. To some degree this reflects common social backgrounds. But more important, it demonstrates the need for some principle or organization to hold government together. Republicans pursue their political, governmental, and career objectives as part of the Republican team; Democrats do likewise.

Finally, the third parties (Conservative, Liberal, and Right to Life) have given those who are disaffected with the two major parties a chance to participate in politics, and have increased the visibility of certain political philosophies and policy issues.

In sum, although the political parties of New York do not provide responsible party government, they do make substantial contributions to our political life.

Conclusion

This overview of politics in New York State focused on the origins and current status of the struggle between downstate Democrats and upstate Republicans for control of state government and public policy. In subsequent chapters, authors will elaborate, challenge, and introduce new perspectives on this central theme of our state's political life. It already should be clear, though, that parties and elections are not the only factors that influence the making of public policy. Thus, in Parts II and III of this volume, we will turn to the more specialized worlds of the state's governmental apparatus and the various interest groups surrounding it.

NOTES

1. For a brief readable history, see David Maldwyn Ellis, *New York State and City,* Ithaca: Columbia University Press, 1979.

2. The term is George Washington Plunkitt's. See William L. Riordan, *Plunkitt of Tammany Hall,* New York: Dutton, 1963.

3. O'Rourke won the tiny upstate counties of Greene, Hamilton, Delaware, Sullivan, and Washington.

4. Robert Marcus, "How Many New Yorks?" *Empire State Report* (April 1983): 48. Also see Lee Miringoff and Barbara Carvalho, *The Cuomo Factor: Assessing the Political Appeal of New York's Governor,* Poughkeepsie, New York: Marist Institute for Public Opinion, 1986.

5. Frank Lynn, "The Dimensions of the State's Divided Loyalties," *New York Times,* 19 September 1982. In 1984, Walter Mondale beat Gary Hart overwhelmingly in New York City—enough to win the state's Democratic presidential primary by a whopping 45 percent for Mondale to 27 percent for Hart and 26 percent for Jesse Jackson.

6. In the only statewide primary of 1986, that for the Democratic nomination for U.S. Senate, 55 percent of the primary vote came from New York City.

7. Parts of this section are drawn from Peter W. Colby, "Illinois Politics and the Ideal of Responsible Party Government," in Edgar G. Crane, ed., *Illinois: Political Processes and Governmental Performance,* Dubuque, Iowa: Kendall/Hunt, 1980), pp. 177-85.

8. E.E. Schattschneider, *Party Government,* New York: Holt, Rinehart & Winston, 1942, p. 1.

9. From a report of the Committee on Political Parties of the American Political Science Association. See Supplement to the *American Political Science Review,* 44 (September 1950).

10. "Strengthening the Political Parties," (Position paper adopted by the Committee for Party Renewal in 1980 and presented to both national party committees).

11. *Washington Post National Weekly Edition,* 23 July 1984, p. 23.

12. The 1986 party enrollment figures: Democratic, 3,820,085; Republican, 2,602,782; Conservative, 110,485; Liberal, 62,540; Right to Life 21,606; blank, void, and missing, 1,461,281.

13. Frank Lynn, "New York G.O.P. Sees Power Shift within the Party," *New York Times,* 6 November 1980, p. A-1.

14. John K. White, telephone interview with Joseph M. Margiotta, 29 May 1981.

15. Dick Behn, "Liberals and Conservatives: The Importance of New York's Two 'Third' Parties," *Empire State Report,* April 1977, p. 164.

16. J. Austin Ranney, "The Concept of Party Responsibility," in *Illinois Political Parties,* Lois M. Pelekoudas, ed. Urbana: University of Illinois Institute of Government and Public Affairs, March 1960, p. 15.

17. Riordan, *Plunkitt of Tammany Hall,* p. 13

18. William J. Keefe, *Parties, Politics, and Public Policy in America,* 2d ed., Hinsdale, Ill.: Drydan Press, 1976, p. 51.

A State of Politics

by

Paul A. Smith

Mr. Smith is Professor of Political Science
at the State University of New York at Binghamton.

EDITORS' NOTE: *This chapter describes the distinctive political culture of New York: the identifications, expectations, and support New Yorkers exhibit towards state government and the styles of our politicians. Portions of this essay have been adapted from Mr. Smith's chapter on New York in Alan Rosenthal and Maureen Moakley, eds.,* The Political Life of the American States *(New York: Praeger, forthcoming).*

PAUL A. SMITH

Politics are alive and well in New York, and whether for good or ill, political activity is accorded plenty of attention and importance—a common element in the life of what is otherwise a very diverse state.

To say New Yorkers are interested in politics is neither very useful nor necessarily very accurate. As elsewhere in America, there are some citizens of the state who are quite indifferent to political affairs and others who view politics with an active distaste. Therefore, we are considering something not that every New Yorker feels or does but rather that which characterizes the political life of the state, perhaps sufficiently to distinguish it from other states.

The Concept of Political Culture

For our purposes, the concept of "political culture" is the most helpful. Central to anthropology, culture has a variety of meanings but usually refers to a society's patterns of behavior that are transmitted from generation to generation; or, in the definition of Margaret Mead, it is "the systematic body of learned behavior." [1] This definition focuses on patterns of action, but anthropologists also indicate that these patterns are accompanied by beliefs and attitudes. In other words, culture involves not only what people do but also what they think and value. Obviously, patterns of culture do not spring up overnight, nor are they here today and gone tomorrow. Representing enduring effects of historical experiences, they bring together the past and present. The culture concept thus sensitizes us to the existence of features of a society that we might otherwise ignore because they are too pervasive and we are too close.[2]

However, because the concept is so all-encompassing and open-ended it lacks precision as an analytic tool. To overcome this problem, political scientists have first looked at particular aspects of political culture, such as its *sources, manifestations,* and *effects,*[3] and second, have broken the concept down into more specific subcategories. Here we shall concentrate on the manifestations of the state's political culture.

In describing political culture, political scientists have tended to emphasize not patterns of *behavior* but what are called "orientations" to behavior, the phenomena of attitudes and beliefs.[4] In the words of a leading scholar, "The political culture of a society consists of a system of empirical beliefs, expressive symbols, and values which defines the situation in which political action takes place." [5] Thus their political culture tells us how people feel and think about such things as authority, the roles of government, and proper ways to act politically. We shall address these subjects through analytic subcategories of political *identifications, expectations,* and *support.*[6]

Yet these "orientations" to politics cannot be isolated from actual political behavior, for patterns of action provide dynamic confirmation for a culture's existence. We shall consider these ways of acting through the subcategory of political *style.* By style is meant distinctive patterns of action that have intrinsic normative or value aspects. In short, the manner or style in which politicians act is something that members of the culture value and support and usually expect.

Putting all this together and applying it to New York politics, the following elements comprise New York's political culture:

Identifications. What political units do New Yorkers identify with? Do they associate themselves with the state, a city, or some region? And are their identifications positive or negative?

Expectations. What do New Yorkers expect from politics and government, especially from state government? Are these expectations of good things or bad?

Support. How positive or negative are New Yorkers toward their state and its politics? Do they respect the state's government, or are they distrustful or cynical toward it? How do they feel generally about political authority?

Style. What types of behavior do New York politicians exhibit? How closely does this conform to what is expected? Is the style of these politicians and officials argumentative or accommodating, assertive or retiring? Do political leaders in the state tend to come from certain ethnic or social backgrounds, or are they a mixed lot?

As we take up these categories (and questions) one by one, keep in mind that we are trying to portray a *whole* political culture. There is no requirement, however, that this culture be highly integrated. Its elements may or may not fit smoothly together.

Identifications

To the surprise of many, New York is a very diverse state. From afar the state's image is dominated by New York City, but it is hard to know whether that image is more of wealth, high art, and sophistication, or of poverty, corruption, and degradation. And the City's diversity is just one part of the state's—a diversity that begins with geography and extends to occupations and ethnic backgrounds.

Starting from the corporate, artistic, and commercial center of Manhattan, one can travel north through the urban desolation of the south Bronx, and then up the Hudson through the affluent old line suburbs of Westchester county; or east past Brooklyn and Queens through the massive "bedroom" communities of Long Island until, later, the small towns and fishing villages are reached far out on the Island. Traveling northwest from the City, one comes to the heavily wooded and picturesque Catskills, punctuated with posh resorts and the enormous reservoirs that provide water to the City, and later to large areas of dairy farming reminiscent of Wisconsin. Still further west, one reaches the wine country of the Finger Lakes and eventually the industrial cities of Rochester and Buffalo on the Great Lakes. And turning north past Albany or Syracuse brings one to the sparsely populated north country of the Adirondacks and eventually Canada—a region that borders and is very much like New England.

In each of these areas the population is different, both in their origins and what they do for a living. The City, of course, has long been recognized as the ethnic melting pot, the evidence of which remains in the Black, Chinese, Italian, Jewish, German, and other settlements that are still more or less distinct neighborhoods. Yet much of this same diversity is also found upstate, where hundreds of thousands of Irish, Italian, Polish, and Ukrainian immigrants stopped to work in the factories of cities like Binghamton, Utica, and Buffalo. Settlers moving west from New England populated much of the north country.[7]

Not only are these populations different, New Yorkers see each other as different. The upstate-downstate distinction is the most fundamental, with residents of the City perceiving virtually everything north of its boundaries as upstate. Naturally, this perception masks the great diversity we have just mentioned. But in other respects clear distinctions are made close to home. For example, George Washington Plunkitt, of Manhattan's Tammany Hall fame, saw the rest of the state populated by "hayseeds,"[8] yet residents of Queens and the Bronx, two of the five counties or "boroughs" of New York City, identify with their boroughs and even today refer to Manhattan as "the City."[9] But the tendency of all New York City residents to identify with the City rather than the state is long and deeply established. A major opinion poll taken in 1982, for example, found that three out of four New Yorkers agreed that a "serious conflict" existed between upstate and the City. Upstaters view the City not only as badly managed and spendthrift, but also as getting too large a share of the state's resources—a sentiment reciprocated by residents of the City toward upstate areas. How close to the surface these sensitivities are was illustrated in the gubernatorial campaign of 1982, when New York mayor (and candidate for governor) Edward Koch caused a furor by making some disparaging remarks about Albany and rural living and in turn received little electoral support beyond the City and its suburbs.

With all this cultural and perceptual diversity, how can New Yorkers have common feelings of political identification? One way is through powerful mechanisms of cultural integration. For one thing, as the state has fallen on hard times, feelings of identification with it have grown. The financial crises of the 1970s came to a head in the City first.

Although the crisis seemed to arise suddenly, the City's financial condition had been in decline for a long time. During the 1950s and 1960s there was a large immigration of poor Black and Hispanic people, coupled with an emigration of middle classes to the suburbs. Between 1960 and 1980, five hundred thousand—about half—of the City's manufacturing jobs were lost. Yet from 1960 to 1975, while the City's work force and general population were declining, the number of public service employees grew. To pay for this the City had to borrow. From 1970 to 1975 its short-term debt increased more than three billion dollars, and the annual pension payments to City workers grew to more than a billion dollars. In the 1975–76 fiscal year, the City had a deficit of almost two billion dollars. So serious was the City's condition—in the midst of the vast wealth of Manhattan—that its ability to borrow was hamstrung; thus the critical need for federal loans and loan guarantees.

With the establishment in 1975 of the Municipal Assistance Corporation and the Emergency Financial Control Board, direct state (and private) intervention in City borrowing and budgeting became a reality. One lesson was that the City's government could not be relied on to keep its finances in order, but there was another lesson: the economic life of the City and the state were thoroughly intertwined, and in a crisis the state's authority would prevail.

Less than a year later, the long practice of spending beyond its means also caught up with the state. New York was brought face-to-face with the harsh reality of a general economic deterioration. Business, industry, and people—mostly income generators and taxpayers—were leaving the state (and the entire northeast) in favor of greater opportunities in Florida, Texas, and California. The situation was worse in small, stagnant, upstate communities than in the City.[9] It was evident that all New Yorkers were in the same boat and the boat was low in the water. Among the states, New York was no longer *primus inter pares.*

At this juncture both the state and City turned to austere financing and creative advertising. Along with determined moves to make the state more appealing to business and industry came advertising designed to make the state look more attractive. For New York City there was the symbol of the Big Apple, and for the state there was "I Love New York." At first taken lightly, these concepts were publicized so widely and with so much vigor and zest that they have become part of the state's collective consciousness. "I Love New York" was made the theme of a continuing series of song and dance television commercials that present, in integrative symbolism, various attributes of the state, ranging from Broadway theatre to upstate industry, skiing, and camping. The Big Apple turns up as a universal symbol not only of the City but of the state as well.[10]

Thus as New York has struggled to overcome its economic and political adversity, symbols of common identification have been developed and a sense of shared problems and identification has been enhanced. To be sure, conflicts over how the contracting pie of state resources will be divided have been intense, and to say that cultural cleavages, particularly upstate-downstate identifications, have gone away would be to say too much. Nevertheless, in recent years there has been a healing of some of these cleavages, and in any case a greater awareness that it is in the arena of state politics that the vital policy decisions will be made.

Expectations

Implicit in the foregoing is the almost universal expectation among citizens that the state will not stand idly by while its residents confront economic difficulties. The government is there to act, and not just the state government. Political officials at every level, whether they are congressmen, town supervisors, or members of school boards, are expected to produce results. In a large sense, government is seen as a service enterprise.

Naturally, when resources for public action are strained, the expectation that government will do things raises conflicting demands. To put it another way, New Yorkers also expect government to be run for the benefit of particular interests. Certainly, New York City politics is known to be the vehicle for boodle and advancement, and the "where's mine" attitude is common. Indeed, much of the political friction in the City today arises from disappointed expectations by Blacks and Hispanics who believe that it is now their turn.

But these payoff expectations are neither new nor confined to the City. Our old friend George Washington Plunkitt, after waxing enthusiastic about how City government should be used as an opportunity source, found to his chagrin that upstaters treated the state government in much the same manner:

> But just let a Republican farmer from Chemung or Wayner or Tioga turn up at the Capital. The Republican Legislature will make a rush for him and ask him what he wants and tell him if he doesn't see what he wants to ask for it. If he says his taxes are too high, they reply to him:

> "All right old man, don't let that worry you. How much do you want us to take off?"[11]

Inherent in this pork-barrel view of government are expectations that more than good things flow from politics. New Yorkers may differ about how necessary or universal it is, but without doubt residents of old Democratic Tammany Hall Manhattan or Republican Nassau County Long Island (where the political machine of Joseph Margiotta ruled) take it for granted that where there is politics there is corruption. Upstate, the traditions—and expectations—are much more mixed. In many towns and villages the citizens, while perceiving the City and Albany as hotbeds of chicanery, assert a high standard for their own officials. They are expected to shoulder the burdens of government for no personal gain other than a modest salary, the respect of their fellow citizens, and (occasionally) elevation to higher office. In some of the more rural communities, residents perceive their elections and policy-making as "public service rather than politics."[12] Expectations that this "New England" model can be achieved do not go unchallenged, however.[13] They collide in particular with the suspicion that all politicians are corruptible when they leave home and enter the state or national politics.

It bears reemphasis that however pure or venal New Yorkers expect their politicians to be, they expect them to deliver the goods. This is particularly true for state government. With its policies and institutions shaped by generations of active leaders, such as Al Smith, Roosevelt, Lehman, and Rockefeller, the state is today expected to carry out a very large array of functions and services, many of which have a direct impact on every local community. These range from the support of all levels of education, to the protection of health and the environment, to the regulation of business and industry. In short, the state is expected to tax and spend and regulate, and in doing so to involve itself in the lives of its citizens.

Support

With all the conflicts over who is to get what, when, and how from government, it might be supposed that support for state authority is in continual flux.[14] It is true that many citizens feel current irritations over what governments are or are not doing, in part because they are expected to do so much. But this does not affect basic attitudes of support in the same way that enduring conflicts between the state and the City do. In fact, with the state's active intervention in City affairs during the past decade, downstate feelings of general support for state government have been enhanced. And across the state there is little evidence that New Yorkers reject the authority of their political institutions.

However, it is equally true that New Yorkers are not very deferential toward political authorities. We have already seen that given their experiences with corruption and ineptitude, New Yorkers are generally skeptical about the integrity of those active in politics.[15] In much of the City and parts of Long Island cynicism is the dominant feeling toward politics and politicians, even though there is considerable respect for their usefulness. Whether upstate or downstate, government officials are not placed on pedestals. They are seen as human beings, perhaps skillful at what they do, but with ordinary foibles and many temptations. Yet the exercise of authority is regarded as a necessary and legitimate function—one to be supported despite its chances of abuse.

In shaping these attitudes toward political authority, the New York print and broadcast media play a significant role. They are generally competitive and vigorous, and despite the ascendancy of television, it is the newspapers that have set the standards for political journalism—standards that place a high value on exposing the behind-the-scenes reality of governmental affairs. Political authorities are considered fair game for tough questions and for doubts about the accuracy of official pronouncements. Whether covering the marriage of a governor or the budgetary decisions of the state legislature, major newspapers of the state take it as their obligation to tell their readers what is "really" going on. This serves to challenge—if not occasionally to trivialize—the mystique of high places and inevitably affects the attitudes and perceptions of the public.

In sum, while political authorities are accorded no immunity from criticism or dissent, support for political institutions of all kinds weathered the national malaise of the 1960s and 1970s, and political authority is active and firmly established in New York.

Political Style

Now we turn from political attitudes to the realm of behavior—to patterns of action on the part of political leaders and activists. It should come as no surprise that, in general, what is expected and supported by the public is what is delivered by the leaders.

Again, a little history is relevant. As immigrants crowded into the City, and it became evident that politics could be a vehicle for advancement, it was also clear that politicians needed to be energetic, alert to opportunities, and quick to take advantage of them. This produced patterns of competitive, assertive behavior, often laced with graft. At the same time, in typical upstate communities the political style was expected to be—and was—much more restrained. Quiet, reserved, statesmanlike behavior, perhaps inferred from schoolbook depictions of great Presidents, was the standard. Local politicians found success in sober, thoughtful demeanors, and since much of upstate New York was one-party Republican, vigorous inter-party conflict was also lacking. Upon reaching Albany, however, and confronting their Democratic counterparts from the City, upstaters found that some adaptations were in order, just as did those from the City.

The result is a fairly integrated New York style. Assemblymen and senators from all parts of the state recognize that to do well in Albany (or Washington), they must know the issues and be able to debate them; be prepared to fight for their interests, while being flexible enough to form winning coalitions; and have the wit and attractiveness to get the publicity needed to stay in office. As party and intra-party competition has increased, politicians who lack these qualities, or who are lazy or negligent, are usually culled out early. The advent of television coverage both of election campaigns and legislative debates has made politicians at all levels more sensitive to the skills of speaking and debating. Therefore, while the slow-moving, soft-spoken, retiring political leader might at one time have been the model in certain communities, one that is energetic, articulate, knowledgeable, and competitive is now more common.

Corrupt practices, or the pursuit of extra-legal side-payments, also remain part of the New York style, although in much attenuated form and frequency. Especially downstate, the similarities between Plunkitt's turn of the century "honest graft" and Joseph M. Margiotta's late twentieth-century "legitimate political patronage" are fascinating. Margiotta, Republican Party chairman of Nassau County and head of the state's most powerful political machine, was convicted of fraud and extortion in 1981 after a long trial. Appeals, supported by many of the state's top leaders, were made all the way to the U.S. Supreme Court before Margiotta finally went to prison in June, 1983. His basic claim was that he was being convicted for what were common and legitimate practices in local government.

The arguments of these two men, separated by eighty years, make no bones about the fact and desirability of corrupt practices as a normal part of politics.

If we extend the meaning of style to include collective patterns of participation, the most striking characteristic of the state's political style is diversity. Whether young or old, male or female, white or black, Italian or Irish, New Yorkers can be found in leadership positions. The "balanced ticket" is an intrinsic part of campaign strategy. But this does not mean that all groups are equal in participation. In terms of age, sex, race, ethnicity, income, occupation, and so on, the state's political leadership exhibits patterns that are much like those of the nation. Men more than women, whites more than Blacks, lawyers more than other occupations, appear in positions of leadership.

In the extremely active and competitive politics of the City, the Black and Hispanic population is badly under-represented. In fact, just before the September primary in 1981 a federal court ruled that in redistricting the City Council to reflect the 1980 census, the City was in violation of the 1965 federal Voting Rights Act. Although comprising forty-five percent of the City's population, Black and Hispanics held only eight of forty-three council seats, and the new districting held no promise of altering this pattern. All City elections were enjoined, and while this injunction was soon lifted for other elections, the councilmanic contests were not held until November, 1982. Even then the districting was not fully completed in a form acceptable to the federal authorities. Beyond the politics of districting, however, a major reason for this appears to be the difficulty that these new immigrant groups have in matching the high levels of political activity, skill, and organization (that is, style) of the established white—and especially Jewish—segments of the population. Because Blacks and Hispanics are concentrated in the City, the same pattern of under-representation is present in the state legislature. There is some evidence that this pattern is breaking up in the 1980s, but like other elements of the political culture it is not likely to change over night.

A final element that is part of New York's political style is a pattern of behavior that reflects a tradition of reform. Of course, one might suppose that a key reason why New York politicians so often talk about reform is that reform is so often needed! This point has some historical validity, but it is hardly the case today. Instead, the "clean up" cycles of the state's political history have been replaced by more systematic efforts to improve government organization and public policies. Thus over the years the state has pioneered in programs designed to aid the disadvantaged and has "earned the reputation of having the best and most innovative state and local government in the nation." [16]

Actually, the existence of a reform tradition in New York can be connected to other elements of its political culture. These include citizen expectations that government will act to satisfy their needs, and the competitive style of politicians seeking public support through vigorous public debates encouraged by an aggressive press. Of course the realization that the political system is hardly pure or perfect also creates pressure for reform, yet in New York the style of reform goes well beyond simply "throwing the rascals out" and becomes an element of the political culture in its own right.

Conclusions

It is clear that in a number of important respects New York has a distinctive political culture. We have tried to draw a portrait of that culture emphasizing features of political identification, expectations, support, and style. If these features have validity it should be possible to see their effects in the state's political organizations and processes, and in its public policies.

New Yorkers respect the authority of their political institutions and support the right of those in authority to govern. But this right is coupled with the expectation that those in authority will deliver the goods. Much is expected of government in New York, including its vulnerability to corruption and mismanagement. Those who aspire to positions of leadership are aware of these expectations and act accordingly. The result is a style of action that is generally intense, aggressive, competitive, and well-informed. New York politicians are not shrinking violets. They pay attention to what their constituents want and speak up for their interests. And, as with Plunkitt, if they see political opportunities they are likely to take them.

With a decade of hard times, New Yorkers have come to identify more with their state, and perhaps to expect less from their government. Long established City versus upstate loyalties remain to fragment common identifications, but the inaugural words of the Governor Mario Cuomo in 1983 express a major theme: "We must be the family of New York, feeling one another's pain, sharing one another's blessings, equitably, honestly, fairly—without respect to geography or race or political affiliation." New Yorkers have come to realize that other states are moving past them in size and wealth, and that they are heavily dependent on decisions made in Washington. Yet conscious of its historical position as the Empire State, New York retains its political culture of high expectation, assertiveness, and verve in the practice of politics.

NOTES

1. From Margaret Mead's 1958 preface to Ruth Benedict, *Patterns of Culture,* Boston: Houghton Mifflin, 1934, p. vii.

2. Samuel Patterson calls culture a "sensitizing concept" in "the Political Cultures of the American States," *Journal of Politics,* 30 (February 1968), p. 90.

3. Daniel J. Elazar and Joseph Zikmund II, eds., *The Ecology of American Political Culture: Readings,* New York: Crowell, 1975, pp. 5-6.

4. Gabriel A. Almond, "Comparative Political Systems," in Heniz Eulau, Sanuel Eldersveld, and Morris Janowitz, eds., *Political Behavior, A Reader in Theory and Research,* Glencoe, Ill.: Free Press, 1956, pp. 34-42.

5. Sidney Verba, "Comparative Political Culture," in Lucian W. Pye and Sidney Verba, eds., *Political Culture and Political Development,* Princeton, N.J.: Princeton University Press, 1965, p. 513.

6. For a fuller discussion of these categories, see Alan Rosenthal's introductory chapter in Alan Rosenthal and Maureen Moakley, eds., *The Politicial Life of the American States,* New York: Praeger, forthcoming.

7. Daniel J. Elazar describes some of these population movements in *American Federalism: A View From the States,* New York: Thomas Y. Crowell, 1966, pp. 99 ff.

8. William L. Riordon, *Plunkitt of Tammany Hall,* New York: E.P. Dutton, 1963, pp. 21-24. Plunkitt also presents a vivid picture of how residents of Brooklyn identify with that borough rather than Manhattan, pp. 41-44.

9. Michael Barone and Grant Ujifusa, *The Almanac of American Politics 1982,* Washington, D.C.: Barone and Co., 1981, pp. 718-19; and Neal R. Peirce and Michael Barone, *The Mid-Atlantic States of America,* New York: Norton, 1977, pp. 288-95.

10. I realize that there is little systematic evidence for the political cultural effects I am claiming, but the anecdotal, on-the-street evidence is impressive! For example, both in and out of the state, frequent references are made in conversations to I Love New York, and at meetings of the national organizations the Big Apple symbol is commonly used to represent New York delegations.

11. Riordon, p. 12.

12. But in many of these small towns, stable, issueless, one-party (Republican) politics masks a subtle corruption of its own. See Arthur J. Vidich and Joseph Bensman, *Small Town in Mass Society,* Garden City, N.Y.: Doubleday Anchor, 1960, esp. Chs. 5-7.

13. This is a combination of what Elazar calls individualistic and moralistic political cultures. See *American Federalism,* pp. 86-101.

14. The phrase is from the classic work of Harold D. Lasswell, *Politics: Who Gets What, When, How,* New York: Whittlesey House, 1936.

15. It is well to bear in mind that New Yorkers have been been caught up in the same attitudinal trends experienced by the nation as a whole. After all, they consume the same mass media and civics books as the citizens of other states. Nationally, there has been a decline in trust in government from 1958 to 1980. See William H. Flanigan and Nancy H. Zingale, *Political Behavior of the American Electorate,* 5th ed., Boston: Allyn and Bacon, 1983, pp. 171-75.

16. Barone and Ujifusa, p. 718.

Electoral Reform: A History of Unrealized Goals and Unanticipated Consequences

by

Howard A. Scarrow

> Neither social scientists, nor politicians, nor public administrators yet know enough about the social world to avoid repeated error in predicting the consequences of policy moves. A wise policy maker consequently expects that his policies will achieve only part of what he hopes and at the same time will produce unanticipated consequences he would have preferred to avoid.
>
> Charles E. Lindblom

Howard A. Scarrow is a Professor of Political Science at the State University of New York at Stony Brook and is the author of *Parties, Elections, and Representation in the State of New York.*

EDITORS' NOTE: *This essay provides a fascinating look at the electoral laws of our state—as they were intended to work and* as they actually impact the process.

Howard A. Scarrow

In this essay we shall review a number of legislative enactments which were intended to reform the electoral process in the state of New York. The laws selected relate to primary elections; the format of the election ballot; the system of cross endorsement; and voter participation. The purpose of the review will be to compare the outcomes of these reform measures with the expressed intentions and hopes of those who promoted them.[1]

Primary Elections

Prior to the late 1800s, political parties in New York and other states were completely private, unregulated organizations. Accordingly, a party's most important activity, the selection of candidates to contest the various offices of government, was carried out in private meetings held in appropriate geographical areas—e.g., congressional and state legislative districts. Because these meetings were often dominated by "bosses" whose tactics included bribes, fraudulent vote counting, and intimidation of opposing factions, reformers demanded that party nominations be regulated by state law. It was not until 1913, however, that the New York State Legislature—whose members, of course, had benefitted from the unreformed system—finally yielded to these demands by enacting today's system of direct primary elections.

The stated purpose of the law was to remove candidate selection from the whims of the bosses, or even from the wider circle of party activists, and to place it squarely in the hands of party members who had registered their affiliation with the local, government-run board of election. In fact, the reform legislation did not produce that result. First, rank and file party members showed little desire to participate in the selection of their party's candidates; a 20 percent or less turnout in a primary election became the norm. One result of this lack of support was that less than ten years after its enactment, the 1913 law was amended to remove the nomination of candidates for statewide office from the primary election process and to return it to the conventions of the party organizations. Second, for the offices which remained under the primary system, the party organizations continued to hold meetings for the purpose of choosing candidates, just as they had always done. The only difference was that now the selected candidates first had to win a primary election—circulating petitions for ballot access and then polling the most votes on primary day—before their names could appear on the general election ballot in November. But this additional step proved to be no major obstacle;

almost invariably the organization's chosen candidate (the designee) won the primary election by virtue of the fact that no other party member rose to challenge him. Indeed, so non-competitive had primary elections become by the year 1959 that, as an economy measure, the law was changed so that local polling stations did not have to open their doors on primary election day if only one candidate had submitted petitions for each of the offices to be filled. A study completed in 1986 showed New York as having the smallest number of contested primary elections of any American state.[2] This scarcity of competition reflected the ability of the party organizations to have the board of election or the courts find technical errors in a challenger's petitions, as well as the potential ability of the party organizations to use their patronage-generated resources of campaign workers and money to defeat primary challengers. In short, if the purpose of the 1913 primary law was to "open up" the nomination process, either to the citizen voter or to party activists wanting to challenge the established party leadership, the effort must be judged a failure.

In 1967 the legislature voted to return nominations for statewide office to the primary election process. Again the action was in response to demands by reformers that these nominations be removed from the control of party "bosses." There was, however, one important difference between the law enacted in 1967 and the one enacted in 1913. Modelled after the ideal primary law drafted by the National Municipal League, the 1967 law was based on the idea that a political party organization, meeting in convention, should be able to nominate anyone it wished, but that the organization should be held accountable for that choice. Accountability would be enforced by a process under which a disappointed party member would have the right to challenge the convention's choice in a statewide primary election, providing that he had received at least 25 percent of the convention's vote or, failing that, was later able to gather 20,000 signatures on petitions circulated throughout the state. The early experience with this new process showed once again how legislative intent can be frustrated by political realities. Within the Democratic party, aspiring candidates for statewide office decided that they did not want to be labeled "the candidate of the bosses"; therefore, rather than strive to capture the convention nomination, they took steps to avoid it, preferring to capture the nomination in a primary. Within the Republican party the problem was of a different sort. This party had become so used to being disciplined and united, that the new opportunity available to disappointed candidates went unused; the choice of the Republican convention continued to be the party's unchallenged nominee.

But political realities change. In 1980, Alfonse D'Amato took advantage of the new law to successfully challenge the Republican convention's choice of Jacob Javits as its nominee for U.S. Senator; and in 1982, Ed

Koch and Mario Cuomo, rather than trying to avoid being the nominee of their Democratic party's convention, tried to win that backing. Yet, whether fought among Republicans or among Democrats, the ensuing statewide primary contests of the 1980s were not contests between a party organization and an insurgent challenger, as envisaged by the National Municipal League. Rather, they were contests between two individuals, each with his own campaign organization and funding, and each relying on modern campaign technology—polling, computerized mailings, and slick radio and television commercials. The goal of making a party organization publicly accountable for its candidate selections had not been realized.

The major lesson to be derived from New York's experience with its two primary laws is that laws do make a difference, but not in the way originally envisioned by their authors. Neither Governor Cuomo nor Senator D'Amato would occupy their current positions had the 1967 primary legislation not enabled them to challenge the choice of their respective party conventions. Numerous other officials can also be said to owe their political careers to either the 1913 or the 1967 enactment. Yet without modern technology and its ability to give insurgent candidates the wherewithal to defeat candidates favored by the party organizations, it is doubtful that either of the two primary laws by themselves would have lessened the ability of the organizations to control candidate selection. Indeed, it was only after such technology became available in the 1970s that the frequency of primary contests began to increase; and to this day primary contests remain infrequent in small districts and localities where that technology is not cost efficient.

Ballot Format

Prior to 1890, elections in New York were conducted with paper ballots printed by the respective parties, each ballot containing the names of a party's candidates for the various offices. A voter would simply take the ballot of his choice and deposit it in the ballot box. Because the various ballots were of different sizes and colors, a voter's partisan preferences were openly displayed. As a result, reformers demanded the introduction of what was known as the Australian blanket ballot, a single sheet of paper, printed by the government, on which the names of all the candidates from all parties would appear. The election of 1986 was the first to be held using this new ballot format.

Although the stated purpose of the Australian ballot was secrecy of the vote, an unavoidable consequence was that a voter could more easily "split his ticket," voting for some candidates of one party and some of another. In fact, however, over the next fifteen years the incidence of split-ticket voting increased only marginally from what it had been under the previous system of balloting. The reason was that New York opted for a ballot format which facilitated the continuation of straight-ticket voting, that is, party columns with a circle at the top of each column. For this reason, reformers continued their campaign for ballot reform, finally convincing the legislature in 1913 to enact a law mandating the office bloc ballot format. Under this format the names of the candidates and their respective party labels were arranged according to the offices they were contesting. Straight-ticket voting now required as much effort and patience as did split-ticket voting. The consequence was exactly what the reformers had intended; straight-ticket voting dramatically decreased.

How does a reform which has been so obviously successful become undone? The answer: by an additional reform which has an unintended byproduct. Less than ten years after the switch to the office bloc format, the election law was amended to allow for the use of voting machines. Again, good-government reformers urged the change, arguing that vote counting fraud was far less likely to occur when this modern device was used. The problem, however, which never seems to have been recognized, or at least never brought to public notice, was that the amending law specifically required that the names of the candidates of a political party had to be listed in a single horizontal row or in a single vertical column when machines were used. Although the term "office bloc" continued to be used to describe this ballot format, in fact the adoption of the machine represented a virtual return to the party column ballot of old. To be sure, there was no master lever for a straight party vote; but thanks to the vertical or horizontal symmetry, little effort was required for a voter to cast such a ballot. Accordingly, once the machines came into use the incidence of straight-ticket voting increased to what it had been prior to 1914. Machines became compulsory for the entire state beginning in 1938.

Given the specifications of commercially produced voting machines in the 1920s, New York probably had no alternative but to arrange candidate names according to party rows or party columns. Today, however, as counties throughout the state begin to replace their worn-out machines with newer types of voting devices (the machines are no longer being produced), ballot format options are available (e.g., punch cards as used in California) which do not require that symmetry. Be that as it may, when the legislature amended the election law in 1986 to permit counties to purchase new equipment, the clause which had been adopted in 1922, requiring that candidates of the same party be grouped together, was retained. With no public fanfare or acknowledgment, the revocation of the much heralded reform of 1913 was now complete.

Cross-Endorsement Legislation

A second unanticipated consequence of New York's shift from paper ballots to voting machines was the encouragement given to minor party growth. By the 1930s, New York had become one of the few states which still allowed a candidate to appear on the ballot as the nominee of more than one political party. How should such a nominee be presented on the ballot? Under the office bloc paper ballot the names of the respective nominating parties would simply be listed beside the name of the candidate as that name appeared in the appropriate office grouping. With the voting machine format, however—as well as with the pre-1913 party column paper ballot—the candidate's name would appear separately in each of the rows or columns assigned to the respective nominating parties. Thus, to use a contemporary example, a Republican candidate who was also the nominee of the Conservative party and the Right to Life party would have his name appear on the ballot three times, with two important consequences: (1) Conservative and RTL voters could vote explicitly and exclusively for their own party's candidate; and (2) the leaders of these parties could use the voting results to demonstrate how much their support had contributed to the candidate's total vote. For example, both Conservative and RTL leaders boasted that D'Amato's 1980 senatorial victory was made possible only because of their parties' support. Without these two by-products of the voting machine, it is very doubtful if New York's minor parties could survive today. This conclusion is suggested by the fact that during the period when New York used the office bloc paper ballot the state had a virtual two-party system; yet as soon as the voting machine came into use, minor parties resumed the conspicuous role in state politics which they had played under the pre-1913 party column paper ballot format. The 1986 election law amendment, mentioned above, requiring that any new voting device provide for grouping of candidates by party, guarantees that New York's ballot format will continue to provide support for a multi-party system.

Even more important in assuring minor party strength in the state was an amendment made to the election law in 1947. The Wilson-Pakula law stipulated that in order to enter a party's primary a person had to be an enrolled party member. Both the Republicans and Democrats had been bothered by "outsiders" from the American Labor party entering and winning their primaries. The 1947 law was intended to put a stop to that practice and thereby, it was said, to preserve what was still seen as the state's two-party system. In fact, the 1947 enactment produced the very opposite result, as a few discerning legislators at the time predicted it would. The reason was that the amendment included a proviso that when a party's leaders (e.g., Conservative leaders, RTL leaders) gave their written permission, then a non-member of the party (e.g., Republican D'Amato) could enter that party's primary and, if successful, become that party's candidate in the general election. The stage was now set for the minor party leaders to drive hard bargains with the respective major parties, offering nominations in return for policy and/or patronage favors. Without that bargaining power, it is doubtful if New York's minor parties would long survive.

Voter Participation

By the mid 1950s, New York State had one of the lowest rates of voter participation of any state in the country. One of the reasons was that persons living in urban areas were required to register each year, thus necessitating two trips to the polling station every autumn—once to register and once to cast a ballot in November. Responding to the League of Women Voters' demand for reform, in 1954 the legislature eliminated this dual requirement, and substituted today's system of permanent registration; a person's name would remain registered so long as that person voted in an election at least once every two years. Rather than increasing, however, voter participation in presidential and gubernatorial election years continued to drop; only for the odd-year local elections did the easier requirements seem to make an impact. Undaunted, in 1975 the legislature tried once again to encourage voter participation, this time by allowing new voters, or voters whose registration had lapsed, to register by mail. But still the rate of participation in elections continued to decline. Finally, making still another effort to raise turnout, the legislature in 1981 increased to four years the interval in which a person could fail to vote yet still remain registered. This change likewise seemed to have little or no impact. The lesson to be learned from these many efforts was that the behavior of the citizen voter can be only marginally affected by changes in registration requirements.

There was, however, one significant by-product of these various attempts to increase voting participation, an outcome which seems to have been totally unanticipated. For reasons which are not clear, when the new registration form was constructed in 1975 to accommodate registration by mail, an important modification of the form was introduced. In addition to listing the names of the (then) four official political parties and instructing the registrant to check one of the boxes attached to these names, the new form contained an additional box to be checked by registrants who did "not wish to enroll in any political party." The in-person registration form had contained (and continues to contain) no such option, and although a person using that form had always been able simply to leave all the party boxes blank, many would-be "independents" apparently were unaware that they had that choice. This became clear once the new form was introduced; immediately the number of "independents" among new registrants (i.e., persons choosing not to enroll in a party) increased dramatically. An ironic consequence of the attempt to increase voter participation in general elections, therefore, was that the number of persons eligible to participate in primary elections declined.

Conclusion

Demands for reform have been a continuous component of New York State's political history, and there is every reason to expect that they will continue to be heard. Indeed, in the wake of the massive corruption uncovered in 1986 and 1987 in New York City and elsewhere, we may expect those demands to be voiced more stridently than ever. It has been the purpose of this essay to warn against any easy optimism that reform legislation intended to cure corruption or any other perceived problems will necessarily accomplish its intended purpose. As Lindblom has warned, unrealized or partially realized goals, as well as unanticipated consequences, are the more likely outcomes.

NOTES

1. The introductory quotation is from Charles E. Lindblom "The Science of Muddling Through," *Public Administration Review* 19:79 (1959). Much of the material contained in this essay is taken from the author's *Parties, Elections, and Representation in the State of New York,* New York University Press, 1983.

2. David R. Mayhew, *Placing Parties in American Politics,* Princeton University Press, 1986, Appendix A.

State-Local Relations: The City and Upstate

by

Jeffrey Stonecash

Mr. Stonecash is Associate Professor in the Department of Political Science at the Maxwell School of Citizenship and Public Affairs at Syracuse University.

EDITORS' NOTE: *Much of New York State government is local government, and much of what Albany does involves establishing mandates, setting restraints, and providing funding for localities. This chapter describes the political evolution and current operations of the New York system, which emphasizes local operation of program under state determined standards and with partial state support rather than direct state assumption of responsibility.*

Local governments in New York are heavily intertwined with state politics. While Americans espouse the ideal of autonomous local governments responding to local desires, this has limited relevance to New York. The state dictates many local practices and policies. It also devotes over 60 percent of the state budget to state aid. This pervasive state presence, however, is not the product of some distant government casually intervening. It is a result of the political lobbying of local government officials, and local interest and constituency groups.

The Legal Autonomy of Local Governments

In the United States the legal autonomy of local governments from their states has been uniformly affected by the court ruling known as Dillion's rule. In an 1868 case Judge Dillion ruled that local governments are the legal creations of the state and are subordinate to it. The state government may intervene as it sees fit. This ruling was not popular with local officials, and it prompted many local organizations to seek state legislation to grant local governments "home rule," the right to be autonomous in matters purely local in nature.

This movement began in New York in the late 1880s when the state legislature prohibited the passage of laws which constituted intervention in just one city's affairs. This was followed by a series of constitutional provisions (starting in 1923) and legislative enactments designed to increase local autonomy. These actions had little impact, however, because New York courts consistently rule that the state can intervene when a state interest exists, and the state has the prerogative to decide what a state interest is. This leaves the state government essentially free to intervene as it sees fit. The real limits upon state intrusion are not legal but depend on the inclinations of politicians.

State Restraints and Mandates

According to some versions of democratic theory, public policy should be made at the level where policy is executed. Political groups do not pay much attention to theory, however. Many groups have found it convenient to try to get the local policies they wish imposed by the state government. This is relatively efficient politically because it requires winning only one major political battle rather than winning battles in every local government. Interest groups can use their resources of contributions and promises of voting support on a more limited group of politicians.

The most significant restraint the state has imposed on local governments is a set of limits on local property tax rates, borrowing maximums, and usage of the local income tax. These restraints originated during national recessions in the late 1800s and the 1930s, which reduced government revenue dramatically. Governments could not repay their debts, and bondholders, bankers and the financial community wanted to prevent such incidents in the future. In addition, property owners wanted to limit the amount of money that local governments could extract from them through property taxes, the primary revenue source of local governments. In response, the state imposed broad limits on local revenue-raising capabilities. The state also exempts all governmental and private non-profit organizations from property taxes, but cities must still provide services to these institutions. In some of the larger cities of the state, over 40 percent of property is exempt. The impact of these limits and exemptions is to prompt local officials to direct their efforts to securing more state aid.

The other major area of state intervention in local governments involves mandating local practices. These are pervasive in New York, where a recent study found this state has more mandates than any other. Mandates are perhaps the best example of how groups move to a higher level of government to achieve what would be very costly to achieve in every local government. Public employee groups find going to the state legislature to pursue policy goals particularly effective because it allows them to operate in an arena removed from the glare of local publicity. Groups like teachers, police, and fire personnel, who are well funded and have large memberships spread across the state, have the resources to both offer legislators campaign support and threaten them with the ability to use these resources against the legislator in an election. At the same time legislators are generally feeling little pressure from their home constituency. Local newspapers do not cover state legislative battles over personnel laws very much, if at all. The line of least resistance for legislators is clearly to reward the groups leaning on them heavily.

Mandates dictate a wide range of local matters, such as requiring certain positions, hours of work, levels and ranges of pay, pension contributions, eligibility criteria, and retirement pay levels. These cost local governments considerable sums of money while also limiting the way that local governments can use personnel. Local officials complain that the state legislature should provide funds anytime they require any expenditure, while the legislature, of course, prefers to claim credit for rewarding certain groups, and not for raising taxes to pay for these matters.

While many of these mandates are self-serving, many others serve legitimate public purposes. They create uniform policy across the state, as with mandates involving health standards, special education, and uniform accounting and financial reporting practices. Many of these mandates stem from a belief that government should be active in trying to create a unified set of conditions within the state for citizens, a policy stance legislators like to support.

State Urban Policy and the Upstate-Downstate Divison

Assuming support for state action on local concerns, the state may assume direct responsibility for policy areas, or it may provide more aid to local governments so they can deal with problems. In New York the choice has consistently been the latter. Relative to other states, New York allocates a very high proportion of its state budget for state aid, and the state has a relatively low level of responsibility for the total of state and local expenditure. The decision to rely on the approach of state aid is a result of the upstate-downstate division in the state and the sheer size of New York's expenditure responsibilities. The enormous burden that the state would have to pick up if it assumed New York's programs has made the state legislature unwilling to assume responsibility for local programs. Understanding these matters requires some background.

The upstate-downstate conflict is fundamental and long-standing. It stems from a sense by residents of each area that they are quite different from those of the other area. As early as the 1800s the state was conceived as divided into New York City and the rest of the state, essentially those residing in rural areas and the moderate sized cities along the Erie Canal. In 1890 New York City already comprised 25 percent of the population of the state and was overwhelmingly the largest city in the state.

New York City differed from the rest of the state in that its population was composed of a higher percentage of recent immigrants, who were quite receptive to supporting the Democratic Tammany machine. The city spent large sums of money and was perceived by most of the rest of the state as a sinkhole for public funds. Upstate cities, on the other hand, had fewer ethnics, and were the primary base of support for the Republican party. The Republican party became the vehicle for upstate residents to try to limit the influence of New York City on the state. Upstate residents were convinced that if the the city gained control, it would destroy the financial integrity of the state.

With the goal of containing New York City, Republicans engineered two significant political changes in the 1890s which were to fundamentally shape state-local relations throughout the twentieth century. To reduce the representation of New York City in the state legislature, Republicans inserted a clause in the 1894 state constitution which permanently designated the election districts for the two houses of the legislature. This clause limited New York City to a maximum number of districts, and guaranteed districts to every upstate area, regardless of the population size of the districts. As the population of New York City grew more than the rest of the state during the 1900s, the clause meant that the city could not achieve representation in the legislature equivalent to its proportion of the population of the state.

The other change which the Republicans engineered was the consolidation of New York City. In the late 1800s, New York was much smaller geographically than today and was dominated by Democrats. The Republicans thought they could solve some of the financial and administrative problems of the city by consolidating the city with surrounding areas that were predominantly Republican. The latter move was an attempt to create a city dominated by Republicans, who could use the patronage system of the city to build up their party in the city. A legislative coalition in which upstate Republicans provided the crucial votes put this change into effect in 1898.

With the creation of a city of such considerable size, the rest of the state probably became even more conscious of the possibility of a single city dominating the state. This anxiety has persisted in upstate areas, and politicians from this region regularly can gain publicity in upstate newspapers by portraying themselves as defenders of the state budget against the enormous appetite of New York City. The hostility toward the city also made the state legislature unwilling to change the representation arrangement adopted in 1894 until a change was required in the mid-1960s as a result of United States Supreme Court decisions against the inequality of representation.

The denial of full representation to New York City meant representatives from the city could never dominate the formation of state urban policy. The desire of New York City representatives was generally to have the state assume responsibility for funding or provide expensive programs like welfare, housing, and transportation. The Republican party, based primarily upstate, controlled the legislature and refused to have the state assume this role. This situation largely accounts for choosing aid over state assumption of responsibility.

The importance of this manipulation of representation for state urban policy can be seen by examining the potential dominance of New York City during the 1900s. In 1900, immediately after consolidation, the city constituted 47.3 percent of the population of the state. From 1910 through 1950 the city comprised more than 50 percent of the state population, reaching a peak of 55.3 percent in 1940. Since then the proportion has dropped to around 40 percent. If New York City had ever achieved full representation, the division of labor in the state might have been very different. When reapportionment finally was mandated in the mid-1960s, New York City had slipped below 50 percent of the population, and the chance for New York City to dictate state urban policy was lost. The Republican move of 1894 to control the representation of the city through constitutional provisions proved to be very effective.

State Aid Distribution and the Upstate-Downstate Division

While New York City was unable to get the state to assume responsibility for services, the city in conjunction with other urban areas was effective in getting the state to provide aid to all local governments. The struggles over how much aid to provide, and how to distribute it, however, were still products of the upstate-downstate division.

When politicians decide to distribute state aid, they must have some basis for this distribution. The usual criterion for taking private wealth and using it for public purposes is that there must be some need for it: we must educate our population, help the poor, and take care of health and environmental problems. This has created tension in New York State because New York City contains a significant proportion of the total of needs, and because the sheer size of the population in New York City means that the amount of aid going to the city will be very large (even if it is distributed on the same basis to all cities in the state). Leglislators from the upstate area of the state do not like the way this looks to their constituents.

The magnitude of New York City's problems and their relevance for the state budget can be seen by examining the state aid programs. In 1982, the state allocated $9,375,009,606 to the local assistance fund. Of that total, 49.0 percent went for education, while 24.0 percent went for social services (which includes programs for income support and medical services for the poor and aged). Thus, the dominant issue for legislators is the allocation of money to education and social services.

Of a total state population of 17,558,000 in 1980, New York City comprised 7,071,639 or 40.3 percent. In this population, the city had 762,200 AFDC (Aid For Dependent Children) cases, which is one of the major welfare programs. This represents 68.3 percent of cases in the state. The city has a disproportinate share of Medicaid cases, housing problems, and public school children who need remedial education. It also has a large number of crimes, creating pressures for police expenditures.

Despite this presumed hostility to urban needs, the legislature has not constructed programs entirely hostile to New York City. The proportion of state aid going to the city for various program areas is: general revenue sharing (55.0), education (34.4), social services (68.0), health and environment (51.1), mental health (39.3), transportation (34.2), and housing (35.9).

Whether New York City has received what it should is a subjective judgment, but it is clear that the city has not been ruined by its position of political representation in the legislature. Two factors explain this. This first is that legislators in general are sympathetic to allocating aid on the basis of need. This tendency has been helped along in the last 15 years by the ability of mayors and state legislators from the "big six" (Buffalo, Rochester, Syracuse, Albany, Yonkers, and New York City) to form a coalition to work for legislation on common problems. This coalition has become stronger in recent years as upstate cities have experienced the same problems as New York City.

The second explanation for programs favorable to New York City and other urban areas has to do with the split constituencies of the Republican party. By all appearances, the Republican party should have had virtually complete ability to dominate the formation of urban aid programs. The Democrats have controlled both houses of the legislature only one year since 1940 (1965); in fact, much of that time the Republicans controlled both houses and the governor's position. Since the Republican party is based upstate and the Democratic party draws the bulk of its support from New York City (and some upstate cities) this position of dominance might have resulted in a set of policies detrimental to urban interests.

This never happened because any Republican candidate for governor must appeal to an urban constituency to win. The formula for victory for many years was that a Republican had to win a large plurality upstate, and hold down the margin of loss in New York City to avoid being swamped by the Democratic margin there. In laters years, with the increase in the population of the three New York City suburban counties of Westchester, Nassau, and Suffolk, the formula has been amended to requiring big margins upstate and in these areas, while holding down the New York City loss margin. This evidence for this formula is shown in Table 6, which shows the average winning margin by geographical area for winning and losing Republican candidates since 1934. The patterns of margins of victory by area for winning Republicans clearly follow the formula for success. This means that Republican governors have invariably been more liberal regarding urban programs and aid than their legislative party. This was the case with Nelson Rockefeller, who was a strong advocate of legislation to deal with urban problems. Legislative Republicans, primarily from conservative upstate areas, can remain conservative as long as they win majorities in their local districts.

This tension within the Republican party has resulted in a "net" urban policy which is far more liberal than might be anticipated. Upstate Republicans oppose aid programs which they believe will benefit New York City. A Republican governor like Rockefeller, however, had to appeal to urban constituents to get elected, so he sought to produce a coalition of urban representatives from upstate and downstate. He was able to win support primarily by offering everybody more of everything. The legacy of having to win support across the state is a state aid program which provides high amounts of aid to all local governments.

Producing such a coalition requires making concessions, and the conservative groups in the legislature have not been willing to give urban areas everything they want. For example, the amount of aid each school district receives is determined in part by the average number of students in attendance in the district each day. School districts in central cities have problems with absent students, so they lose aid when such students are not in school. These districts would prefer to have aid distributed on the basis of the number of students enrolled. Suburban districts, which have less difficulty with students being absent, are in favor of using average attendance, and they fare better in the distribution of aid under this approach.

The Future of State Aid

New York state is now in the midst of considerable change, which may change the politics of state aid. The dominance of New York City in the state's politics is steadily declining, and the role of the city's

Table 6

MARGINS OF VICTORY BY AREA FOR WINNING AND LOSING REPUBLICAN GUBERNATORIAL CANDIDATES (1934-1982)

AREA	CANDIDATES WHO LOST (5)	CANDIDATES WHO WON (8)
Upstate non-NYC	184,514	493,450
Suburban NYC	42,385	279,048
New York City	−604,521	−17,219

Source: *Legislative Manual*, various years. (1982 results from *The New York Times*).

suburbs is increasing. This is a reflection of the changing role of these areas as a source of votes. In 1934–50, New York City provided 44.6 percent of the two-party gubernatorial votes, and the city's suburban counties provided 10.6 percent. By 1974–82, the city was providing only 30.4 percent, while the suburban counties of Westchester, Nassau, and Suffolk were 21.7 percent of the vote. During this change, upstate remained relatively stable, starting with 44.8 and ending with 48.1 percent. If the suburban areas remain predominantly Republican, future governors are going to feel more pressure to respond to the concerns of upstate and surburban areas and less pressure to be sensitive to New York City concerns. The city will also receive fewer legislative representatives. At the same time, there is considerable pressure upon politicians to reduce the taxation and expenditure levels within the state. New York has lost a large amount of employment and a lot of this loss is being attributed to state tax levels. The combination of these trends suggest that there will be less support for high levels of urban aid in the future.

Yet, there is the potential of a new source of support for urban aid in the future. With declining growth across the state, the urban problems of stagnant tax bases, declining housing, and aging public facilities have spread to cities and suburbs which once thought that urban aid was primarily for New York City. The populations of these areas may become strong supporters of urban programs.

Ed Koch and the New York City Political Tradition

by

Peter W. Colby

EDITORS' NOTE: *The state's largest city has a long tradition of fascinating and colorful politics and politicians. This brief article assesses the current status of city government.*

New York City politics usually is analyzed in terms of one or more of three major issues in the city's political tradition: the degree of pluralism, the pace of ethnic succession, and the cycle of party corruption and reform. This chapter will extend the analysis of these three themes through the long mayoralty of Edward I. Koch and conclude with a look to the future.

Mayor Ed Koch

The 105th Mayor of New York City was trained as a lawyer and began political life as an activist in the anti-Tammany reform politics of Greenwich Village in the early 1960s. Later, as a Congressman from Manhattan, he was known as one of the most liberal members of the United States House of Representatives. In 1977, he led a six-candidate field in the Democratic Mayoral primary with 21 percent of the vote (see Table 7), defeated Mario Cuomo in the runoff for the Democratic nomination, and then easily won the General Election.[1]

He ran as a combination reformer and serious-minded government manager: "After charisma (Lindsay) and clubhouse (Beame), why not competence (Koch)?" Despite a controversial style, problems with major interest groups, and revelations of corruption in his administration, Mayor Koch won reelection easily in 1981 and 1985, and remains very popular today.

To understand the Koch Administration and the future of New York City's political life, one must first review recent history in terms of our three themes: pluralism, ethnic succession, and reform.

Pluralism in the New York Political Tradition

A generation ago, Wallace Sayre and Herbert Kaufman produced an outstanding book describing city politics through the early 1960s.[2] They asked four questions: What are the prizes of politics? Who wants these prizes? How do those who want them seek to get them? Who wins and who loses? They further provided a set of answers, describing a fairly successful pluralistic system.

1. Every program and policy represented a compromise among interested participants who often included party officers, elected and appointed public officials, city bureaucrats, interest groups leaders, and representatives of state and federal agencies.
2. No single elite group controlled the political and governmental system of New York. There were numerous decision centers with cores

Table 7

FIRST DEMOCRATIC MAYORAL PRIMARY RESULTS

YEAR	WINNER'S PERCENTAGE
1961	61%
1965	45%
1969	33%
1973	35%
1977	21%
1981	60%
1985	64%

and satellites defined by authority and interest respectively. They proceeded to make policy through a process of negotiation and mutual accommodation.

3. The system was generally open and responsive to all who tried to participate—municipal unions, civil rights forces, welfare interest, and community groups among those "recently" incorporated.
4. There was a balance of stability and change. Nobody won or lost too much, all remained supportive of the process. Regardless of specific outcomes, all interest groups continued to be active participants seeking a better result tomorrow.

Naturally, Sayre and Kaufman recognized distinctions in the power of various interests, one of the most crucial being the differences between established groups (professional, business, labor, civic, religious, philanthropic, and ethnic) and what were then "newcomer" groups (poverty, welfare, housing, racial, community, school, and neighborhood). Established groups had access to authority and a stable existence, pursuing political goals as but one aspect of their member services and activities. Their political strategies included testifying at public hearings, consulting with agencies and elected officials, providing technical assistance and advice, serving on committees and boards, and influencing appointments and nominations.

Newcomer groups lacked the access, skills, status, and finances to pursue such strategies, and generally provided few "non-political" services to members and supporters. Lacking alternatives, many turned to protest and confrontation to gain media attention and mobilize constituencies. Winning, rather than compromise, was the necessary outcome to prove the worth of the group to its potential followers.

As Donald Haider has perceptively argued,[3] the system described by Sayre and Kaufman survived more or less intact into the mid-1970s. At first during the late 1960s, the city was able to accommodate the needs of *both* established and newcomer organizations because of economic growth, inflation, new local taxes, and huge increases in inter-governmental aid from the state and particularly the federal government. Still, the success of militant tactics of newcomer groups spilled over to established groups—notably, labor and public bureaucracies—and bred even more use of these hard-line approaches. The city government distributed money *and* authority via the creation of the Metropolitan Transit Authority, the Health and Hospitals Public Benefit Corporation, thirty-two school "districts" within the city system, and, later, community boards for input to city government. The central authorities of the city were weakened substantially.

Although by no means left without influence, the established groups' *common interests* in sound city economy, low taxes, and good basic city services were on the retreat. As a former Lindsay Administration official described it:

> Business came to be viewed as a source of taxes, not jobs; liberal politics dominated sound economics. Profits were somehow wicked. New York discouraged tax and other incentives for private enterprise. We worried about rip-offs, the rich soaking the poor, the inequality of wealth.[4]

These trends continued until the 1975 fiscal crisis, despite the declining economy of the early 1970s. Tax increases, more government borrowing, and budget "gaps" (planning deficits as a political strategy to enhance the chances for getting more state and federal aid) were the preferred approaches, rather than that of slowing the growth of city spending.

The days of reckoning arrived from 1975 to 1978, when the city teetered on the brink of bankruptcy as a result of overspending its revenues. Central control was reasserted as established groups—including business, finance, and labor—with a bottom-line common interest in the general welfare of the city formed a coalition through the Municipal Assistance Corporation, and the Emergency Financial Control Board. The new institutions held the critical power to approve city operating and capital budgets, and to ratify all labor contracts. "A whole new layer of government had been created to contain the multiple pressures to spend."[5]

With startling rapidity, a new governing philosophy emerged,[6] and after the 1977 mayoral election, the new philosophy found a champion in the city's new mayor, Edward I. Koch. Simply put, Koch "reversed the pattern of most New York City politicians since the end of the Second World War by publicly allying with the revenue providers rather than the service demanding sectors of his constituency."[7] In terms of policy, cutting spending and promoting new building and other economic development assumed highest priority. The local economy and the city government's fiscal health improved. In part, this was due to national and especially international factors, but it was at least in part due to Koch's policies. There were no new taxes, certain business tax rates were reduced, no increases in property taxes were approved. Capital improvements were undertaken to stimulate the local economy and rebuild an aging infrastructure. The budget, which grew between 10 and 15 percent annually in the years 1970 to 1975, was actually reduced in the years 1975 to 1980.[8]

As the quantity and quality of city services declined, the poor, as the heaviest users of those services, suffered most. Further redistributive policies were cut more than other areas.[9] The newly emergent groups were cut out of the deal—an affront to their leaders and a cost to their constituents in such policies as tuition at the City University, transit fare increases, social service cutbacks, and reductions in school spending. The public employee unions also suffered, experiencing layoffs, job losses through attrition, wage freezes, and investment of union pension funds in city bonds.

The newcomer groups acquiesced to this situation because of widespread acceptance of the reality of the fiscal crisis and the consequent shifting of public opinion to embrace the new governing philosophy. Although the city's improving economy has made it possible for the city to meliorate these consequences, particularly in mayoral election years, the new priorities appear firmly ensconced over a decade later.

Ethnic Succession and the New York Political Tradition

Politics in New York can also be seen as a pattern in which one ethnic group after another moves to the city, grows in numbers, becomes active in politics, and eventually succeeds to positions of power and influence with all the attendant rewards of city jobs and contracts, public facilities and programs for the neighborhood, and feelings of pride and identification that come from seeing one of their own in leadership positions.[10] In this way, ethnic groups can also be interest groups. Today the facts of life are that the established groups in the city are largely White, and the emergent groups are largely Black and Hispanic. The overlapping cleavages of race and interest tend, of course, to greatly intensify the usual conflict over the tangible prizes of politics.

For some time, the most public manifestation of the ethnic succession battle has been the confrontation between the city's 1.1 million Jewish population and the 1.8 million Black population.[11] This is ironic because in the 1950s and 1960s Jews were the Blacks' closest allies, providing much of the financing and organization skills for the early civil rights movement. As the civil rights movement evolved to more immediate economic goals (affirmative action) and a more radical style (Black power), the alliance collapsed, most visibly in the 1968 city school strike when the Jewish-led teachers union clashed with Black neighborhood activists over community control.

Today, Jewish politicians like Mayor Koch dominate elective office in the city—a fairly recent phenomenon, since the first Jewish mayor was not elected until 1973. Still, Blacks are eager for their turn. In Brooklyn, for example, a Jew succeeded an Italian as borough president and county leader only in the 1980s. Yet, nearly one-half of Brooklyn's 2.6 million people are Black or Hispanic, including two-thirds of the school-age population. Eighty percent of the senior citizens are White. It should be observed that few Hispanics visualize their role as that of helping Blacks assume power, while waiting several decades for still another succession.

Reform and the New York Political Tradition

The basis of political party organization in New York is the county, and in New York City, the counties are the five boroughs of the Bronx, Manhattan (New York County), Queens, Brooklyn (Kings County), and Staten Island (Richmond County). A powerful county leader can, though the office of the Borough President, directly influence the operation of what's left of county government in the city, and have a voice in citywide affairs through the powerful Board of Estimate. On a citywide basis, political influence is based on a shifting coalition of the five county organizations. On a more local level, state assembly districts, of which there are sixty in the city, form the grassroots components of county organizations.

In city politics, the Republican party is nearly totally irrelevant. Thus, battles over issues, class, race, personalities, and ethnicity take place within the Democratic party. As elsewhere, the power of party "machines" is in a considerable state of decline, owing to the end of immigration, the welfare state, media politics, civil service, and reform of election laws and city operations. The triumph of Manhattan reformers over Tammany Hall machine politicians in the early 1960s was, to many New Yorkers, the end of clubhouse politics.[12] Still, especially in the outer boroughs, a leadership position in the party does provide access to policy makers, and some influence over jobs and contracts as well.

Today, New York City employs over 200,000 individuals, and in a single year enters into contracts with over 40,000 businesses—contracts worth around $4.5 billion. It is hardly shocking that a little corruption would sneak into the process. However, the revelations of the mid-1980s exposed wrongdoing of a scope and magnitude that few could accept as an inevitable cost of city operation. Although the details are not of interest, at the bottom of city government, among the workers, over 1,600 were charged with corruption during Mayor Koch's first two terms of office.[13]

Public attention began to focus on this issue in 1985, when about one-half of the city's sewer inspectors, one-half of its electrical inspectors, and one-fourth of its public housing superintendents were arrested.

Then came corruption at the top: The Queens Borough President was implicated and committed suicide, the Bronx Democratic leader was convicted, and several of Mayor Koch's top city commissioners were forced from office amid formal charges or allegations of wrongdoing.

New York has a long tradition of various elements in the city pulling together periodically to support a "fusion" candidate uniting many diverse interest in a common cause to reform city government when corruption within the governing party became widespread. By the late 1980s, many voices were suggesting that the tradition should be revived.

Mayor Koch and the Future

As mayor, Ed Koch has presided over a return to fiscal solvency and emerged as a champion of the working and middle-class homeowners of Staten Island and the farther reaches of the Bronx, Brooklyn, and most of Queens. He won reelection overwhelmingly in 1981, and repeated the feat in 1985 despite having antagonized minorities, labor, and liberals by his policies, his symbolic stands opposing affirmative action, his rallying the city against the transit strike, and his advocating the death penalty.

His opposition in 1985 included a white liberal, the two-term City Council President Carol Bellamy, and a black state senator, Herman "Denny" Farrell. Bellamy scored best in Manhattan and adjacent areas of Brooklyn, Farrell in the minority neighborhoods of the Bronx, Manhattan, Brooklyn, and Queens. Beyond these limited pockets of opposition, Koch won over 70 percent of the vote in every other assembly district, overwhelming his opponents in the city's middle-class neighborhoods, far from Manhattan. It is fairly clear where the heart of Koch's pro-business, anti-tax, tough-on-crime appeal lies. However, it must also be noted that Koch dropped below 40 percent of the vote in only four of the sixty districts; Bellamy scored above 40 percent in only two; and Farrell was above 40 percent in just three districts. The victory was truly citywide.

On the surface, those interested in a return to a more open pluralistic politics, more liberal policies, an acceleration of Blacks and Hispanics up the ladder of ethnic succession, and a revival of reform-oriented political activity may have a long struggle ahead. At the highest level, the mayor's office, it appears likely that Mayor Koch or a candidate of similar style and priorities is most likely to continue in office. In an overwhelmingly Democratic city, mayors are most likely to emerge from a Democratic

Table 8

NEW YORK CITY DEMOCRATS BY RACIAL/ETHNIC GROUP

GROUP	PERCENTAGE
White	57.1%
Black	27.1%
Hispanic	12.0%
Other	4.1%

Based on data from *Empire State Report Weekly,* June 24, 1985.

primary where one must lead the field with at least 40 percent of the vote in a possibly multi-candidate first round or face a one-on-one runoff. As Tables 8 and 9 make clear, the votes are not there for a candidate with appeal only to a Black or Hispanic constituency. Mayors will continue to be elected by White Catholic and Jewish voters in the foreseeable future.

On the other hand, there are indeed two New Yorks. One is fairly prosperous and includes a growing number of middle-class Blacks and Hispanics, many moving up the ladder with government jobs just as others did in the past. However, the poor New York is desperately poor and a very large group: one in four New Yorkers lives below the poverty level; two-thirds of city school children are Black or Hispanic, and 60 percent drop out before graduation; one-third of public school children will be on public assistance at some time during their school years; thousands of children live in shelters for the homeless; and the percentage of female-headed households in the Black community has increased from 21 percent in 1960 to nearly 50 percent today. The flashpoint between the two New Yorks is crime, and the Bernhard Goetz subway shooting and Howard Beach incidents speak volumes about the true feelings between haves and have-nots, and about the related racial tensions between Black and White.

Table 9

NEW YORK CITY DEMOCRATS BY RELIGION

GROUP	PERCENTAGE
Catholic	44.0%
Protestant	28.1%
Jewish	24.1%
Other	4.1%

Based on data from *Empire State Report Weekly,* June 24, 1985.

At some point, the old emergent groups of the 1960s are going to re-emerge with renewed militancy seeking a greater share of the public policy pie. Yet they will confront an establishment determined not to forget the fiscal crisis and the free-spending programs and loss of governmental control that fueled the near-bankruptcy. Striking a new balance between these forces will be a difficult challenge for the city's political leadership in the 1990s.

NOTES

1. In New York City, the leading candidate in the party primary must win at least 40 percent of the vote to move directly to a general election against the nominees of other parties. Otherwise, the top two candidates compete in a runoff ten days after the primary.

2. Wallace Sayre and Herbert Kaufman, *Governing New York City,* New York: Russell Sage, 1965.

3. Donald Haider, "Sayre and Kaufman Revisited: New York City Government Since 1965," *Urban Affairs Quarterly,* 15, 1979, pp. 123-45.

4. Ken Auletta, "New York: the Liberals' Vietnam," *Washington Monthly,* 10, 1978, p. 45.

5. Robert W. Bailey, *The Crisis Regime,* Albany: State University of New York Press, 1984, p. 188.

6. Peter W. Colby, "Public Policy in New York State Today," in Peter W. Colby, ed., *New York State Today,* Albany: State University of New York Press, 1985, p. 228.

7. Paul Kantor and Stephen David, "The Political Economy of Change in Urban Budgetary Politics," *British Journal of Political Science,* 13, 1983, p. 271.

8. Charles Brecher and Raymond Horton, "Retrenchment and Recovery: American Cities and the New York Experience," *Public Administration Review,* March/April 1985, pp. 268-69.

9. *Ibid.,* p. 272.

10. See Nathan Glazer and Daniel Patrick Moynihan, *Beyond the Melting Pot,* 2nd edition, Cambridge, Mass.: M.I.T. Press, 1970; and Daniel Patrick Moynihan, "Patterns of Ethnic Succession: Blacks and Hispanics in New York City," *Political Science Quarterly,* Spring 1979, pp. 1-14.

11. See Dorothy Rabinowitz, "Blacks, Jews, and New York Politics," *Commentary,* 66, 1978, pp. 42-47; and Michael Kramer, "Blacks and Jews: How Wide the Rift?" *New York,* February 4, 1985, pp. 26ff.

12. James Q. Wilson, *The Amateur Democrat,* Chicago: University of Chicago Press, 1966.

13. Nicholas Pileggi, "The New Corruption," *New York,* November 11, 1985, pp. 42ff.

A Short History of New York's Two Major Parties

by

Karen Markoe

Ms. Markoe is Professor of History in the Humanities Department at the State University of New York Maritime College in Fort Schuyler, Bronx, New York.

EDITORS' NOTE: *Often the best way to understand the present is to study the past. In this essay, the author describes the three historical party systems of New York and the events and people that have shaped the Republican and Democratic Parties of today.*

KAREN MARKOE

Although minor parties often have existed in New York State as they do today, a vital two-party political system has been the dominant characteristic of state government for nearly two hundred years. Like their national counterparts, New York State's two major parties have been spreading umbrellas under which assorted political viewpoints have sought shelter. Despite the absence of clear ideological differences (there is no consistent conservative versus liberal split), Federalists, Whigs and modern Republicans have leaned toward conservative, business politics. The opposition Democrats, earlier called Democratic-Republicans or just plain Republicans, have been more attentive to downstate immigrants and working people throughout the state.

Reform has been a strong feature of the parties during various stages of their evolution, manifesting itself in different ways. Republican reform, and Federalist and Whig reform before it, have come with a strong dose of *noblesse oblige,* as in the state career of Theodore Roosevelt. Democratic reform, and certainly Democratic rhetoric, have had more proletarian roots. The forward looking governorship of Al Smith is an example. Bear in mind that these are generalizations which break down under close scrutiny. Thus, Franklin Roosevelt fulfilled Hamilton's criteria of being both "rich and well born." Yet Franklin Roosevelt was a Democrat. Nevertheless, broad generalizations are useful in making sense of the muddy political waters of New York State's two party systems.

Another generalization is the strong influence of New York's political leaders in the national arena. In this century alone, New York State governors have played an extraordinary role in United States politics. These include Theodore Roosevelt, Charles Evans Hughes, Alfred E. Smith, Franklin Roosevelt, Herbert Lehman, Thomas Dewey, and Nelson Rockefeller.

Both parties have contributed to the talent pool, but not equally in each period of history. For despite the persistence of a two-party system, seldom have the two parties alternated holding power every two or four years. Instead, one party dominated an entire era to be succeeded, sometimes decades later, by the party waiting in the wings.[1] From the end of World War I to the middle of World War II, the governorship was in Democratic hands for all but two years. From 1944 to 1975, the State House was controlled by Republican governors, except for four years.[2] It appears that currently the governorship is again in a Democratic era.

Often the New York State legislature has worked against the governor, miring the state in political stalemate. Early in the nineteenth century, for example, Federalist legislatures often ruled with Democratic-Republican governors[3] and in this century even extremely popular Democratic governors—Franklin Roosevelt and Herbert Lehman are two—have been forced to share power with Republican controlled legislatures. But this state of affairs is less disruptive to the political process than it might appear, especially when the state is led by a strong executive; and the state has been blessed with a great number of forceful and visionary governors.

The Emergence of Political Parties

Although something resembling parties was in existence in colonial New York, these entities were simply factions that coalesced around political families such as the Livingstons, Schuylers and DeLanceys. They were not parties in the modern sense of the word. It is to George Washington's first term in office that we must look for the beginning of the two-party system both in the state as well as the nation.[4]

The first two parties were the Federalists and the Democratic-Republicans. The recognized head and ideological leader of the Federalists was an adopted son of New York, Alexander Hamilton. As Washington's trusted Secretary of the Treasury, Hamilton supported measures to strengthen the national government at the expense of the states. John Jay, the first chief justice of the United States, was the only Federalist governor of the state. Other leading Federalists included Philip Schuyler and Robert Livingston. While there were simply too many Federalists for them all to be "rich and well born," it is true that most of the large property holders in New York were Federalists. Federalists, often accused of aristocratic leanings, did, in fact, distrust democratic principles.

The opposition Democratic-Republicans supported the states rights, agrarian views of Thomas Jefferson and James Madison. George Clinton,

EVOLUTION OF THE TWO MAJOR PARTIES
IN NEW YORK STATE

FIRST PARTY SYSTEM	SECOND PARTY SYSTEM	THIRD PARTY SYSTEM
Democratic-Republicans vs. Federalists (1790s–1820)	Democrats vs. Whigs (1834–1854)	Democrats vs. Republicans (1854–Present)

New York's first governor, was a devout Jeffersonian, and extremely popular among the state's lower classes.

The differences in outlook between the two parties were exacerbated by foreign policy issues. Hamilton's financial program necessitated a British connection, while Democratic-Republicans led by Jefferson, were "well-wishers" of the French Revolution. The well-publicized marriage of George Clinton's daughter to "Citizen" Genet, representative of the French revolutionary government in the United States, accentuated party differences, even within the confines of state politics.

George Clinton nurtured the political ambitions of Aaron Burr, who had a promising career before running for vice-president on Jefferson's ticket in 1800. Due to an omission in the Constitution (later corrected by the twelfth amendment which prescribed separate ballots for president and vice-president), and a display of perfect party discipline by Democratic-Republican electors, Burr tied with Jefferson for president in the electoral college. Hamilton's was the leading voice in the selection of Jefferson over Burr for President in 1800. The long standing personal and political enmity between Hamilton and Burr resulted in Jefferson's election, and the subsequent death of Hamilton, New York's greatest Federalist, as a result of a duel with Burr in 1804. Thereafter, Burr's strange career as an adventurer, and his trial for treason (although he was found not guilty) short-circuited the political ambitions of one of the state's most colorful figures.

These leadership losses notwithstanding, New York politics, in the early nineteenth century was filled with men of extraordinary talent. The most influential was De Witt Clinton, nephew of the state's first governor. He served as mayor of New York City in the early part of the century, while simultaneously holding state office, first as a member of the senate and then as lieutenant-governor. In 1817, he was elected governor for the first time, polling better than 95 percent of the vote. His administrations had an enormous impact upon the state. Clinton was largely responsible for introducing the spoils system into New York politics, and particularly for making the Tammany Society a powerful political machine of the Democratic-Republicans. The state's public school system took its first tentative steps under the watchful eye of De Witt Clinton. But he is best known for his vigorous support of the project linking the Great Lakes to the Hudson River and New York City, the Erie Canal. Despite strong opposition from within Tammany, and Martin Van Buren's upstate followers, Clinton and his canal remained exceedingly popular.

Meanwhile, following the War of 1812, the Federalist Party, which had been hostile to the war with England, was viewed by the country at large as vaguely treasonous. The Federalists soon disappeared from the national scene. However, in New York, the Federalists held on longer than elsewhere, keeping up the semblance of opposition to the Democratic-Republicans until 1820. But Democratic-Republicans found little joy in their dominance of state politics. The party became increasingly factionalized in the two decades following the War of 1812. Each faction was united less by issues than by devotion to a leader and the spoils that success at the polls would bring.

The major anti-Clinton faction was led by New York's master politician of the early nineteenth century, Martin Van Buren, whose supporters were known as Bucktails because they sported the tails of deer in their hats. Van Buren was a strong advocate of the spoils system as a means of promoting party discipline. Bucktail leaders, collectively known as the Albany Regency, merged into the radical wing of the Democratic party (later known as Barnburners). Radical leaders such as Van Buren, Silas Wright and William Marcy,[5] with a strong following of farmers and laborers, were parsimonious in spending for public improvements and slow to grant charters for banks. They stood against the extension of slavery into the territories. The radicals were opposed by the conservative Hunkers (accused of "hunkering" after office), like Horatio Seymour, who, eager to retain a national outlook, were cautious on the emerging slavery issue and earnestly promoted canal building and bank charters.

The Whig Party Challenges Andrew Jackson

During the presidency of Andrew Jackson, full-fledged national and state parties arose to counter the strong leadership of "King Andrew." Taking their name from the historic opposition party to the King of England, the anti-Jacksonians called themselves Whigs. In New York State, led by the brilliant editor, Thurlow Weed, the Whigs built upon the political opposition to the secretive Masonic Order, the Anti-Masons. Whigs were usually "haves," in favor of internal improvements, protective tariffs and a strong banking system. On the national level, Henry Clay's American System was the clearest expression of Whig belief. Meanwhile, Van Buren became the leader of the Jacksonians who soon dropped Republican from their name in favor of the simpler Democrat. Both nationally and in New York State, the second American party system was born.

In 1838, Weed engineered the election of his protege, William Seward, to the governorship. The Whig triumph, however, was short-lived. Widespread opposition to the Whigs' penchant for spending huge sums for canals and railroads soon returned the Democrats to power. By the late 1840s, the political division between Whig and Democrat had grown murky. Both parties contained dissident factions, and large groups of voters joined third-party movements, especially the anti-immigrant American or Know-Nothing Party. A particular New York political issue involved large numbers of tenant farmers who worked their lands under archaic lease-holds. These farmers voted for candidates running under anti-rent banners.

In 1848, a national issue split the Democratic Party. The subject was the Wilmot Proviso, which was designed to exclude slavery from any lands acquired from Mexico. The Hunkers opposed the Proviso; the Barnburners supported it. Barnburners, responding to a call from a rising star in the New York organization, Samuel Tilden, met at Utica in June, 1848, to form their own party. They nominated Martin Van Buren for president and John A. Dix for governor. Later that summer they joined forces with delegates from eighteen states to form the Free Soil Party. The Free Soilers of 1848 in both membership and ideology foreshadowed the Republican Party of the next decade.

Meanwhile, the split in Democratic ranks resulted in a Whig victory in the state and the nation in 1848. In 1849, William Seward became a U.S. Senator from New York. When President Zachary Taylor died the following year, Vice-President Millard Fillmore, a New York Whig from Cayuga County, became president. His support of the 1850 Compromise, and particularly the hated Fugitive Slave Law, caused a schism in the state party. Weed and Fillmore went their separate ways. Pro-Fillmore conservatives, known as Silver Grays, the color of the hair of their leader, Francis Granger, walked out of the Whig Party rather than be dominated by "Woolly Heads," as Weed and Seward men were called.

Because of the lack of Whig cohesion in 1852, Democrat Horatio Seymour was elected governor. *Herald Tribune* editor Horace Greeley proclaimed the death of the Whig organization. However, in the state, the Whigs managed to stay alive for another two and a half years. The decision to keep the party going while it was being abandoned all over the nation proved to be enormously significant. As late-comers to the ranks of the new Republican Party, the New York leaders temporarily forfeited much of the influence that they had been used to wielding in national political councils.

The Establishment of the Current Two-Party System

Although the issue of slavery was decisive in determining new party alignments, other issues also stirred strong emotions in the 1850's. One was nativism, brought on by the influx of a large number of immigrants, particularly Irish Catholics, to New York City. Another was temperance reform, encouraged by the 1851 Maine prohibition law. Party lines, however, were redrawn permanently over the issue of the Kansas-Nebraska Act. This act repealed the 1820 Missouri Compromise, which had prohibited slavery in the Louisiana Territory above 36° 30′. The imbroglio over Kansas-Nebraska destroyed the Whigs and created the free soil Republicans. Within the state, the new Republican Party was dominated by Seward and Weed. Free soil Democrats joined the party in large numbers.

Despite strong misgivings among Democrats, especially among the Soft-shell faction, the remaining New York Democratic Party acquiesced to the expansion of slavery in the territories. In 1856, the voters decided in favor of the Republicans and Preston King became New York's first Republican governor. However, Weed was unable to prevent Seward's loss to Lincoln as the party's standardbearer at Chicago in 1860. Still the Republicans began their political life in the state with high hopes and the talents of extraordinary men including the editorial triumvirate Horace Greeley *(Tribune)*, Henry Raymond *(Times)*, and William Cullen Bryant *(Post)*.

The state's current two-party system, Democratic and Republican, was firmly in place by the Civil War. Although both parties have evolved to accomodate themselves to changing state issues, there is a strong element of consistency in each party's base of support. Republicans benefited from their identification with a big business economy. Democratic voting rolls were expanded by immigrants, especially downstate, whose needs the party faithfully represented.

Following the Civil War, the industrial revolution nourished political corruption and bossism in state governments everywhere. New York was no exception. Special interest politics rather than genuine democratic rule defined the Gilded Age. Publicly both parties loudly condemned corruption, while both were manifestly corrupt. Tammany boss William Marcy Tweed and Republican boss Roscoe Conkling were firmly in control. Tweed's scandalous rule, even in an age of excess, was too blatant to ignore. The *Harpers Weekly* cartoons of Thomas Nast and the disclosures of reformer Samuel Tilden helped put Tweed in prison.

Tweed's downfall was followed by two decades of able Democratic governors, but Republicans led by spoilsman Conkling generally controlled both the state senate and the assembly. While Grant was president, Conkling dispensed thousands of federal jobs to state Republicans. Nationally, Conkling headed the Republican faction known as the Stalwarts, whose chief rivals were the Half-Breeds led by James G. Blaine. Stalwart Collector of the New York Customs House, Chester A. Arthur, was given second place on the national ticket in the 1880 election. When President James Garfield was assassinated, Arthur became president.

In 1882, a solid reform candidate, Democrat Grover Cleveland, was elected governor of the state. A Republican member of the state legislature, Theodore Roosevelt, joined Cleveland to promote civil service reform. When Cleveland was elected president in 1884, he was succeded by David B. Hill, an able and honest boss. But the hard times brought on by the Panic of 1893 ended the Democratic era and forestalled the party's complete ascendancy for the next fifteen years.

The two-party equilibrium with executive and legislative power split between the parties produced a period of stalemate that on the national scene has been referred to as "the politics of dead center." Still there were sporadic advances made in the last decades of the nineteenth century, especially in the areas of civil reform, conservation, railroad regulation, and factory reform.

The Twentieth Century

The Progressive era did not leave New York behind. Progressives were to be found in both parties; Republican Theodore Roosevelt and Democrat Robert Wagner are clear examples. Indeed, New York was a leading Progressive state, despite the existence of anti-reform politicians such as Boss Thomas C. Platt, who dominated the state's Republican Party in the waning years of the nineteenth century. Platt engineered passage of the Greater New York bill, which joined Brooklyn to New York City in one huge metropolis. He allowed Roosevelt the gubernatorial nomination in 1898, despite Roosevelt's maverick tendencies. Two years later Platt was instrumental in kicking Teddy "upstairs" to the vice-presidency. From that position, Roosevelt became president when William McKinley was assassinated.

Roosevelt's sometime Progressivism was outstripped by Charles Evans Hughes, an apolitical Republican governor who gained popular recognition as a result of his skillful investigations of the state's gas and insurance companies. For four years, Hughes, disregarding the protests of party leaders, secured labor legislation and appointed investigative commissions that were central to the programs of Progressive reformers. His ascension to the U.S. Supreme Court left a partial void, but reforms continued, guided through the legislature by two outstanding Tammany men, Robert F. Wagner in the senate and Alfred E. Smith in the assembly. Prior to U.S. entry into the First World War, these two Democrats made New York the leader in labor reform.

The state's reform impetus continued despite the conservative reaction that the nation experienced in the 1920's. Al Smith made New York a model of reform. Soon afterward, much of the New Deal was anticipated during Franklin Roosevelt's tenure as New York's governor in the early days of the Depression. When Roosevelt became president, he was succeeded as governor by another reformer, Herbert Lehman, who worked well with the new president. From New York City, Mayor Fiorello La Guardia, a nominal Republican, whom Democrats voted for on a Fusion ticket, was a strong supporter of the New Deal.

Certain generalizations can be made about the two-party system in New York State in the quarter century following the end of World War II. For one, there were many more Democrats enrolled in the state than Republicans. That fact notwithstanding, elective offices usually went to Republicans. From 1956 to 1970, New York was the seventh most Republican state in the nation and the most Republican among the ten most important states measured according to their social and political influence.[6] As in earlier eras of its history, postwar politics were dominated by nationally recognized political leaders. Foremost among them were Republicans Thomas Dewey and Nelson Rockefeller. Rockefeller was governor for fifteen years, longer than any other person except the state's first governor, George Clinton.

In the most recent past, Democrats have managed to keep control of the executive branch. This is in keeping with the state's proclivity to alternate long stretches of one party's rule with long stretches of the other's, at least in the governorship.

The state, of course, does not operate in a vacuum. The fortunes of the national parties, sometimes, but not always, are a determinant of state politics. However, strong state leaders of either party can and do overcome national trends.

It appears that the influence of party politics in this state and others is on the decline. Astute political observers cite several reasons for the decline including: government welfare in the place of the largesse that was once offered by the parties; television, which allows candidates to appeal directly to the voters without the intermediary of the party functionary; and in New York, a recent (1966) direct primary law which allows candidates who receive at least 25 percent of the party's convention vote to run in the primary.[7]

Still, the two-party system is very much in place. The Democratic Party of Mario Cuomo is the lineal descendant of the party of George Clinton. It still retains its flavor as the people's party, although the states' rights orientation of the Jeffersonians did not survive the First World War. The Republican Party bears some resemblance to its two forebearers, the Federalists and the Whigs. Nelson Rockefeller's predilection for business interests and positive government had much in common with the philosophies of Federalist Alexander Hamilton and

Whig William Seward. Indeed, Seward was one of the founders of the modern Republican party.

The current two-party system has survived much longer than its predecessors and it continues to show great strength despite the declining influence of the political parties themselves. From this vantage point it appears that New York State in its third century of existence will continue its adherence to a two-party system, a system which has brought an extraordinary number of talented leaders to the service of the state and nation.

NOTES

1. This is the case primarily with the governorship. The state legislature has been more consistently Republican.

2. Beginning in 1938, New York governors were elected for a term of four years. The only Republican governor in the earlier period was Nathan L. Miller, who was elected in 1920. The only Democratic governor in the later period was Averell Harriman, who was elected in 1954.

3. Federalists won in 1809, 1812, 1813 and 1814.

4. Some historians refer to the division on the adoption of the Constitution between supporters (Federalists) and opponents (Anti-Federalists) as the first two party system. I have chosen to follow the lead of V.O. Key and others who have not. See, for example, William Nisbet Chambers and Walter Dean Burnham, *The American Party Systems,* New York: Oxford University Press, 1967, p. 5.

5. Marcy is perhaps best remembered for a line in a speech that he delivered in the U.S. Senate: "To the victor belongs the spoils of the enemy." The term "spoils system" derives from this.

6. Gerald Benjamin, "Patterns in New York State Politics," in Robert H. Connery and Gerald Benjamin, editors, *Governing New York State: The Rockefeller Years,* New York, Proceedings of the Academy of Political Science, May, 1974, p. 31.

7. Oren Root, *Persons and Persuasions,* New York: Norton, 1974, pp. 237–8.

The Tail Wagging the Dog: Multi-Party Politics

by

Robert J. Spitzer

Mr. Spitzer is Chairman of the Political Science Department
at State University College at Cortland, New York,
and author of *The Presidency and Public Policy,*
a study of presidential policy-making in Congress.

EDITORS' NOTE: *In New York, minor parties have played and continue to play a key role in state politics. This chapter describes why minor parties have found relative prosperity in the Empire State, how they have been able to exercise considerable leverage over the Republicans and Democrats, and what all this means for the state and its citizens.*

Robert J. Spitzer

> I believe that the people of the state of New York are finding that the minor parties are the tail that wags the dog, and are seeking to impose their candidates on the major parties.
>
> Mayor Edward I. Koch
> New York City, 1982
> Quoted in the *Ithaca Journal,*
> August 26.

Any basic textbook in American politics will inform the reader that America has a two-party system. Despite periodic regional and national third-party thrusts,[1] party politics have been dominated indisputably by the Democrats and Republicans. Why, then, is Mayor Koch worried about minor party "blackmail" in New York?

The answer begins with the basic acknowledgment that the structure of federalism in the United States has engendered not merely one national party system, but 51 party systems: one at the national level, and one for each of the 50 states. The U.S. Constitution left to each state the responsibility of formulating and regulating its own electoral structure. Thus, many states have evolved unusual if not unique party practices, and New York's system is certainly one of the more esoteric. But aside from illustrating how federalism engenders electoral permutations, the case of New York also demonstrates the decisive importance of electoral/legal structures in shaping party politics, and the key role minor parties can play, especially when the two major parties compete actively, as they do in New York.

History

New York has witnessed the emergence of no less than a dozen minor parties during the twentieth century.[2] Of this dozen, three maintain an automatic slot for all elections on the state ballot through 1986. These three, in order of formation, are the Liberal Party, the Conservative Party, and the Right to Life Party. (Figure 2 depicts a copy of the state's party enrollment form, giving the enrollment choices available to voters through 1986.)

The oldest of these, the Liberal Party, was an offshoot of the American Labor Party. The latter was formed by a group of socialists and trade unionists seeking a way to support President Roosevelt and other liberal-leftist candidates without working through the corrupt Democratic Party,

Enrollment No. VOID
Name of Voter VOID
Registration No. VOID
Address
Date VOID
City or Town
Ward/Assembly District
Election District

I hereby state that I am in general sympathy with the principles of the party which I have designated by my mark hereunder.

VOID

DEMOCRATIC	REPUBLICAN	CONSERVATIVE	LIBERAL	RIGHT TO LIFE
○	○	○	○	○

VOID

INSTRUCTIONS

Make a cross x mark or a check ✓ mark with a pencil or pen in the circle under the emblem of the party with which you wish to enroll. Persons not wishing to enroll in a political party are to sign the form unmarked. Marks in more than one circle, will void the enrollment.

VOID VOID

Signature

Figure 2. New York State Party Enrollment Form

then dominated by Tammany Hall.[3] The success of the Labor Party (ALP) in bargaining with the major parties was such that it attracted more radical elements, and in 1943 many of the original founders, including Alex Rose, broke away and formed the Liberal Party. Dominated by Rose until his death in 1976, the Liberal Party has generally sided with liberal Democratic candidates, though it did support a number of moderate Republicans in the 1960s.

The Conservative Party was also founded as a result of dissatisfaction with a major party. After his election as Governor in 1958, Nelson Rockefeller dominated New York's Republican Party until 1974, when he resigned to become Vice-President. But Rockefeller's brand of liberal Republicanism was distasteful to many traditional conservative Republicans, especially in the business and professional class, and a group of them combined in 1961 to offer a conservative alternative to Rockefeller Republicanism. They also hoped to pressure the Republicans to move to the right.[4] The Conservatives have generally identified with conservative Republicans, especially after Rockefeller's departure.

The Right to Life Party (RTLP) was the most recent addition to New York's multi-party system. But whereas the Conservatives and Liberals were founded by political activists and business leaders, the RTLP began inauspiciously among a book discussion group in the home of a Merrick, Long Island housewife. The party's grassroots beginning was prompted by attempts in the State Legislature to liberalize the state's abortion law. Those attempts succeeded in 1970, and the concerns of these formerly apolitical individuals accelerated when the Supreme Court ruled in 1973 *(Roe v. Wade)* that women had a right to a safe, legal abortion.[5] Unlike its other, minor party counterparts, the RTLP is predicated on a single issue—that of opposition to abortion. The salience of this issue for some New York voters was evidenced when, in 1978, the RTLP succeeded in establishing its place on the New York ballot. The method by which the RTLP and New York's other minor parties established themselves and extended their influence over the state's electoral landscape reveals both the potency of electoral structures, and the fragility of pure two-party politics.

New York's Electoral Structure

To understand how electoral structures encourage parties in New York, one must begin with the initial establishment of a party. According to state election law, a political party may establish an automatic ballot line for all New York elections by fielding a candidate for governor who receives at least 50,000 votes in the general election.[6] If this threshold is reached, the party is guaranteed a ballot position in all New York elections for the next four years (until the next gubernatorial election). If no automatic ballot slot exists for a party or candidate, an individual seeking statewide office must obtain at least 20,000 petition signatures (signature requirements are less for non-statewide offices). Any registered voter may sign an independent candidate's petition, regardless of the voter's party affiliation, unless the voter has already signed a competing candidate's petition. In comparison with ballot access requirements in other states, New York's is one of the most demanding. Despite this fact, determined and organized third parties can endure in New York where they cannot in other states by virtue of another characteristic of state law. Thus, once a party does gain automatic ballot access, it must work to keep that slot and enhance the party's influence. The key provision of New York election law that helps the minor parties is the cross-endorsement rule. It says, very simply, that parties may nominate candidates already endorsed by other parties. The votes a candidate receives on all his/her lines are then added together in the final count to determine the winner. Only two other states have this provision—Vermont and Connecticut. But in Vermont, the lack of close party competition between the major parties precludes the likelihood of minor parties providing the margin of difference. Connecticut possesses a high minimum in gubernatorial races (20 percent of the vote) as a requirement for party recognition.

The cross-endorsement system has a number of consequences for the New York Party system, the sum total of which cause New York to resemble, in certain respects, European multi-party systems. *First,* this provision removes a major impediment to voters casting votes for minor parties—that is, the "wasted vote" syndrome. Voters frequently have preferences for third party candidates, but refrain from voting for them because of the feeling that they are throwing away their vote on a candidate or party that cannot win. But according to the cross-endorsement rule, votes cast for a candidate anywhere on the ballot are added to the candidate's total.

Second, one can easily calculate how many votes a party contributes to a candidate by observing the vote count on each line. Many quickly point out that a candidate would receive about the same total number of votes whether he/she appeared on one line or several, but candidates *perceive* that every line helps, especially in this politically competitive state. And who is to say that minor parties make no contribution under any circumstances? Evidence of the importance candidates attach to multiple party endorsements can be seen in the frequency of cross-endorsements. In 1978, for example, 145 of 210 state legislators had more than one ballot line endorsement.

Third, minor parties may go beyond merely offering an additional line by offering the *only* line for a candidate denied a major party line. While not a common occurrence, there have been instances of major party candidates denied a major line who have gone on to win election on a minor party line. In 1969, then incumbent Republican New York Mayor John Lindsay was defeated in the Republican primary by John Marchi. But Lindsay was nevertheless re-elected by running on the Liberal Party line. It was later said that no Liberal Party activist seeking a municipal job went without work. In 1970, the Conservative Party succeeded in electing one of its own, James Buckley, to the U.S. Senate in a three-way race against the Democratic nominee, Richard Ottinger, and a liberal anti-Nixon Republican, Charles Goodell.

Fourth, minor parties can run their own candidates, or endorse others, to punish major party candidates by depriving them of votes. In 1966, the Liberal Party ran the popular Franklin D. Roosevelt, Jr. for Governor, instead of endorsing the Democratic candidate, Frank O'Connor. Incumbent Nelson Rockefeller was viewed as being vulnerable to defeat that year, and the over half-million votes garnered by Roosevelt deprived O'Connor of the election (he lost by 392,000 votes). Alex Rose, then the leader of the Liberal Party, commented later that the move to nominate someone other than the Democratic nominee was sparked at least partly by a desire for retribution against Democratic leaders who were so sure of victory with or without Liberal support that they brushed aside attempts by Rose to have input in the process of nominating the Democratic candidate.[7]

Finally, minor parties can nominate candidates before the major parties to try and influence the choices of the major parties. Recent New York politics is replete with examples. In 1982, the Liberal party moved early to nominate Mario Cuomo for Governor. Many felt that this influenced the subsequent Democratic primary between Cuomo and New York Mayor Ed Koch in Cuomo's favor because Democrats feared that if Cuomo lost the Democratic primary, his name would still appear on the November ballot, and as a result Democratic-Liberal votes would be split as in 1966, allowing Republican Lewis Lehrman to be elected. In 1980, an unknown town supervisor from Hempstead, Long Island, Alfonse D'Amato, received a critical early boost in his campaign for the U.S. Senate by receiving the nomination of the Conservative Party. He then went on to defeat incumbent Jacob Javits in the Republican primary and win election in November.

Major party anxiety over this "tail wags dog" syndrome has recently led leaders of both major parties to propose that the cross-endorsement provision be wiped from the books. A Democratic party resolution considered briefly by party leaders denounced cross-endorsements in saying: "The process has led to many cases where the people able to dispense such cross-endorsements obtain influence out of all proportion to the people they represent." [8] Similar sentiments have been expressed by the Republicans.[9] Despite this current discontent, the major parties learned to live with insurgent parties and factions (they first appeared on the scene at the turn of the century), which generally arose in reaction to disclosures of corrupt and autocratic major-party practices. Minor parties thus provided a vent for reformist zeal. But those minor parties that survived soon made their peace with the major parties. If major party bosses had succeeded in suppressing dissident reformist parties, enhanced public outrage might have cost the bosses control of their own party machines. The possibility of this occurring caused party leaders to at least tolerate the existence of these dissident elements.

These five factors outline a significant degree of electoral potency for minor parties; and it is evident that the major parties decry the extent of influence. Successful moves to change the system have been blocked, however, by a state legislature populated with representatives who have benefited from the system.

Minor Party Leverage

New York's third parties are interested in maximizing their influence, but their primary goal is not supplanting one of the major parties, since

New York's system allows them to acquire rewards and influence without actually winning elections on their own. *First,* minor parties will trade their lines and their support for patronage, usually in the form of jobs, as the Liberals received after Lindsay's re-election. In 1978, Republican gubernatorial candidate Perry Duryea sought the Conservative Party line in his unsuccessful bid to unseat Hugh Carey. Since Duryea's conservative credentials were less than sterling, he struck a deal with Conservative Party leaders that allowed the Conservative Party to nominate one of their own, William Carney, for the U.S. Congress from the First Congressional District (Duryea's home area) in exchange for granting Duryea the Conservative line. Carney was later elected after winning the Republican primary.[10] Though not a typical patronage reward, the Carney example illustrates the kind of patronage bargaining integral to New York party politics.

Secondly, minor parties may exchange their ballot lines for ideological/policy support. The RTLP in particular is motivated by the desire to impel state lawmakers to curtail liberalized abortion practices. As party leaders have made clear, they are less interested in running their own candidates, and much more interested in endorsing major party candidates who can be persuaded to advance the right-to-life position in government in exchange for the RTLP line. The party's stated goal is to end abortions, not elect candidates.[11]

Prospects and Implications: or, Am I in New York, or Postwar Paris?

The 1982 gubernatorial elections illustrated the continuing attractiveness of New York's electoral system to minor parties. No less than four new or revived parties placed gubernatorial candidates on the ballot (see Figure 3). None of the four succeeded in garnering the magic 50,000 vote minimum. Among the five established parties, the RTLP suffered the greatest setback, as its candidate for governor received just over 52,000. This dropped the RTLP ballot position to the fifth slot, below the Liberal party, from 1983 to 1986. This electional dip caused RTLP leaders to seek a more well-known gubernatorial candidate for 1986. They turned first to the Republican-Conservative nominee, Westchester County Executive Andrew O'Rourke. But O'Rourke declined the endorsement, despite his own opposition to abortion, based on the belief that a RTLP endorsement would actually cost him more votes than it would gain.[12] The RTLP turned next to a Democrat, Nassau County District Attorney Denis Dillon. Dillon initially declined the offer because "they approached me on the basis of saving the party." Though unwilling to jeopardize his political career for the RTLP, he finally accepted so that he could "talk about the

City of Ithaca, Towns of Danby, Ithaca & Ulysses

1 GOVERNOR & LIEUTENANT GOVERNOR (Vote Once)	3	4 COMPTROLLER (Vote for One)	5 ATTORNEY GENERAL (Vote for One)	6 UNITED STATES SENATOR (Vote for One)	7 JUSTICE OF THE SUPREME COURT 6th Judicial District (Vote for Any Two)	8	9 REPRESENTATIVE IN CONGRESS (Vote for One)	10 STATE SENATOR (Vote for One)	11 MEMBER OF ASSEMBLY 125th (Vote for One)
1A DEMOCRATIC Mario M. Cuomo Alfred B. DelBello		4A DEMOCRATIC Raymond F. Gallagher	5A DEMOCRATIC Robert Abrams	6A DEMOCRATIC Daniel P. Moynihan	7A DEMOCRATIC Salvatore A. Fauci	8A DEMOCRATIC William Tucker Dean	9A DEMOCRATIC Matt McHugh	10A DEMOCRATIC Richard J. Shay	11A DEMOCRATIC John J. Winkelman
1B REPUBLICAN Lew Lehrman James L. Emery		4B REPUBLICAN Edward V. Regan	5B REPUBLICAN Frances A. Sclafani	6B REPUBLICAN Florence M. Sullivan	7B REPUBLICAN D. Bruce Crew	8B REPUBLICAN Albert E. Tait, Jr.	9B REPUBLICAN David F. Crowley	10B REPUBLICAN Lloyd S. Riford, Jr.	11B REPUBLICAN Hugh S. MacNeil
1C CONSERVATIVE Lew Lehrman James L. Emery		4C CONSERVATIVE Edward V. Regan	5C CONSERVATIVE Frances A. Sclafani	6C CONSERVATIVE Florence M. Sullivan	7C CONSERVATIVE Salvatore A. Fauci	8C CONSERVATIVE Albert E. Tait, Jr.	9C CONSERVATIVE David F. Crowley	10C CONSERVATIVE Lloyd S. Riford, Jr.	
1D RIGHT TO LIFE Robert J. Bohner Paul F. Callahan		4D RIGHT TO LIFE John A. Boyle	5D RIGHT TO LIFE Kevin P. McGovern	6D RIGHT TO LIFE Florence M. Sullivan			9D RIGHT TO LIFE Mark R. Masterson		
1E LIBERAL Mario M. Cuomo Alfred B. DelBello		4E LIBERAL William Finneran	5E LIBERAL Robert Abrams	6E LIBERAL Daniel P. Moynihan			9E LIBERAL Matt McHugh		
1F FREE LIBERTARIAN John H. Northrup David Hoesly		4F FREE LIBERTARIAN William P. McMillen	5F FREE LIBERTARIAN Dolores Grande	6F FREE LIBERTARIAN James J. McKeown					
1G SOCIALIST WORKER Diane Wang Peter A. Thierjung				6G SOCIALIST WORKER Steven Wattenmaker					
1H NEW ALLIANCE Nancy Ross Lenora B. Fulani									
1I UNITY Jane Benedict Angela M. Gilliam	3I INDEPENDENT Lew Lehrman James L. Emery								11I CITIZENS Tim Joseph

Figure 3. General Election Sample Ballot (1982)

lives being killed by abortion."[13] Dillon waged a vigorous campaign, and received 130,802 votes. This total surpassed that of the Liberal party, returning the RTLP to the number four ballot slot through 1990. The RTLP as a whole did not fare as well, however, as the party fielded fewer candidates than ever for congressional and state legislative contests.

Despite the RTLP's cloudy prospects, New York's minor parties were again a central issue in statewide politics. The principal political furor of the 1986 gubernatorial race revolved around whether and under what circumstances Governor Mario Cuomo (Democratic-Liberal nominee) and O'Rourke would debate each other. The main bone of contention concerned the matter of which minor party candidates could participate. Both agreed to include Dillon, but Cuomo urged that the New Alliance Party candidate Lenora Fulani be included as well. O'Rourke balked, however, claiming that the nascent leftist party had ties to extremist groups and was anti-semitic. Fulani was ultimately excluded, but the attendant publicity probably helped her receive over 24,000 votes in the election (more than four times the vote polled by the New Alliance gubernatorial candidate in 1982).

It would be a mistake to conclude from this account that major party leaders had acquired new respect for the minor parties. Rather, the squabble was widely understood as an attempt by front-runner Cuomo to sidestep a debate with O'Rourke for as long as possible, because of Cuomo's overwhelming lead in the polls (he ultimately received 61.9 percent of the vote—the highest winning percentage of any New York governor). Still, it is important to note that minor parties were the pawns in this mini-campaign-drama. Sometimes the tail wags the dog; but more often, the dog wags the tail.

Finally, what does this near-multi-party system offer for the voters of New York? As previously mentioned, many major party leaders and others have come to vilify the current system,[14] fearing, in the extreme, a political process paralysis characterized by institutionalized factionalism brought about by too many parties—as occurred during the French Fourth Republic after World War II.[15] These fears have been heightened by the spread of single-issue politics, of which the RTLP is an obvious example, and the generalized "decline of parties."[16] On the other hand, the New York system may offer, apart from the virtues or vices of particular parties, a feasible avenue to reinvigorate party politics[17] by providing voters with a greater variety of party and, therefore, policy options. A vote for a candidate on the RTLP line, for example, is clearly an "issue vote," single-issue or no. Moreover, the presence of more parties can only help diversify an electoral landscape considered by most voters to be uninteresting at best. Few could deny that the multi-party system sparks greater interest in the electoral process.

E.E. Schattschneider observed many years ago that competition was the hallmark of a vigorous party system, and that democracy was unthinkable without vigorous parties.[18] The current national electoral malaise leans clearly toward the side of decay and disinterest. If there is a risk of overreacting on the side of either too little or too much electoral activity, we might better err on the side of the latter; and it seems only appropriate that the Empire State lead the way.

NOTES

1. See, for example, Daniel Mazmanian, *Third Parties in Presidential Elections,* Washington, D.C.: Brookings, 1974.

2. New York minor parties, and their years of official ballot status: Prohibition (1892-1922); Socialist Labor (1896-1904); Socialist (1900-1938); Independent League (1906-1916); Progressive (1912-1916); American (1914-1916); Farmer Labor (1920-1922); Law Preservation (1930-1934); American Labor (1936-1954); Liberal (1946-); Conservative (1962-); and Right to Life (1978-).

3. Robert Karen, "The Politics of Pressure," *The Nation,* September 20, 1975, pp. 236-37.

4. Robert A. Schoenberger, "Conservatism, Personality and Political Extremism," *American Political Science Review,* September 1968, p. 869.

5. Robert J. Spitzer, "The Right to Life Movement as a Third Party," Nelson A. Rockefeller Institute Working Paper, No. 4, September, 1982.

6. Ballot position is determined by gubernatorial vote. The party whose gubernatorial candidate receives the largest vote appears first on all New York ballots, followed by the other parties, according to the amount of gubernatorial vote. If a party does not field a gubernatorial candidate, it forfeits the line.

7. Karen, "The Politics of Pressure," p. 236.

8. Maurice Carroll, "State Democrats Attack Cross-Endorsement Policy," *New York Times,* January 29, 1982, p. B-2. See also Milton Hoffman, "Major Parties Might Lose Top Ballot Positions," *Ithaca Journal,* August 26, 1982, p. 10.

9. Frank Lynn, "Conservatives and a Political Gamble in New York," *New York Times,* January 26, 1982, p. B-7. See also Maurice Carroll, "Minor Party Once Again Has a Major Effect on Politics," *New York Times,* March 14, 1982, p. E-7.

10. Alan Ehrenhalt, ed., *Politics in America, 1982,* Washington, D.C.: Congressional Quarterly, 1982, p. 804; and Michael Barone et al., *The Almanac of American Politics,* New York: Dutton, 1979, p. 580.

11. Robert J. Spitzer, *The Right to Life Movement and Third Party Politics,* Westport, CT: Greenwood Press, 1987, Chapter 2.

12. Frank Lynn, "Right to Life Candidate Tries to Make Abortion an Issue," *New York Times,* September 21, 1986.

13. Lawrence Neumeister, "Dillon: Victory is Not Main Issue," *Cortland Standard,* October 27, 1986. The RTLP first established its ballot line in 1978 when its gubernatorial candidate, Mary Jane Tobin, received 130,193 votes.

14. Howard Scarrow, *Parties, Elections, and Representation in the State of New York,* New York: New York University Press, 1983, Chapter 2.

15. One symptom of the continued concern about the minor parties was seen in 1986, when the liberal *New York Times* called in an editorial for the dissolution of the Liberal party, citing its factional disputes and apparently declining influence.

16. William Crotty, *American Parties in Decline,* Boston: Little, Brown, 1984.

17. For more on this argument, see Spitzer, *The Right to Life Movement and Third Party Politics,* Chapter 4. See also Mazmanian, *Third Parties in Presidential Elections,* Chapter V.

18. E.E. Schattschneider, *Party Government,* New York: Holt, Rinehart and Winston, 1942, p. 208 and passim.

A Profile of Senator D'Amato

by

Alan Emory

Alan Emory is the Washington correspondent for the *Watertown Daily Times.*

EDITORS' NOTE: *This chapter examines the constituency-oriented approach Alfonse D'Amato brings to his job of U.S. Senator.*

Alan Emory

Senator Alfonse M. D'Amato is not inclined to play favorites. Among his recent targets have been the Reagan Administration's Office of Management and Budget (he calls it the Office of Disinformation); trustees of the Museum of the American Indian, whom he sees participating in a "power grab"; the White House; and, on occasion, his New York Senate colleague, Democrat Daniel Patrick Moynihan.

The feisty D'Amato has launched his second six-year term in the manner of an office-holder who has few political cares, a counter-puncher daring his adversary to throw the first punch. He is fiercely resentful of what he considers slights on his senatorial position or character. While he and Moynihan have a workable working relationship and mutual political respect, D'Amato frequently seethes privately at what he regards as Moynihan's less-than-equal treatment of him as a fellow New York senator.

On the surface D'Amato does not appear to have changed much from his first term. He still moves and talks fast, his conversation is staccato, he raps out orders like a machine gun with an endless supply of ammunition. And, yet, on closer inspection, one finds that the pace has slowed, almost imperceptibly. His commands to his staff seem just a touch less insistent.

Alfonse D'Amato likes being called "the pothole senator," even though the label was fixed on him in a less-than-flattering context in the 1986 campaign. In his second term, D'Amato says he is "more at ease" with the people in government. A high D'Amato aide comments that his boss "may work just as hard, but it doesn't seem as frantic." He targets his energy more efficiently than he did before.

D'Amato tells interviewers he will continue to focus on New York State's problems and on issues affecting the state, and, if that seems "overly parochial," he is not ashamed of paying the price. "They call me a special-interest representative for the people of the state," he told a reporter. "I admit to that." With a landslide reelection victory behind him, he reflects with satisfaction on a "certain measure of respect" he has gained. "So many of us came in as a result of the Reagan landslide (in 1980)," he says. "In my case if President Reagan had not made such a strong run I would not have been elected. Now, when people are looking at you and wondering why you took a position at variance with their interests or politics, they have a better appreciation of the things I fought for."

D'Amato's big win, he points out, coincided with Governor Mario M. Cuomo's record victory margin, although D'Amato describes himself as a "conservative Republican from liberal Democratic New York."

Although D'Amato insists that, as a U.S. senator, he is not in a position to become the real leader of the New York State Republican party, he was more active earlier than anyone else in trying to round up an opponent for Moynihan. He insists he did not "encourage" Manhattan U.S. Attorney Rudolph W. Giuliani to make the race, that he did not try to "recruit" a candidate, and that he did not want to create any "estrangement" between himself and Moynihan by his campaign activities. D'Amato argues, "I have never said, 'You should' or 'You shouldn't do it.'" He said he had given Giuliani a "very candid assessment" of the New York Senate situation, telling him that a race against Moynihan would be difficult, that the Democrat was "very formidable, very well-known and a respected senator."

He makes clear that he is not going to say anything against Moynihan—at least in public—because that would have a "totally negative" impact on their relationship and, by implication, for programs and projects in which New York State has an interest in Washington. "It's tough enough to deal on a day-to-day basis," he says. According to tradition, an incumbent senator campaigns for the nominee of his party, but does not attack his colleague from the state, even though they have opposing political affiliations.

On the legislative front, D'Amato concedes that in some specialized fields in which he has taken on major responsibilities, such as securities and housing, he is "still learning"; but in his second term, complex matters such as stocks and bonds and commodity futures regulation have become easier, and "it's fun dealing with these issues now." D'Amato's position has become even more important in the aftermath of the Black Monday market crash of October 19, 1987.

One of the most dramatic conflicts between D'Amato and Moynihan arose when Reagan decided to put American flags on Kuwaiti tankers, a move that D'Amato immediately criticized, but which seemed to win the initial support of Moynihan. On May 28, 1987, D'Amato offered an amendment to a pending bill to delay the tanker reflagging. Several Democrats opposed the move, but Moynihan was the one who infuriated D'Amato, who claimed to reporters that he had been "savaged" by Moynihan. D'Amato did not mention Moynihan by name, but he removed any doubt when he cited a Moynihan comment on the Senate floor that the D'Amato proposal amounted to seeing "the Persian Gulf become a Soviet lake." When Moynihan later switched sides, insisting his views were consistent, D'Amato declared abruptly, "The record doesn't indicate that. . . . Senators can have a change of heart . . . there is nothing wrong in admitting an error." To D'Amato attacks on his position reflected a lack of "any kind of bipartisan cooperation in efforts important to this nation" and indicated "legitimate needs are being sacrificed on the of political trench warfare." However, D'Amato twice voted for filibusters that made it impossible for the Senate to vote on the reflagging issue. D'Amato says that the proposals were Democratic moves to embarrass President Reagan, and, while he refused to "eat crow for the Republicans," and, in fact, accused the White House of pursuing a "befuddled, inconsistent policy," he said he would not allow himself to be used to embarrass the administration without a constructive alternative.

One of D'Amato's major frustrations has been with Reagan's budget experts. In a heated blast on the Senate floor during debate on what would have been the first major housing bill in seven years, the New Yorker said, "I have almost never seen the Office of Management and Budget negotiate in good faith." He doesn't let the White House off the hook, either. "I have called them repeatedly," he told the Senate. "They have no idea, nor do they give us any signal."

Says D'Amato, "I get a little tired hearing the rhetoric that this is a big spending program, that we are just pushing out that money. It is unrealistic to assume that our cities, towns, counties and other localities are no longer in need of these programs." With Senator Alan Cranston (D-California), a liberal with whom D'Amato is often in conflict, in his corner on the housing issue, D'Amato accused the administration agency of "twisting the figures when they see fit, cutting the programs they may disagree with, shirking their responsibilities by failing to communicate forthrightly with the committees and the members attempting to work something out, but really looking to see how they can sabotage those programs they are opposed to."

The housing issue brought D'Amato into direct confrontation with fellow conservatives like Senator Phil Gramm (R-Texas), who called the housing bill "just a little bit more pork . . . the last sausage that is coming out of the sausage machine." D'Amato replied that the programs might displace low-income families who need "decent, affordable housing (so) it does not make much sense to come into an area, tear it down, build a shopping center or a hotel or another complex." D'Amato lights into his fellow conservatives for talking about the needs of older citizens, and then approving few housing units for them. He advises them, "Go home to your districts and tell them how you are concerned about the senior citizen when you will not provide what is necessary to give them an opportunity to live a decent, productive life."

In still another explosion, D'Amato has accused the leadership of the Museum of the American Indian (MAI) of a "power grab" policy that says, "The heck with the public, the heck with the American Indian." D'Amato was irate because his attempts to negotiate a solution to the museum problem that would keep the facility in New York, rather than having it moved to Washington, had been stalemated over a disagreement on where in New York the museum should be located. Although he and Moynihan had differed over the museum site, D'Amato finally threw up his hands and agreed to go along with whatever site appealed to a majority of the New York leadership. That turned out to be the U.S. Custom House in Manhattan. D'Amato notes sarcastically that leaders of the Museum of the American Indian had first claimed the Custom House was "uniquely suited for a museum," only now to back a move out of the state, and had said the Custom House would lead to a windfall in new fund-raising, only now to say the arrangement would not work because of a lack of money.

D'Amato feels that the Iran-Contra scandal has made President Reagan's last months in office more difficult, but insists that neither he nor "the things I consider important" have felt the impact. "It never has affected me, even when he was riding the greatest tide (of popularity)," he told an interviewer recently. "They don't go hand in hand." "People are rather disappointed in the way a mission was bungled that was not adequately explained form the beginning, " he told the *Watertown Daily Times* and *Empire State Report.* "People are not furious, not angry. They are sorry the presidency has been damaged. Most of them still have a high regard for the man. They see this as having interfered with an outstanding administration. Reagan's advisers could have cushioned him tremendously. It has diminished what would have been a tremendously successful stewardship."

D'Amato has had frequent differences with the White House on key foreign policy questions, but declares, "If you think I am going to put my head in the sand, I would not be true to my country or to the people who elected me."

For the future, D'Amato intends to concentrate on answers to the twin problems of drug and alcohol abuse, warning that "we are not going to solve it all with legislation and dollars," and stressing the need to aid countries "plagued with the drug culture," while cutting off aid to, and ending favorable treatment of, countries that refuse to suppress drug production and distribution. "We must cajole, harass and beat on the administration," he says, "let them know we are serious."

The 1986 Gubernatorial Election

by

Lee M. Miringoff and
Barbara L. Carvalho

Mr. Miringoff is Assistant Professor of Political Science and Director of the Marist Institute for Public Opinion at Marist College in Poughkeepsie, New York.

Ms. Carvalho is Director of Research and Data Analysis at the Marist Institute for Public Opinion at Marist College in Poughkeepsie, New York.

EDITORS' NOTE: *This analysis is based in part on The Cuomo Factor: Assessing the Political Appeal of New York's Governor* (Marist Institute for Public Opinion, Marist College, Poughkeepsie, New York, 1986).

The 1986 reelection of Mario Cuomo as Governor of New York State represented a referendum on his incumbency rather than a hotly contested give-and-take between Cuomo and his Republican opponent, Westchester County Executive Andrew O'Rourke. Although O'Rourke may have outsung Cuomo at the Legislative Correspondent's Association dinner early in the campaign, as the summer months passed it was clear that the electorate was singing Cuomo's reelection tune.

If 1982 marked a dramatic and sudden shift in voter sentiment to the then relatively unknown Lieutenant Governor Mario Cuomo, 1986 represented a confirmation of the unprecedented popularity Cuomo had built during his first term as governor. During his initial run for the statehouse against Ed Koch in the 1982 Democratic primary, and later, against Lew Lehrman in the general election, Mario Cuomo demonstrated an ability to understand and define the substance of a political issue, to develop positions which were consistent with his outlook, and to communicate his views effectively. During his first term as governor, Cuomo further defined his positions and established his role. Through the positions he took and his ability to articulate his stands, Cuomo fashioned a balanced approach to government which matched the concerns of contemporary voters. He repeatedly outlined his conception of a positive role for government, one that involved a new blend of progressive values about government's place in society and pragmatic approaches to public policy.

New York voters have responded positively to Cuomo's approach as governor. In a Marist Institute for Public Opinion poll (MIPO) conducted in June 1983, several months after Cuomo assumed office, 57 percent of the state's voters approved of the job he was doing. A year later, his rating had risen to 59 percent. In June 1985, 69.6 percent of state voters saw Cuomo as doing either an "excellent" or a "good" job in office. In June 1986, as he looked ahead to his reelection campaign, his approval rating was 70.6 percent.

MIPO survey data reveal that New Yorkers have consistently seen Cuomo as a good leader for New York State, as taking clearly defined positions on issues, as having compassion for the needs of the poor and the elderly, as having policies that are fiscally sound, and as being someone who speaks on behalf of traditional family values. On each of these issues, more than two-thirds of the electorate have rated Cuomo positively.

In addition, Cuomo's appearance at center stage in national politics following his keynote address at the Democratic National Convention in San Francisco in 1984 has not tarnished his standing among New Yorkers. New York voters do not, for the most part, believe Cuomo has paid too much attention to national politics and not enough attention to New York State. Cuomo has successfully raised issues that extend beyond the borders of New York and has related those issues to the concerns of the New York electorate.

As the 1986 campaign approached, it was clear that not only did the electorate assess Mario Cuomo favorably but that the composition of those who were receptive to his approach was significant. Since his election in 1982, Cuomo has established new bases of support in state politics. His popularity extended beyond the traditional Democratic stronghold of New York City, where he received a 72.3 percent approval rating in a June 1986 MIPO statewide poll, to the suburbs surrounding New York City (Nassau, Westchester, Suffolk, and Rockland counties) where he received a 71.6 percent approval rating. Even in upstate New York, the traditionally strong Republican area, Cuomo's approval rating was 68.9 percent.

Cuomo's success has been highlighted by his political appeal to suburban voters throughout New York State, and especially in the four-county suburban region surrounding New York City. These suburban communities have undergone tremendous growth and development over recent decades, and now constitute about one-quarter of the state's electorate. As a result, the New York electorate can no longer be considered politically divided into rural-conservative upstate and urban-liberal New York City. But who are these suburban voters and what are their political attitudes? What is the relationship Mario Cuomo has with them?

Conventional wisdom suggests that suburban voters are steadfast Republicans and ideological conservatives, who oppose, for the most part, extensive government intervention into domestic policy. But Democrat Cuomo has achieved significant popularity in the suburbs and has gained the approval of these voters by stressing a positive role for government in domestic policy. Cuomo is not, however, a political anomaly. Gradual changes in the population and economy of the region have made this new, vital partner in New York State politics more heterogeneous, more politically independent and less conservative on government's role in domestic policy than is generally thought. For example, the region's electorate today can be characterized by the weakening party attachments of its voters. The proportion of Independents to enrolled Democrats and Republicans in the suburbs has increased dramatically in recent decades. Independents currently represent 23.1 percent of registered voters in the region, up from 9.89 percent in 1956. Although the trend towards growing independence has occurred throughout the New York electorate, it has been especially evident in the suburbs.

In addition, the weakening of party attachments is even more pervasive than these enrollment figures alone suggest. Comparisons between party enrollment and party identification show that even among voters enrolled in a political party, Independent identification is widespread. Although the party enrollment in the suburbs is reported as 31.2 percent Democratic, 43.4 percent Republican, and 21.2 percent Independent, voters in the region express their party identification as 25.3 percent Democratic, 32.9 percent Republican, and 39.8 percent Independent. Independent identification is almost twice the Independent enrollment. Also, a majority of voters who identify with either the Democratic or Republican parties do not see themselves as strongly committed to that party (Table 10).

Table 10

NEW YORK SUBURBAN RESPONDENT'S PARTY REGISTRATION, PARTY IDENTIFICATION, AND STRENGTH OF PARTISANSHIP (MIPO, OCTOBER 1985)

Party Registration*

"Are you currently registered to vote as a Democrat, Republican, Independent, Conservative, or Liberal?"

Democrat	31.2%
Republican	43.4%
Independent	21.2%
Conservative	2.4%
Liberal	1.2%
Other	0.7%

Party Identification

"Do you consider yourself to be a Democrat, a Republican, or an Independent?"

Democrat	25.3%
Republican	32.9%
Independent	39.8%
Other	1.9%

Strength of Party Identification**

"Do you consider yourself to be a strong Democrat/Republican or not a very strong Democrat/Republican?"

	Strong	Weak	Unsure
Democrat	44.7%	51.2%	4.1%
Republican	39.6%	55.0%	5.4%

*Note: These survey estimates are consistent with the enrollment figures compiled by the New York State Board of Elections. Their 1986 enrollment figures, collected in the fall of 1985, were: 31.9% Democrat, 42.2% Republican, 22.9% Independent, 2.1% Conservative, 0.6% Liberal, 0.4% Right to Life.

**Asked only of Democrats and Republicans.

The attitudes of the new suburban voter are evidenced on a variety of public policy issues, as well (Table 11).

Suburban voters now have a new political outlook. They constitute the swing group in New York State politics. They are a part of the electorate that is up-for-grabs.

Mario Cuomo, for his part, recognized the growing role of this group of New York voters, understood the current views of this electorate, and raised issues of concern to these voters. Regarding the suburban voter, Cuomo commented, "They read more and they are politically independent. . . . As for the suburbs, I think of them as thinking, eclectic and discrete. I do not think of them as conservative or Republican." So that in the wake of the 1984 elections, for example, Cuomo observed that this Democratic debacle did not constitute a conservative trend. "(The media) converted one headline into another. They converted the headline 'Reagan wins the Suburbs Big' into ' Conservatism wins the Suburbs Big,' and they are two different things. . . . I can win the suburbs. Anybody who believes the things I believe and makes them clear will win the suburbs."

To a significant degree, Cuomo's expanded political appeal in the suburbs allowed him to pursue a record-setting strategy in 1986. As his Director of Communications, Gary Fryer, noted: "When you examine the possibility of winning by a large majority, (the suburbs) are essential. We have enjoyed for better than three years some abnormally high numbers in these areas . . . that provides for us an enormous base upon which to build a candidacy. It allows us to pay more attention to upstate while basically trying to maintain the popularity we have in those areas as opposed to trying to create it. So, in that respect they become key to a large victory, but they are important to any victory."

Cuomo's across-the-board appeal eroded the traditional ideological and partisan distinctions, as well. He received an 80.1 percent approval rating among self-styled political liberals, 68.6 percent among middle-of-the-roaders, and 66.7 percent among conservatives at the onset of the campaign. By party, 80.8 percent of Democrats, 65.2 percent of Independents, and 61.6 percent of Republicans gave Cuomo either an "excellent" or "good" rating. Cuomo's ability to appeal beyond mainstream Democrats has been particularly fortuitous for him because it has occurred at a time when the electorate as a whole is increasingly selective and less partisan in its approach to politics. With fewer voters firmly rooted in either political party, the potential for landslides is heightened.

It was in this context that Andrew O'Rourke set out to upset Mario Cuomo. It was too tall an order. When voters were asked early in the campaign to assess Mario Cuomo and Andrew O'Rourke, the differences between the two candidates in name recognition and popularity were stunning (Table 12). Subsequent polling revealed a similar pattern, with one

Table 11

NEW YORK SUBURBAN RESPONDENT'S VIEWS ON THE ROLE OF GOVERNMENT AND CANDIDATE POSITIONS (MIPO, OCTOBER 1985)

"Using the numbers 1 to 5, with 1 meaning strongly agree and 5 meaning strongly disagree, please tell me how you feel about each of the following statements."

	Agree (1 & 2)	Neutral (3)	Disagree (4 & 5)
"Government should not get involved in programs for housing, health care, and jobs and should let each person work things out on his own."	22.3%	15.4%	62.3%
"Government should concern itself with narrowing the income differences between the rich and the poor in this country."	52.7%	16.8%	30.5%
"Everyone is sharing in the economic recovery."	24.1%	32.2%	43.7%
"Government should spend more time improving and protecting the environment."	71.9%	15.4%	12.7%

"Would you be more likely or less likely to vote for a candidate who does each of the following? If it makes no difference to you, please say so."

	More Likely	No Difference	Less Likely
"A candidate who wants to increase federal aid to cities."	62.2%	24.9%	12.8%
"A candidate who wants to increase spending for mass transportation."	61.3%	28.6%	10.1%
"A candidate who advocates increased spending for job training for the unemployed."	74.9%	11.4%	13.7%
"A candidate who advocates increasing government programs for the poor and the elderly."	76.6%	10.0%	13.4%
"A candidate who wants to balance the budget by cutting social programs."	22.7%	6.8%	70.6%
"A candidate who wants to cut taxes by cutting government services."	27.7%	8.4%	64.0%

Table 12

GUBERNATORIAL CANDIDATES' STATEWIDE NAME RECOGNITION (MIPO, JUNE 1986)

	Favorable	Unfavorable	Unsure/ Never Heard
Mario Cuomo	81.3%	15.1%	3.6%
Andrew O'Rourke	18.3%	10.3%	71.4%

Table 13

GUBERNATORIAL CANDIDATES' STATEWIDE NAME RECOGNITION BY REGION AND PARTY REGISTRATION (MIPO, OCTOBER 1986)†

	Favorable	Unfavorable	Unsure/ Never Heard
Mario Cuomo			
October 1986*	77.4%	16.9%	5.6%
September 1986*	80.3%	14.8%	4.9%
June 1986	81.3%	15.1%	3.6%
Andrew O'Rourke			
October 1986*	25.7%	28.2%	46.1%
September 1986*	29.2%	15.3%	55.5%
June 1986	18.3%	10.3%	71.4%
By Region*			
Cuomo			
Upstate	77.6%	16.4%	6.1%
New York City	77.2%	17.1%	5.8%
Suburbs	77.4%	17.9%	4.7%
O'Rourke			
Upstate	22.1%	31.8%	46.1%
New York City	21.1%	28.8%	50.1%
Suburbs	38.4%	20.6%	41.0%
By Party*			
Cuomo			
Democrat	88.4%	7.2%	4.3%
Republican	61.7%	31.0%	7.2%
Non-Enrolled	85.0%	7.9%	7.1%
O'Rourke			
Democrat	19.0%	34.3%	46.7%
Republican	36.2%	21.9%	41.9%
Non-Enrolled	18.9%	28.4%	52.7%

†Unless otherwise noted
*Likely Voters

noteworthy development. As the electorate became more familiar with Andrew O'Rourke, his negative rating grew more rapidly. Cuomo's image, in contrast, remained positive and relatively steadfast (Table 13). When it came to specific image questions, O'Rourke's inability to establish a positive image was revealed. Issue by issue, Cuomo was clearly pitching a shutout (Table 14).

The odds against O'Rourke were steep from the beginning. Had he focused on a single issue or two, like crime or taxes, he might have become associated with those voters who felt strongly about those two issues. This could have created some interest in the O'Rourke campaign, although it is unlikely that the inroads into Cuomo's lead would have been substantial. Instead, O'Rourke's campaign largely focused on the need to debate and on a cardboard likeness of Cuomo which he carried around with him while campaigning. The electorate was never moved to vote for O'Rourke on the basis of his calls to debate, and it was not convinced when O'Rourke pictured Cuomo as incompetent.

Mario Cuomo began the 1986 campaign riding an enormous wave of popularity, coupled with substantial name recognition and financial advantages. By election day, little had changed. Cuomo's defeat of Andrew O'Rourke by 65 percent to 32 percent reflected strong voter approval of Cuomo's first term rather than the introduction of major new approaches

Table 14

GUBERNATORIAL CANDIDATES' STATEWIDE IMAGE
(MIPO, SEPTEMBER 1986)

"I'm going to read you a list of issues which may face the next governor. For each one please tell me which candidate you think will do the better job, Mario Cuomo or Andrew O'Rourke."

	Cuomo	O'Rourke	Both	Neither	Unsure
"provide leadership for the state"	69.6%	14.1%	1.2%	0.6%	14.5%
"manage state government"	65.9%	15.2%	1.1%	0.9%	16.9%
"get jobs for people"	58.8%	16.6%	1.4%	2.2%	21.0%
"hold down taxes"	50.5%	17.4%	0.9%	5.9%	25.3%
"reduce crime"	52.4%	18.2%	1.5%	4.2%	23.7%
"address the needs of the poor and the elderly"	61.5%	11.7%	1.4%	3.2%	22.2%

by Cuomo during the campaign. Mario Cuomo achieved the largest victory for a gubernatorial candidate in New York State history, surpassing Grover Cleveland's 1882 winning share. Voters throughout the state and across party lines gave Cuomo unprecedented marks on his first term in office as he carried all but a handful of New York's sixty-two counties.

These numbers notwithstanding, Cuomo's reelection campaign was not without its rough spots. Frequent skirmishes with the press contributed to the view of Cuomo as being "thin-skinned," and led to several critical pieces about him in the national press and elsewhere.

In Mario Cuomo's initial campaign for governor in 1982, he successfully shaped the political agenda by focusing voter attention on the issue of President Reagan's economic policy. In that election, Cuomo's strategy of attacking Reaganomics and its supply-side theories was well-founded, given that a majority of New Yorkers disapproved of the policy. If 1982 was a referendum on President Reagan's economic policy and how voters' choices closely matched their feelings about the economy, then 1986 should be viewed as a referendum on Mario Cuomo's incumbency—and New Yorkers voiced overwhelming approval.

The End of Liberalism?

by

John K. White

EDITORS' NOTE: *After years in which "New Deal liberalism" has dominated the speeches of politicians in New York State, the political rhetoric has been drastically altered. This article places the altered rhetoric in context with other recent political developments affecting the parties in New York State.*

More than 150 years ago, the poet Ralph Waldo Emerson wrote:

> If there is any period one would desire to be born in—is it not the age of Revolution; when the old and the new stand side by side, and admit of being compared; when the energies of all men are searched by fear and hope; when the historic glories of the old, can be compensated by the rich possibilities of the new era? This time, like all times, is a very good one, *if we but know what to do with it* [emphasis added].[1]

During the 1980s New York's political parties entered an era of change—revolutionary change. The elevation of a one-time movie actor to the presidency, and a town supervisor to the U.S. Senate, in 1980 marked the new political era. "New right" conservatives like Ronald Reagan and Alfonse D'Amato were in vogue, while the "old liberalism" that once dominated both parties was on the wane. Shortly after the 1980 results were in, *New York Times* reporter Frank Lynn wrote that the Reagan and D'Amato victories "rang down the final curtain on the Dewey-Rockefeller-Javits era of liberal Republicanism in New York."[2] New York City Mayor Ed Koch, a man with sensitive political antennae, heard the signals of change before most of his colleagues. In 1979, he branded his fellow Democrats as "knee jerk liberals," telling the *New Yorker:*

> I don't believe in half their crap. That government has to become bigger. That government is better if it does more. It's the New Deal out of the thirties—that government solves problems. I once believed that. I have *contempt* for government [emphasis added].[3]

The old liberalism has become so passé that the once-mighty Liberal party—whose endorsement was deemed a matter of political life or death to Democrats—fell into disrepair. Intra-party bickering, and benign neglect from Democratic governor Mario Cuomo, hastened its downfall. By 1985, even the *New York Times* questioned Liberals' purpose: "If in the shadow of a conservative era, they are truly intent on promoting liberal values, should they not bring their energy and dedication into the ranks of the major parties?"[4] A year later, the bottom dropped out as the party placed dead last in the race for governor. Mario Cuomo, the Liberal candidate (and the Democrat's also), did not receive enough votes to beat the Right-to-Life candidate. Henceforth, the Liberals will be listed *last* on the 1988 and 1992 election ballots—behind the Right-to-Lifers.

An old adage has it, "The more things change, the more they stay the same." While things have changed for the Liberal party, Democrats and

Republicans have been little affected—at least according to figures that give the Democrats 3,820,085 registered voters; Republicans, 2,602,782; Conservatives, 110,485; Liberals, 62,540; and Right-to-Lifers 21,606. Another 1,461,281 chose not to identify with any party. These data represent very little change since the start of the decade.

But how things have changed! Instead of using the political parties as catalysts for reform, New Yorkers have transcended them. The contrast between the last two Democratic landslides, Lyndon Johnson's in 1964 and Mario Cuomo's in 1986, makes the point. Johnson and Cuomo devastated their Republican opposition, winning 68.6 percent and 64.6 percent of the statewide vote, respectively. In each case, the Democratic totals *exceeded* the vote for the Republican candidate.[5] Cuomo's percentage, in fact, was the largest amassed by a reelected governor in New York history—easily beating previous record holder Grover Cleveland, and causing Cuomo partisans to boast, "*Move Over Grover*."[6]

But the similarity between the two Democratic landslides ended there. Lyndon Johnson had "coattails" that reached to the lowest offices on the ballot. The result was a Democratic recapturing of both houses of the New York State Legislature, something the party had not been able to do since 1958.

Mario Cuomo's "coattails" were non-existent. His large vote made *no difference* to his fellow Democrats. The popular governor did not influence a single outcome in the Republican-controlled state Senate, where not one seat changed parties. And in the state Assembly, the Democrats added just one seat to their majority. These results, coupled with Cuomo's unwillingness to come to the aid of his party, left many Democrats unhappy. Senate minority leader Manfred Ohrenstein said of Cuomo: "He embarked on a strategy to win by a huge margin, and he did it. Not everyone liked the strategy. It is a controversial strategy, but it worked enormously well."[7] A spokesman for the defeated Democratic U.S. senatorial candidate Mark Green was bitter: "[Cuomo] didn't do enough to help him. The real test of leadership is guiding and building and helping the party, not building up superfluous margins. It wasn't a team effort."[8]

But not all of this was Cuomo's fault. Alfonse D'Amato and Ned Regan won by impressive margins, yet failed to help their fellow Republicans. The unwillingness of so many New Yorkers to follow a party line was transfigured into a perverse version of the child's game "einny, meany, miney, mo." Democrat Cuomo polled nearly 2.7 million votes, only to be immediately followed by Republican Regan's 2.2 million. Democrat Robert Abrams won 2.4 million votes, followed by a massive switch to Republican D'Amato, who received 2.3 million. Voters then did a quick two-step—siding more often than not with their Republican state senator, then supporting their Democratic representative in the state Assembly.

A Rhetorical Realignment, Not a Partisan One

Clearly, there is no party realignment akin to the one of more than a half century ago. An influx of immigrants, the Great Depression, and the personal magnetism of Franklin D. Roosevelt transformed the New York Democratic party from minority to majority status.[9] Roosevelt's New Deal became grafted onto the upstate/downstate split. Upstaters were steadfastly Republican; downstaters, loyally Democratic. Remnants of the old fissure remain. But the haphazard results of the 1986 election indicate considerable change in New York politics. And no party has been able, in Emerson's phrase, "to know what to do with it."

What *has* happened in state politics is a "rhetorical realignment." Beginning with Ronald Reagan's election in 1980, the tone of political conversation changed. Instead of promising to increase the size of government, politicians in both parties now suggest ways of limiting its growth. Instead of raising taxes, most Republicans and more than a few Democrats are scrambling to cut them.

The rhetorical "newspeak" is particularly evident in the comments of Democratic leaders. House Speaker Tip O'Neill said in 1982: "You just can't go the old New Deal road. The 1980s are a time of change, and the Democratic party has to respond to the people."[10] In 1987, Democratic U.S. Senator William Proxmire suggested revoking the Glass-Steagall Banking Act, a landmark New Deal law that established the Federal Deposit Insurance Corporation.[11] Others echo O'Neill and Proxmire. A 1986 report issued by the Democratic National Committee proclaimed a "Democratic Creed," a set of political commandments that could have been handed down from Ronald Reagan himself: "the freedom to make personal choices is at the heart of the American dream"; "individuals must be responsible for their own lives"; "opportunity is the key to a free society"; "a growing economy is the foundation of a society that is both dynamic and just"; "achievement and progress are central to the expectations of Americans"; "strong state and local governments are essential"; "America must be strong to deter aggression and keep the peace."[12]

The altered rhetoric was not confined to the Democratic political establishment. Many voters were quickly adapting to the "newspeak." In 1986, Democratic pollster Stanley Greenberg asked ordinary Americans what John F. Kennedy meant when he declared in his famous 1961 Inaugural Address, "Ask not what your country can do for you, ask what you can do for your country." Some of the answers were truly startling. One said: "He's trying to remind the American people that they should try to be more responsible for themselves, and not be dependent on somebody taking over their responsibilities, such as providing you with benefits whenever you need it. . . . Once you get on that track, why should you go back, because government is taking care of all your responsibilities." Another said: "I believe we are doing what we can for our country. We are not accepting any government programs and so-called handouts by being middle class.[13]

Rhetorical conservatives are winning elections in New York. Rather than playing "einny, meany, miney, mo," New Yorkers are selective: choosing rhetorical conservatives from both parties. Those who do not speak the new conservatism, like 1986 Democratic senatorial candidate Mark Green, are rejected by voters.

The New Deal Refusenik

No one is better at playing the new game of rhetorical conservatism than Mario Cuomo. The day after the 1984 presidential election, Mario Cuomo told an interviewer:

> One of the Senators . . . is supposed to have said, "We have read all of Governor Cuomo's speeches and they are New Deal." I laughed. What are you when you reduce public employees by 9,000? What are you when you say [that] need should be the criterion [for welfare benefits]? What are you when you come out for a tax cut? What are you when you refuse to raise the basic taxes? What are you when you spend more on your defense budget, which we call corrections, than any governor in history?[14]

The answer to Cuomo's litany of questions is *reelected*—overwhelmingly. Cuomo's aversion to the tag "New Deal liberal" has earned him a new appellation: the New Deal refusenik. Addressing the nation's editorial cartoonists in 1987, Cuomo asked, "What's a New Deal liberal?" He proceeded to devise a true/false test: (1) A New Deal liberal spends a lot of money on social problems", and (2) a New Deal liberal is mushy-headed, soft, and weak on defense.

Those who would answer "true" to both questions would fail Cuomo's test. In each instance, Cuomo contends the answer is false. On defense, Cuomo retorts: "Roosevelt was a New Deal liberal, but didn't he win World War Two? Truman made the bomb. Kennedy almost started a war in Cuba and chased the Russians away he was so bellicose. We kicked Johnson out because of the Vietnam War." To whom are you referring if you answered "true" to the defense question? Says Cuomo, "McGovern."

On social programs, Cuomo points to himself as the antithesis of the stereotypical New Deal liberal. This is not without justification. During his first term, Cuomo balanced the books using Generally Accepted Accounting Principles—an achievement lauded by Republican Comptroller Ned Regan. Tax rates were reduced to their lowest point in twenty-seven years. Theresa Funiciello and Sanford Schram report in a later chapter in this book that from 1975 to 1985 state support for welfare recipients fell from 110.1 percent to 64.3 percent of the poverty level. In 1984, the governor withheld $20 million earmarked for staff at state institutions for the mentally ill.

But it is in dealing with criminals that Cuomo points to with some pride as his anti-liberal legacy. During his first term, 10,200 more New Yorkers were put behind bars. In fact, Cuomo spent more than $600 million to construct new prisons. This is in sharp contrast with one of Cuomo's predecessors, Republican Nelson Rockefeller. Rockefeller regarded the construction of the State University of New York as his most imposing legacy. Others might add the imposing Nelson A. Rockefeller Empire State Plaza to the list. Ironically, Rockefeller felt that his greatest mistake was advocating a get-tough, put-the-users-in-jail, anti-drug law. Cuomo, on the other hand has poured thousands of pounds of concrete into the building of prisons—more than 10,000 new prison cells. Without a doubt, prisons have become the greatest physical legacy of the Cuomo years.

It is no wonder that nearly one-half of those who supported Reagan in 1984 backed Cuomo in 1986.[15] These voters, understandably, saw little conflict between the two. One young New Yorker who admired Reagan and Cuomo said of the governor, "He gives people the same feeling about New York that Reagan gives people about America."[16] Cuomo even took the tag line of Reagan's 1984 commercials, "Leadership That's Working," as his own. Some dub him "the ethnic Ronald Reagan." The Democratic political consultant Robert Squier says, "One of the things that qualifies Mario Cuomo to be considered for president of the United States is that he gets his Teflon from the same place Reagan does."[17]

Cuomo's "Teflon" has received an extra coating from the historical perception in New York that it is the *Republican* party that "taxes and spends, taxes and spends." Ronald Reagan used that shibboleth against the Democrats with telling effect in 1980 and again in 1984. But Nelson Rockefeller and John Lindsay were just as prone to do what Reagan accused the Democrats in Congress of doing. Rockefeller once told an audience, "You could plop me down in a town of two hundred people, and the first thing I'd do is try to start solving their problems." One voter, somewhat less than enthralled with this approach, wrote the governor, "Thank God our town is too small for your plopping."[18]

In his acceptance speech for a second term, Cuomo deftly reminded voters of the Republican's profligate ways.

> For sixteen years, from 1959 to 1974, the Republicans dominated the government in Albany. During that period they took us from twenty-second in the United States in terms of per capita taxes, to first. They raised the state income tax to a nearly incredible 17½ percent rate. In the process we lost hundreds of thousands of jobs. . . . By 1983 we were still suffering from the after effects of sixteen years of crippling Republican tax increases.[19]

No wonder *Washington Post* columnist David Broder calls Cuomo "Mario Machiavelli."[20]

The End of Liberalism?

Mario Cuomo likes to say, "You campaign in poetry, but you govern in prose."[21] Clearly, in New York the poetry has changed, but has the prose? From fiscal year 1982-83 to fiscal year 1985-86, disbursements from the state's general fund increased 30 percent.[22] Patrick J. Buchanan, the Director of Communications for the Reagan White House in 1985, attacked Cuomo's proclivity to spend: "Mario Cuomo's incessant invocations of the poor, the downtrodden, [and] the ill almost invariably turn up as preambles to budget requests that would augment the power of his own political class—the Welfare statists."[23]

Ironically most New Yorkers have not abandoned the "old liberalism." Sixty-two percent of the state's suburbanites say Mario Cuomo "believes in active government intervention in health care, housing, and employment"; 77 percent agree he is "especially sympathetic to the problems of the poor and the elderly"; 78 percent perceive him as a spokesman for "traditional family values."[24] Such perceptions conform with majority sentiments.

But the governing elite, including Cuomo, have a different view of what voters want. In a July 1986 memorandum uncovered during the Iran-Contra affair, Lieutenant Colonel Oliver North told his superior, John M. Poindexter, "We live in a world of perceptions, not realities."[25] To the governors, the perception is that voters want tight-fisted, fiscally conservative government. To Mario Cuomo, the perception is so real that it has become a political reality of sorts. Cuomo, therefore, vociferously challenges the notion that he is a "New Deal liberal."

But the voters are ahead of the politicians. Their support for Cuomo derives from the perception that he is both a conservative and a liberal. Voters like the fact that he has built so many jail cells, and they also support him in his role as a liberal spokesperson for the welfare state. Mark Twain, upon hearing reports of his death, pugnaciously denounced them as "premature." As the public opinion data cited in this chapter suggests, any declaration of liberalism's demise in New York State would be equally premature.

NOTES

1. Ralph Waldo Emerson, "The American Scholar," address delivered before the Phi Beta Kappa Society at Cambridge, Massachusetts, 31 August 1837. Reprinted in Albert R. Ferguson, ed., *The Collected Works of Ralph Waldo Emerson,* Cambridge, Massachusetts: Belknap Press, 1971, p. 67.
2. Frank Lynn, "New York G.O.P. Sees Power Shift within the Party," *New York Times,* 6 November 1980, p. A-1.
3. Quoted in Ken Auletta, "Profile: Mayor Edward I. Koch," *New Yorker,* 10 September 1979, p. 79.
4. "This Liberal Party's Over," *New York Times,* editorial, 20 October 1985, p. E-20.
5. The official statewide returns for 1964 show Democrat Lyndon Johnson receiving 4,913,102 and Republican Barry Goldwater with 2,243,559—resulting in a difference of 2,669,543 votes. Official returns in 1986 gave Democrat Mario Cuomo 2,775,229 and Republican Andrew O'Rourke 1,363,810—resulting in a difference of 1,411,419 votes.
6. Cleveland received 58.4 percent of the total vote in 1882.
7. Michael Oreskes, "Cuomo's Solo Campaign Drive Leaves Undercurrent of Discontent in Party," *New York Times,* 6 November 1986, p. B-12.
8. *Ibid.*
9. Former governor Alfred E. Smith, a Catholic whose mother emigrated from Ireland, helped the Democrats begin their ascendancy to majority status with his appeal to the immigrants. But the Democratic majority became secure under Franklin Roosevelt's New Deal.
10. John Kenneth White, interview with Thomas P. O'Neill, Jr., Washington, D.C., 22 September 1982.
11. Nathaniel C. Nash, "For Proxmire, The Fleece Goes On," *New York Times,* 28 September 1987, p. B-6.
12. *New Choices In A Changing America: The Report of the Democratic Policy Commission to the Democratic National Committee,* Washington, D.C.: Democratic National Committee, p. 2.
13. Stanley B. Greenberg, "Plain Speaking: Democrats State Their Minds," *Public Opinion,* Summer 1986, p. 48.
14. Fred Barnes, "Meet Mario the Moderate," *New Republic,* 8 April 1985, p. 18.
15. *New York Times,* exit poll, 4 November 1986. Of those who said they voted for Reagan in 1984, 46 percent backed Cuomo and 49 percent supported O'Rourke.

16. Chuck Lane, "Ronnie's Kids," *New Republic,* 3 December 1984, p. 22-23.
17. Miriam Powell, "Nine Great Myths About Mario Cuomo," *Mother Jones,* February/March 1987, p. 27.
18. Joseph E. Persico, *The Imperial Rockefeller: A Biography of Nelson A. Rockefeller,* New York: Simon and Schuster, 1982, p. 201.
19. Mario M. Cuomo, Acceptance Speech to Democratic State Convention, 3 June 1986.
20. David Broder, "Mario the Mysterious," *Washington Post,* 14 January 1987, p. A-23.
21. Barnes, "Meet Mario the Moderate," p. 18.
22. *1985-86 New York State Statistical Yearbook,* Albany, New York: Nelson A. Rockefeller Institute of Government, p. 350.
23. Gerald M. Boyd, "Buchanan Labels Cuomo a 'Reactionary Liberal,'" *New York Times,* 16 June 1985, p. A-1.
24. Marist Institute for Public Opinion, survey, October 1985, reported in Lee M. Miringoff and Barbara L. Carvalho, *The Cuomo Factor,* Poughkeepsie, New York: Marist College, 1986, pp. 88-89.
25. "In Their Own Words: How the Iran-Contra Affair Took Shape," *New York Times,* 28 February 1987, p. 8.

A Democrat Reflects on Parties and Elections

by

Edward I. Koch

Mr. Koch was elected Mayor of New York City in 1977
and was reelected in 1981 and 1985.
He had previously served as a United States Congressman.
In 1982, he was endorsed for Governor by the
Democratic Party State Convention,
but he lost the Democratic primary election to Mario Cuomo.

EDITORS' NOTE: *In these brief remarks, the Mayor of New York City offers his views on parties and elections in the state, with emphasis on the decline of party organizations. These remarks are excerpted from an interview with Mayor Koch conducted by Professor John K. White of SUNY at Potsdam on March 11, 1988.*

EDWARD I. KOCH

I believe that the Democratic party of New York State is in very good shape because Governor Cuomo has been such a dominant force. He has the support of all the county chairmen, and the Democrats have won most of the important statewide contests in recent years.

In the city of New York, the Democratic party is in terrible shape. My working relationships with several of the county leaders are not good. The party organizations at the county level are fractionated—both ideologically and personally. For example, I do not get along with the county leader in Brooklyn (Howard Golden) because we do not agree on many substantive issues, and he has some personal animus towards me as well.

The fact that I do not have good relationships with the county leaders does not prevent me from winning elections. The bottom line is that the county leaders cannot deliver elections—neither assure your victory or defeat. That stopped a long time ago when Mayor Robert Wagner ran against the county leaders and defeated them. The county leaders may help you get your nominating petitions signed so as to get on the ballot, but they do not assure your election. You get elected primarily on your own. It really does not matter if the party organization likes you, because they do not influence enough voters in the primary to support you. Of course, it's helpful to have their campaign workers handing out your literature. It is the independents who are Democrats by way of enrollment, who vote in the primaries in as large a number as the party faithful, who will decide the outcome. Even the party faithful are not so faithful anymore.

This fragmented party organization has been helpful to me. The first time I was elected (in 1977) I got 51 percent of the vote. I was not the favorite—I was sixth in a field of seven. The second time I was elected (in 1981) voters looked at my record, and I received 75 percent of the vote. The third time I was elected I got 78 percent of the vote. So what is wrong with a fragmented party organization? Nothing.

Since the Democratic party has absolutely no impact on my ability to win elections, it consequently has no impact on my professional obligations. Democrats have no input, for example, into the selection of judges. They have very little input into the selection of any personnel in government that are non-civil service and are appointed by me. (Tom Manton, the Queens Democratic chairman, says he is "batting zero" on City Hall patronage, even with such lesser jobs as temporary typists and drivers.)[1] The county leaders despise this. One of them, in fact, is not going to support me for reelection in 1989 because he has received no patronage from me.

I do not miss having the support of the party organization. I have always been a political loner in the sense of taking on controversial issues ahead of my time. Ultimately, the public catches up and supports me. Would I prefer a party system that is less fractionated? The answer is I'm not sure. I have nothing to give them. Suppose they were a well-oiled machine, instead of being as sloppy as they are in terms of delivering votes? I don't think I would be comfortable with that. Currently I do not have to respond to their demands for patronage, and they don't like it; many reporters don't believe that is the case, but it is a fact.

I know that Ned Regan says that there has been "the evil intersection of the power of the New York City Board of Estimate to approve no-bid contracts with the Democratic borough clubhouses." (See "A Republican Reflects on Parties and Elections", following this chapter.) My response to him is that there are a lot of decisions made by the Board of Estimate—I know of no corrupt one. I don't believe that the members of the Board of Estimate are corrupt, as Donald Manes (the late Democratic leader of Queens) was or Ivan Boesky (the Wall Street financier) was. They were corrupt. Regrettably, a number of people in all levels of government as well as in the private sector are corrupt. We have our fair share of corrupt people in government who have been independently elected, or appointed, or hold civil service jobs.

I did not know that Donald Manes was corrupt—that he had sold his office. But the fact that the Republican party is so enfeebled in the city, and the Democratic party is so fractionated, had nothing to do with the scandals. The Parking Violations Bureau has 550 people in it, and two people were found to be corrupt. One was Geoffrey Lindenauer; the other was Lester Shafran. That can happen anywhere. Both were in prior administrations. They were promoted, not by me, but by my Transportation Commissioner. I ran government on the basis that commissioners could hire and fire anybody they wanted to, as long as they did not engage in discriminatory hiring practices.

With hindsight, I have changed this. Now with any position that pays more than $40,000, the commissioner cannot hire that person without an interview with me. Prior to offering the job, the commissioner must convince me that this is the best person available. This is a new safeguard. Just by having to bring the candidate to see me puts them on notice that they must come up with the best.

Strong party organizations would not reduce corruption. Let me give you an example of why I think the premise is wrong. Donald Manes came to see me and wanted Lester Shafran to be elevated to be first deputy commissioner of transportation. I told him that I wasn't going to do anything until after the 1985 election for Mayor. Manes was a strong supporter of mine in that reelection campaign. When Manes submitted Shafran's name, First Deputy Mayor Stan Brezenoff told me he was not the best available. I then said, "Take someone who is better." Manes was furious and complained to the deputy mayor and commissioner. Word got back to me of Manes's anger, and I told him through Stan Brezenoff, using an expletive, to buzz off.

Let's assume that the city is controlled by powerful county leaders. I don't know if a Mayor could engage in the kind of conduct I have just outlined and not worry about being reelected. Would another Mayor, controlled by a strong party organization, react as I did? I don't know.

NOTES

1. Frank Lynn, "Being at Odds with Leaders May Aid Koch," *New York Times,* 13 March 1988, 33.

A Republican Reflects on Parties and Elections

by

Edward V. Regan

Mr. Regan is Comptroller of the State of New York. He serves as Administrative Head of the Department of Audit and Control.

EDITORS' NOTE: *These remarks are based upon an interview with Comptroller Regan conducted by Professor John K. White of SUNY at Potsdam on October 14, 1987. Here, the Republican Comptroller of New York State deplores the current condition of the state's Republican party—especially its ineffective response to the scandals in New York City.*

There is no state Republican party— it is dormant. I have said this repeatedly, not only to the press, but to Tony Colavita [the Republican State Chairman]. Even dormant organizations can coalesce around a cause. But the Republican party has ceded its role as the "loyal opposition." Nowhere is this more apparent than in New York City. We have had almost two years of continuous scandals there—all of them centered in the Democratic clubhouse. Federal prosecutor Rudolph Giuliani says, "The real problem is rooted in the distribution of jobs through political patronage." There has been an evil intersection of the power of the New York City Board of Estimate members to approve no-bid contracts with the Democratic borough clubhouses. The scandals are beyond public acceptability. Voters are angry. It is time to take a strong position against the Democratic clubhouse politics which have dominated for too long. But our party says nothing.

Last year I was speaking to a neighborhood group in Queens, and I was confronted with the following statement: "Most of us in this room are Democrats, but we need an active Republican party in this city. Where are you?" It is a question I hear repeatedly from New Yorkers, so many of whom want the status quo challenged. Yet when I publicly criticized our party for saying nothing, I received a telegram from one Republican leader in the city complaining to me about criticizing him. And my response to him is, "How many times did you ever send a telegram to the Democratic leader complaining about judgeships for sale?" My fellow Republicans were quick to yell at me, and except for that, they have been unable to find their own voice as a party.

One reason for this sad state of affairs is the relationship that has developed between Democrats and Republicans in New York City. Sam Rayburn [the former Democratic Speaker of the House of Representatives] said it best: "To get along, go along." To some extent it is understandable. In New York City, party registration is five to one against the Republicans. Republicans win only occasionally there: John Marchi [State Senator from Staten Island], Guy Molinari [Congressman from Staten Island], Roy Goodman [State Senator from Manhattan], Guy Velella [State Senator from the Bronx], Bill Green [Congressman from Manhattan], Marty Knorr [State Senator from Queens], Bob Straniere [Assemblyman from Staten Island], and Susan Molinari [the only Republican New York City Council member] are among the rare exceptions to the rule. There has not been a sustained challenge to Democratic control. In fact, the situation is so bad that sometimes candidates have just walked into Republican headquarters and have received the party's nod.

If Republicans want to get a few good jobs for their people, or receive cross endorsements from the Democrats for their judicial candidates, they have to cooperate with the Democratic hierarchy. To get along, you go along. I understand that. That is government, that is politics, that is business, that is life.

But our party has carried that maxim to an extreme. It has refused to speak out in opposition to the scandals. Roy Goodman, Guy Molinari, Guy Velella, and I have been vocal, but our party has largely done nothing. The loyal opposition is expected to say something. But nobody yells. Silence. The situation cries out for strong voices and dedicated institutions to keep a bright spotlight on those who would steal taxpayer's money. City officials have to know that, come election time, they will be facing serious opponents who are going to raise the controversial issues and publicly ask the hard questions.

Ironically, it was the news media, not the Republican party, that has played the role of the loyal opposition. But crusading newspapers, television reporters, and editorial writers cannot manufacture a story; they have to have someone saying and doing something. There must be a legitimate newsworthy event. The Republican party did not provide them with any "news." Other than the opposition by those I mentioned earlier, we did nothing.

I say these things because I am proud to be a Republican and want my party to play a strong role in New York City. But I do not equate party loyalty with acquiescence and silence when it comes to the scandals that were tearing the city apart. It is because I believe in what our party has to offer that I am distressed that we are not responding to a clear call to repeatedly confront and disavow the stealing, bartering, and favoritism that takes place in New York City.

The Republican party's lack of organization in New York City is not indicative of the rest of the state. There are numerous county organizations that are very strong. One of the strongest Republican organizations in the nation is in Nassau County. They put up good candidates for office, and they are in there slugging. Even in Albany County, where the Democrats have a two to one registration advantage, the Republican party organization is vocal in its opposition.

But statewide the Republican party is still a minority: it has elected Alfonse D'Amato and myself, and there is a Republican State Senate. But we have lost the last four gubernatorial elections. And the statewide organization is in disarray.

I am a revisionist, like so many other people in this country. We no longer see the party bosses—the tough Sam Rayburns—and the tenacious political parties. The party bosses, like Sam Rayburn and Lyndon Johnson [as Senate leader], would never have allowed the chaos that presently exits in the Democratic presidential race to occur. They would have never permitted a Gary Hart to run for president. Democratic and Republican party bosses would have never permitted $200 billion a year federal deficits. They had a long view and would exercise some discipline over their fellow legislators over the pork barrel. Strengthening the political parties would be a very healthy thing for this country.

PART II

Government

The Government of New York State Today

by

Peter W. Colby and John K. White

EDITORS' NOTE: *This chapter provides a formal introduction to the legal structure and basic organization of New York State government. The intention is to offer readers the background necessary to more easily understand the more analytical chapters that follow.*

As the New York legislature reconvened in January 1988 to begin another year of legislating, Governor Mario Cuomo proposed a budget of $44.2 *billion* to meet the needs of the state's large population (17,558,072 in 1980). This budget and the demands placed on state government by its citizens exceeds that of many countries. It is not surprising, then, that our state has a rather complex governmental structure. In this chapter we will review the familiar divisions of executive, legislative, and judicial branches of state government, and conclude with a brief look at local governments in the Empire State—counties, cities, towns, villages, and special purpose units such as school and fire districts.

The Executive Branch

The executive branch is headed by the governor, who must be at least thirty years old, a citizen of the United States, and a resident of New York for at least five years. Prior to 1938, the term of office varied from one year to two years; that year, an amendment to the state constitution extended the term to four years. Mario Cuomo serves now as the state's chief executive and commander in chief of its military and naval forces. He is required by the state constitution to submit an annual budget to the legislature that includes recommendations for legislation and suggested appropriations for departments and programs. The governor can veto bills; convene the legislature for special sessions; appoint and, under certain conditions, remove non-elected state officers; and grant reprieves, commutations, and pardons.

The lieutenant governor is elected for the same term as the governor and must possess the same qualifications for office. The lieutenant governor's only constitutional responsibility is to serve as president of the state Senate, a largely ceremonial task performed by presiding over the Senate during the legislative session and voting to break the rare tie. Otherwise, the lieutenant governor is "standby equipment"; he or she can become governor only in the event of the impeachment, resignation, absence, or death of the incumbent.[1] Any other duties the lieutenant governor may have are designated by the governor. The current lieutenant governor is Stan Lundine, and one of his primary tasks was managing New York State's application to the U.S. Department of Energy for the supercollider project. Past lieutenant governors have had other tasks given to them by the governor, such as the chairing of state councils.

The comptroller and the attorney general are the other two elected officials who serve in the executive branch. The current comptroller, Ned

Regan, is the state's chief fiscal officer and administrative head of the Department of Audit and Control. Attorney General Robert Abrams is the state's top legal officer and head of the Department of Law. He is responsible for the prosecution of all legal cases involving the state and its officers and department heads.

The governor, comptroller, and attorney general head just three of New York State's *twenty* executive departments.[2] The heads of the remaining seventeen coordinate policy for and activities in specific areas, and are usually appointed by the governor with the advice and consent of the state Senate. The principal exception is the commissioner of education, who is selected by the Regents of the State University of New York. The executive branch is characterized by a strong governor who has considerable power to appoint and to determine the state's budget.

The relationships of the departments to the elected officials, as well as to the corporations, commissions, committees, and agencies of the executive branch, are shown in Figure 4.

The Legislative Branch

The legislature is the law making branch of state government. It is a bicameral—that is, two-house—elected body composed of the Senate and the Assembly. The state constitution authorizes a Senate of varying numbers, now 61, and an Assembly of 150 persons elected for two-year terms from districts scattered across the state. Each member of the legislature must be a United States citizen; a resident of New York state for at least five years; and, in most cases, a resident of the Senate or Assembly district that he or she represents for at least one year preceding the election.

The lieutenant governor is Senate president, but the senators choose a temporary president for a two-year term. Traditionally, the temporary president is the ranking member of the majority political party.[3] It is the duty of the temporary president to supervise the business of the Senate, appoint its committee members, name its employees, and perform or delegate to another member the duties of Senate president during the lieutenant governor's absence.

One member of the Assembly is chosen by the other members to preside over the lower house as its speaker for a two-year term. The speaker possesses powers similar to those of the temporary president of the Senate.

The powers reserved to the legislature by the state constitution are varied and extensive. Among the most important is the ability to propose laws within the limits set by the U.S. Constitution and certain federal statutes and treaties. Proposed laws, called bills, may be introduced in

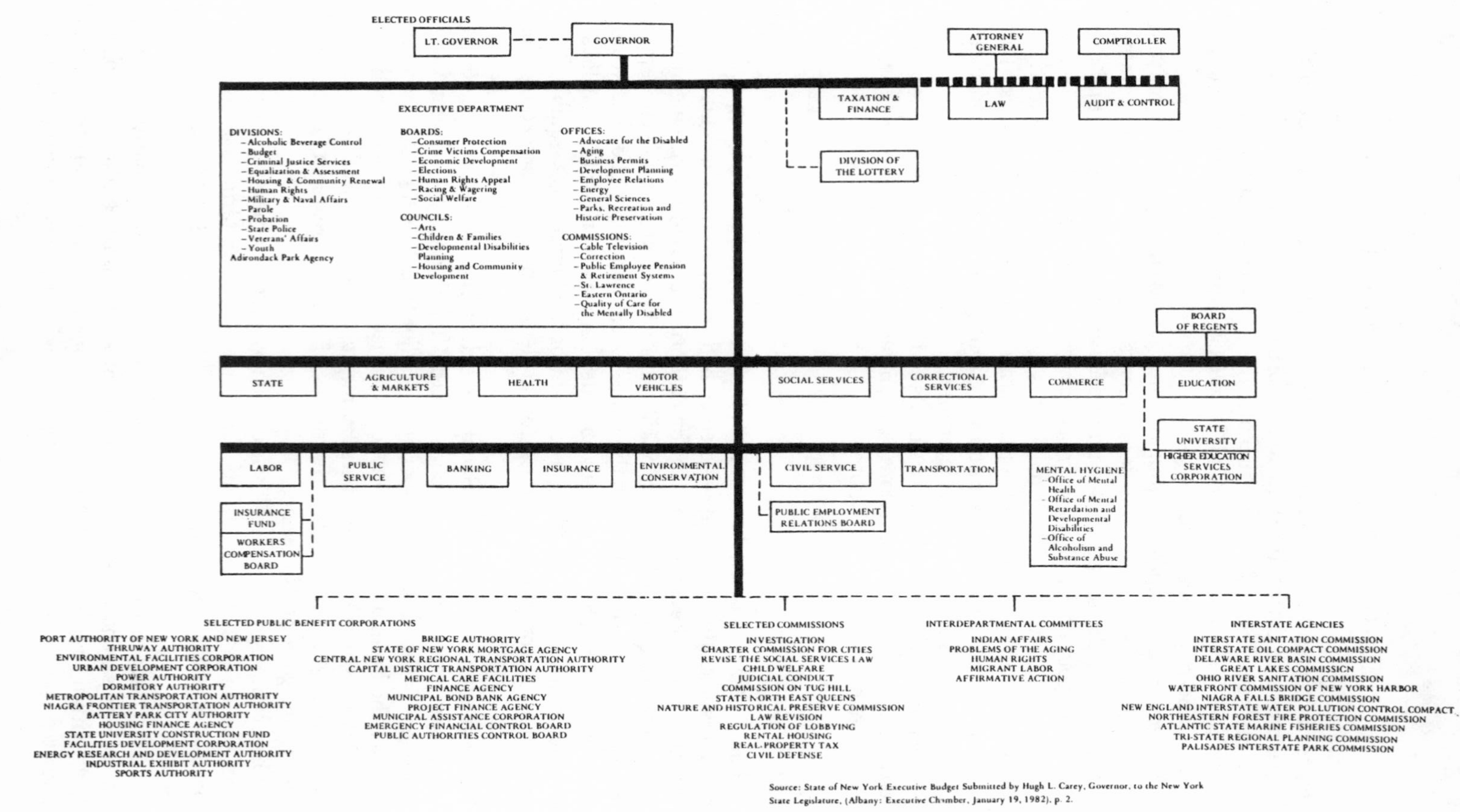

Figure 4. The New York State Bureaucracy

either house. A bill passed by one house must be approved in exactly the same form by the other before it can be sent to the governor for signing into law (see Figure 5).

Among the primary responsibilities of the legislature is the appropriation of money for the operations of state departments and agencies; allocating funds to assist local governments; defining acts of commission or omission that constitute crimes, and setting penalties for violators; promoting the public welfare, including the indigent, mentally ill, and unemployed; and clarifying, amending, or repealing laws that are confusing or outdated.

The legislature has several other powers that originate in the state constitution. One is the ability of two-thirds of the Assembly together with two-thirds of the Senate to override a gubernatorial veto. However, the legislature has overridden relatively few vetoes, thereby contributing to an environment that encourages compromise among the Senate, Assembly, and governor.

Only the Senate has the power to confirm gubernatorial appointments of non-elected state officials and court judges. The constitution provides that such appointments are to be made by the governor subject to the "advice and consent of the Senate," which approves or disapproves a nominee after a hearing on his or her qualifications.

In sum, the legislature serves as a check upon the governor, and helps ensure that the interests of the state's citizens are represented.

The Judicial Branch

The state constitution defines the organization and jurisdiction of New York's judicial branch, one of the busiest and most complex in the nation. It has approximately 1,100 full-time judges, 2,500 part-time judges, and more than 9,500 non-judicial employees. The structure and jurisdiction of the courts in the New York judicial system are shown in Figure 6 and Table 15.

The chief judge of the Court of Appeals is the chief judicial officer of the state. Sol Watchler, the current chief judge, was appointed by Governor Cuomo in 1985 for a fourteen-year term that will expire on January 2, 1999. Watchler serves as chairman of the Administrative Board of the Courts, which consists of the presiding justices of the four appellate divisions of the Supreme Court. The Administrative Board establishes administrative standards and policies for the court system.

The organization of the courts is based upon the cases each is empowered to adjudicate. The three principal court categories are the appellate courts, trial courts of superior jurisdiction, and the trial courts of lesser jurisdiction. Trial courts are those with original jurisdiction. They

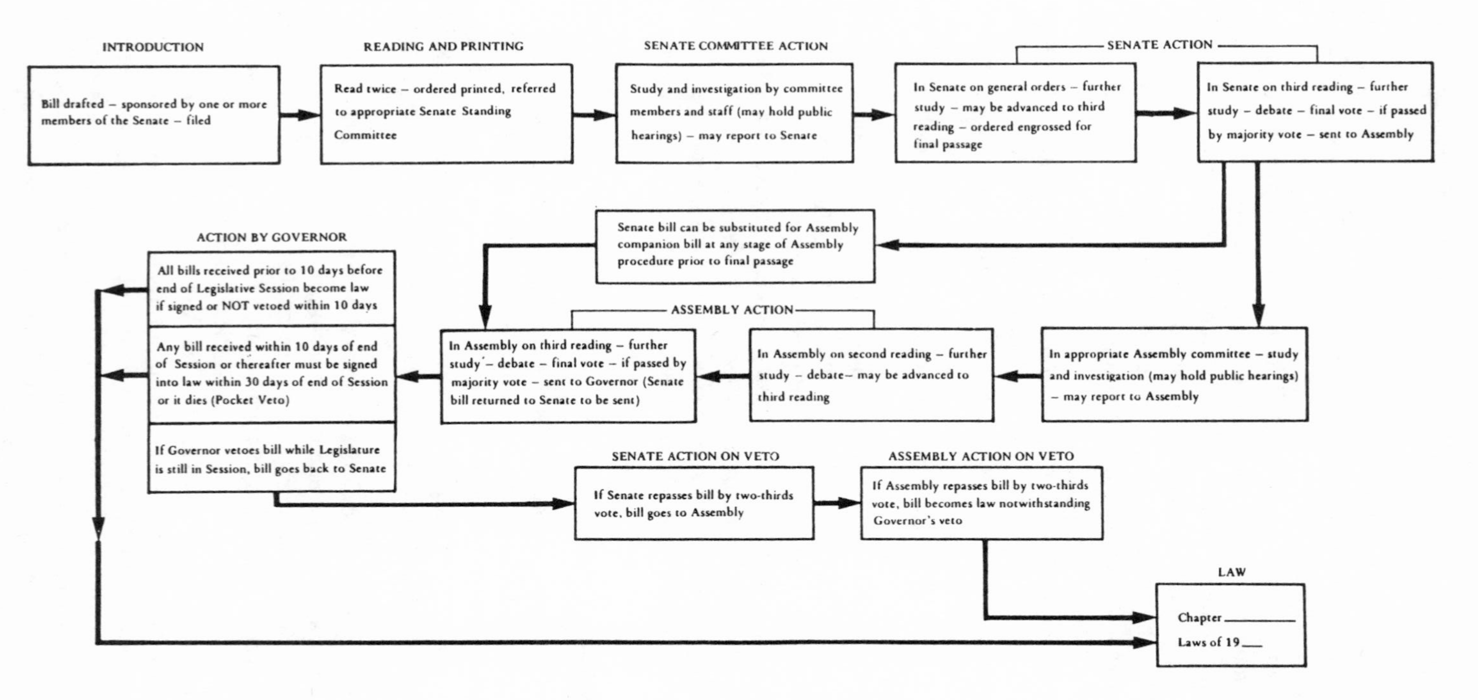

Figure 5. Course of Bill Through New York State Legislature

THE JUDICIARY

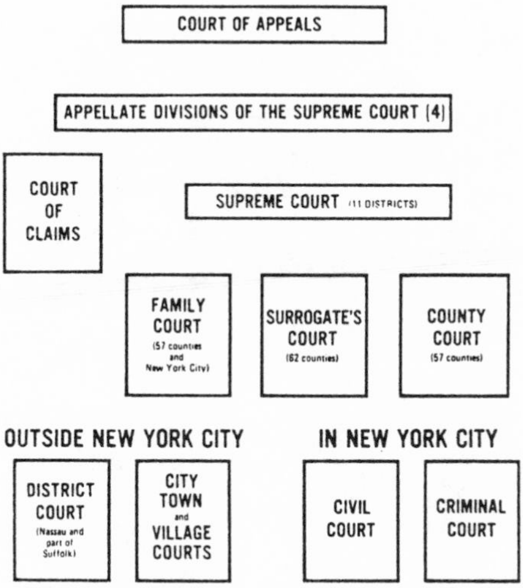

COURT OF APPEALS

APPELLATE DIVISIONS OF THE SUPREME COURT (4)

COURT OF CLAIMS

SUPREME COURT (11 DISTRICTS)

FAMILY COURT (57 counties and New York City)

SURROGATE'S COURT (62 counties)

COUNTY COURT (57 counties)

OUTSIDE NEW YORK CITY

DISTRICT COURT (Nassau and part of Suffolk)

CITY TOWN and VILLAGE COURTS

IN NEW YORK CITY

CIVIL COURT

CRIMINAL COURT

Figure 6. The Judiciary

are empowered to hear the initial case in most court proceedings. Appellate courts reconsider decisions of other tribunals in the state.

The Court of Appeals is New York's highest court. In addition to the chief judge, it includes six associate judges, who are also appointed by the governor for fourteen-year terms. The governor does not have a free hand in making the selections, but receives a list of recommendations from the Commission on Judicial Nomination. The choice must be approved by the state Senate. The Court of Appeals reviews cases from the other appellate courts and, in some instances, from the courts of original jurisdiction. Its findings are generally limited to questions of law.

In 1981 there were four appellate divisions of the Supreme Court, one in each of the state's four judicial departments, which comprise all eleven judicial districts. There are seven appellate justices apiece in the first and second departments, and five apiece in the third and fourth, who are designated by the governor from among Supreme Court justices to serve five-year terms. In the first two departments, appellate courts review criminal and civil cases from the criminal and civil courts of New York City; cases from the other district, city, town, and village courts are heard in the appropriate county court.

New York State's Supreme Court, which functions in each of the eleven judicial districts, has unlimited jurisdiction. Despite this, it usually hears

Table 15

NEW YORK STATE COURT SYSTEM CHARACTERISTICS

COURT	NO. OF JUDGES	HOW SELECTED	TERM
Court of Appeals	7	Gubernatorial appointment with advice and constent of Senate.	14 years.[1]
Appellate Division	24 permanent; no. of temporary justices varies.	Gubernatorial designation from among duly elected Supreme Court justices.	Presiding justice: 14 years, or balance of term as Supreme Court justice.[1] Associate justice: 5 years, or balance of term as Supreme Court justice.[1]
Appellate Term	Varies	Designation by Chief Administrator of Courts, with approval of presiding justice of the Department, from among duly elected Supreme Court justices.	Varies.
Supreme Court	282	Elected.	14 years.[1]
Court of Claims	44	Gubernatorial appointment with advice and consent of Senate.	9 years or, if appointed to fill a vacancy, the period remaining in that term.[1]
Surrogate's Court	62	Elected.	14 years in New York City.[1] 10 years outside the City.[1]
County Court	104	Elected.	10 years.[1]
Family Court	106	Mayoral appointment in New York City. Elected outside the City.	10 years or, if appointed to fill a vacancy, the period remaining in that term.[1]
Civil Court of New York City	120	Elected.	10 years.[1]
Criminal Court of New York City	98	Mayoral appointment:	10 years or, if appointed to fill a vacancy, the period remaining in that term.[1]
District Court	49	Elected.	6 years.[1]
City Court	154	Most elected; some acting judges appointed by Mayor or Common Council.	Varies.[1]
Town Court	Approx. 2,000	Elected.	4 years.
Village Court	Approx. 570	Elected.	Varies.

[1]Mandatory retirement at age 70.

only those cases outside the authority of other courts, such as civil cases involving more than $10,000. It also adjudicates most felony cases in New York City and the rest of the state.

The Court of Claims is a statewide court whose primary jurisdiction involves claims for monetary damages involving the state and a claimant, or two other conflicting claimants. Its judges are appointed by the governor for nine years. Some Court of Claims judges are empowered to adjudicate other civil and criminal matters that would normally come before the Supreme Court.

There are four courts of lesser jurisdiction outside New York City—district, city, town, and village courts—that handle minor civil and criminal matters.

The complex structure of the state's court system is a reflection of the numerous tasks that the judiciary is asked to perform, including the fair and prompt resolution of all civil claims, family disputes, criminal matters, juvenile delinquency cases, and disputes between citizens and the government. The courts are also asked to determine the legality of wills, adoptions, and divorces; to provide legal protection for children, the mentally ill, and others entitled to the special safeguards of the court; to regulate the admission of lawyers to the bar and their legal conduct; and to review administrative decisions to admonish, censure, or remove judges. It is the duty of the courts to decide the constitutionality of current laws, as well as settling disputes concerning how bureaucracies apply them. This is a complex and challenging task.

Local Government

Much of the business of government in New York State is carried out through local governments (see Table 16). Counties, cities, villages, towns, schools, and special districts legislate and implement policies for the specific needs of their own populations.

COUNTIES

Counties were established by the state legislature to perform specific functions on behalf of the state. Excluding New York City, the state is divided into fifty-seven counties. The city's five boroughs are vestigial counties for certain purposes, although they are not organized as such nor do they operate as county governments. Originally modest in function, county government during the past half century has undergone a major transformation in its function, form, and basic nature. Counties are no longer mere subdivisions that perform assigned functions but municipal corporations with sufficient legal and fiscal power to provide a wide range of services. Counties were, in a sense, ready-made "regional" govern-

Table 16

CURRENT OPERATING EXPENDITURES OF ALL LOCAL GOVERNMENTS IN NEW YORK STATE, BY TYPE OF EXPENDITURE, SELECTED YEARS 1971-1984
(millions of dollars)

	1970	1980	1981	1982	1983	1984
All Local Governments	$11,732.2	$25,495.1	$26,625.2	$28,368.4	$30,189.2	$32,454.5
Education	4,571.5	9,231.9	9,808.6	10,588.3	10,588.3	11,886.9
Social Services[1]	2,671.8	5,025.3	5,260.5	5,304.8	5,802.3	6,155.1
Public Safety	1,165.7	2,480.8	2,742.1	3,028.9	3,306.0	3,611.7
General Government	632.2	1,276.5	1,299.5	1,490.9	1,625.5	1,735.3
Highways	386.4	965.5	1,055.6	1,181.6	1,263.2	1,297.4
Sanitation	290.4	797.3	883.5	973.4	1,058.9	1,135.7
Public Health	824.4	1,332.9	1,227.3	1,347.1	1,580.0	1,740.6
All Other	1,189.8	4,384.8	4,347.9	4,453.3	4,626.0	4,891.6
New York City[2]	$ 6,020.8	$11,810.3	$12,109.1	$13,283.9	$13,965.7	$15,224.2
Education	1,674.4	3,042.3	3,202.2	3,512.7	3,396.7(b)	3,819.6
Social Services[1]	1,798.4	2,894.1	3,066.6	3,381.0	3,592.1	3,974.9
Public Safety	770.2	1,480.8	1,647.5	1,836.6	2,013.6	2,204.7
General Government	308.2	513.0	487.0	606.1	676.0	722.0
Highways	55.8	359.8	383.5	456.4	527.4	495.8
Sanitation	194.5	430.2	473.5	517.9	570.0	603.2
Health	598.5	718.7	578.5(a)	626.7	770.8	840.0
All Other	620.7	2,371.3	2,270.3	2,346.4	2,419.0	2,564.0
Rest of State[3]	$ 5,711.4	$13,684.8	$14,516.1	$15,084.5	$16,223.5	$17,230.3
Education	2,897.1	6,189.6	6,606.4	7,075.6	7.530.7	8,067.3
Social Services[1]	873.4	2,131.2	2,193.9	1,923.8	2,210.2	2,180.2
Public Safety	395.5	1,000.0	1,094.6	1,192.3	1,292.4	1,407.0
General Government	324.0	763.5	812.5	884.8	949.5	1,013.3
Highways	330.6	605.7	672.1	725.2	735.8	801.6
Sanitation	95.9	367.1	410.0	455.5	488.9	532.5
Public Health	225.9	614.2	648.8	720.4	809.2	900.6
All Other	569.1	2,013.5	2,077.6	2,106.9	2,207.0	2,327.5

Note: Detil may not add to totals due to rounding.

[1]The State and Federally funded portion of the Medical Assistance program is not reflected in the Social Services category for New York City (starting in 1980) and for participating counties during the transition period (1980m through 1982) and for all counties thereafter (with the exception of Erie County). Starting in 1984, Erie County is now reporting net Medical Assistance expenditures in the same manner as all other counties. Payments to vendors are now processed directly by the State through the Medical Management Information System (MMIS).

[2]New York City has installed a new accounting system; therefore, certain functional categories for 1980 through 1984 may not be comparable to the corresponding data of prior years.

[3]In 1970, the detail includes payments for all applicable personal services, equipment and other expenses. Fringe benefits (except Education) are included under All Other unless the benefits were expended out of specific funds (i.e, water, sewer, library, hospital, etc.) For 1980 through 1984, the detail includes payments for all applicable personal services and contractual expenses. Expenditures for equipment (except certain equipment expenses in Education) are not included as in previous years. Employee benefits (except Education) are included in All Other. Expenditures for special districts in 1980 through 1984 are included in Public Safety, Sanitation, Highway and All Other. In 1970, they are included in All Other.

[a]Reflects a decrease in New York City's subsidy to the Health and Hospitals Corporation.

[b]Starting in 1983 the State assumed full responsibility for funding the senior colleges of the City University of New York. Accordingly, the financial transactions of the senior colleges are no longer reflected in this category.

Source: New York State Office of the State Comptroller.

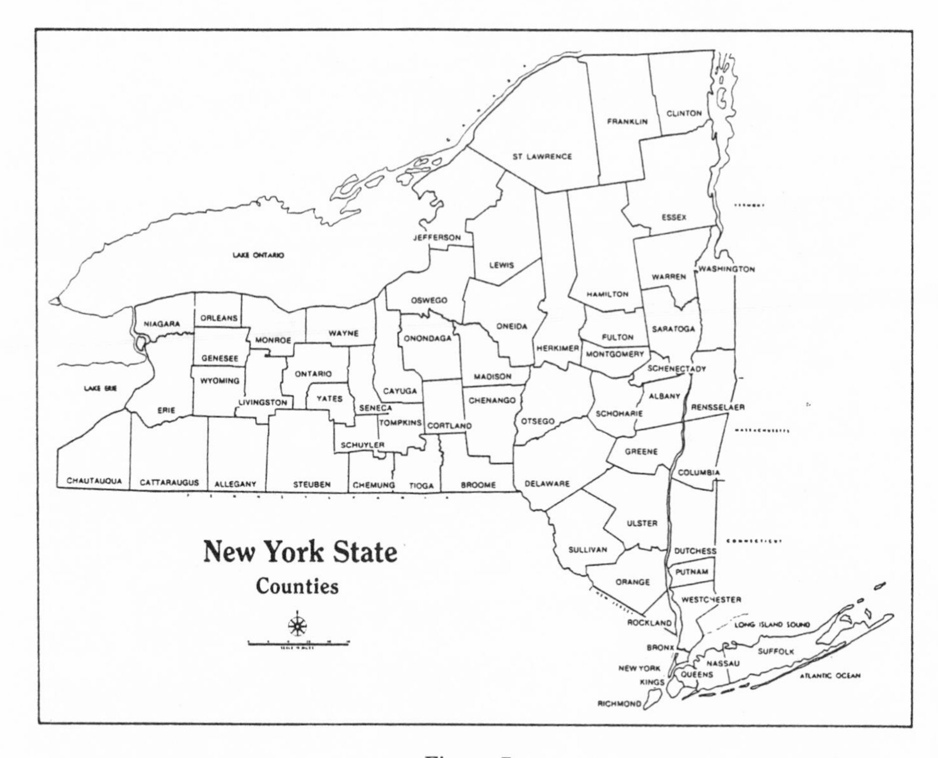

Figure 7

ments that overlap but do not necessarily supersede the jurisdictions of cities, towns, and villages within their borders.

CITIES

As population clusters developed into urban areas during the nineteenth century, the need for government services prompted the legislature to incorporate cities. Aside from their similar origins, it is difficult to ascertain common purposes among cities or generalize about their structure, because the charters granted to them differ widely.

There is no general law concerning municipal incorporation. No statutory standards exist concerning how populous or how large an area must be to be granted recognition as a city by the state legislature. Nor is there a discernable progression from village to city designation. The legislature may incorporate a community of any size as a city (see Table 17). In 1980, 48 of the state's 62 cities had populations smaller than that of the largest village, and 176 of the state's 554 villages had populations greater than that of the smallest city.

Table 17

FORMS OF GOVERNMENT AND POPULATIONS FOR CITIES IN NEW YORK STATE

	1980 POPULATION	FORM OF GOVERNMENT
1. Albany	101,727	Mayor-Council
2. Amsterdam	21,872	Mayor-Council
3. Auburn	32,548	Council-Manager
4. Batavia	16,703	Council-Manager
5. Beacon	12,937	Commission
6. Binghamton	55,860	Mayor-Council
7. Buffalo	357,870	Mayor-Council
8. Canandaigua	10,419	Council-Manager
9. Cohoes	18,144	Mayor-Council
10. Corning	12,953	Mayor-Council
11. Cortland	20,138	Mayor-Council
12. Dunkirk	15,310	Mayor-Council
13. Elmira	35,327	Council-Manager
14. Fulton	13,312	Mayor-Council
15. Geneva	15,133	Council-Manager
16. Glen Cove	24,618	Mayor-Council
17. Glens Falls	15,897	Mayor-Council
18. Gloversville	17,836	Mayor-Council
19. Hornell	10,234	Mayor-Council
20. Hudson	7,986	Mayor-Council
21. Ithaca	28,732	Mayor-Council
22. Jamestown	35,775	Mayor-Council
23. Johnstown	9,360	Mayor-Council
24. Kingston	24,481	Mayor-Council
25. Lackawanna	22,701	Mayor-Council
26. Little Falls	6,156	Mayor-Council
27. Lockport	24,844	Mayor-Council
28. Long Beach	34,073	Council-Manager
29. Mechanicville	5,500	Commission
30. Middletown	21,454	Mayor-Council
31. Mount Vernon	66,713	Mayor-Council
32. Newburgh	23,438	Council-Manager
33. New Rochelle	70,794	Council-Manager
34. Niagara Falls	71,384	Council-Manager
35. North Tonawanda	35,760	Mayor-Council
36. Norwich	8,082	Mayor-Council
37. Ogdensburg	12,375	Council-Manager
38. Olean	18,207	Mayor-Council
39. Oneida	10,810	Mayor-Council
40. Oneonta	14,933	Mayor-Council
41. Oswego	19,793	Mayor-Council
42. Peekskill	18,236	Council-Manager
43. Plattsburgh	21,057	Mayor-Council
44. Port Jervis	8,699	Mayor-Council
45. Poughkeepsie	29,757	Council-Manager
46. Rensselaer	9,047	Mayor-Council
47. Rochester	241,741	Council-Manager
48. Rome	43,826	Mayor-Council
49. Rye	15,083	Council-Manager
50. Salamanca	6,890	Mayor-Council

Table 17—Continued

51. Saratoga Springs	23,906	Commission
52. Schenectady	67,972	Mayor-Council
53. Sherrill	2,830	Council-Manager
54. Syracuse	170,105	Mayor-Council
55. Tonawanda	18,693	Mayor-Council
56. Troy	56,638	Council-Manager
57. Utica	75,632	Mayor-Council
58. Watertown	27,861	Council-Manager
59. Watervliet	11,354	Council-Manager
60. White Plains	46,999	Mayor-Council
61. Yonkers	195,351	Council-Manager
62. New York City	7,071,030	Mayor-Council

Source: Local Government Handbook (Albany, New York: Department of State, 4th edition, 1987), pp. 87–87.

As a practical matter, the legislature does not create a city in the absence of compelling demands from the locality for incorporation. This usually takes the form of a locally drafted charter submitted to the legislature for enactment.

TOWNS

Everyone in New York who resides outside a city or an Indian reservation lives in a town. Towns are the state's most numerous units of local government.

"Town government" ranges in size from Hempstead, with a 1980 population of 738,517 (more than twice that of the City of Buffalo) and taxable property valuation in 1978 of more than $11 billion, to Montague with 32 residents in 1980 and taxable property valuation in 1978 of more than $3 million. Between these two towns are some 930 others. Some provide many municipal services; others do little more than maintain a few roads.

New York State courts have recently determined that towns are, in fact, municipal corporations. The courts had ruled previously that towns were "involuntary subdivisions of the state, constituted for the purpose of the more convenient exercise of governmental functions by the state for the benefit of all its citizens."[4] Towns have incorporated the latest court rulings into their statutes.

> A town is a municipal corporation comprising the inhabitants within its boundaries, and formed with the purpose of exercising such powers and discharging such duties of local government and administration of public affairs as have been, or, may be conferred or imposed upon it by law.[5]

Table 18

LOCAL GOVERNMENT DISTRICTS AND AUTHORITIES
IN NEW YORK STATE
1984

School Districts	733
Town Fire Districts	837
Town Fire Protection Districts	1,011
Town Lighting Districts	1,599
Town Sewer Districts	985
Town Drainage Districts	487
Town Water Districts	1,330
Town Refuse and Garbage Districts	172
Town Park Districts	127
Town Consolidated Health Districts	78
Other Town Districts	164
County Districts	139
Public Housing Authorities	178
Other Public Authorities	64
Urban Renewal Agencies	124
Industrial Development Agencies	163

Source: New York State Office of the State Comptroller: *Special Report on Municipal Affairs, 1984* as reported in *New York State Statistical Yearbook,* p. 385.

Towns were granted full status as local governments when, in 1964, they were constitutionally granted home rule powers.

VILLAGES

Most New Yorkers think of villages as small, rural communities. But number of inhabitants alone does not determine that one community becomes a village and another a town. In New York a village is a legal concept; it is a municipal corporation.

Villages were formed within town boundaries to provide services for clusters of people: first, in rural areas; later, in suburbs around large cities. Many have public service responsibilities that do not differ substantially from cities, towns, and counties. Like their other local government counterparts, village officials face the full range of municipal obligations and challenges.

The rapid growth of suburban towns beginning in the late 1930s and accelerating after World War II emphasized the need for alternatives to villages. To provide services, suburbs made increasing use of the town improvement district. This had a profound effect on village growth. Although more than 160 villages were formed from 1900 to 1940, only 13 new ones were incorporated during the succeeding forty years, and several others have been dissolved.

There were 553 villages in New York State in 1980. Most were in areas surrounding the larger cities. They ranged in size from tiny Dering Harbor, with a population of 16, to the Village of Hempstead, with 40,404 residents. Most villages have populations under 2,500, although 21 had more than 20,000 residents.

SPECIAL PURPOSE UNITS

In addition to the municipal corporations discussed above, another group of public entities provides a number of specific services. These special purpose units include school districts and fire districts (see Table 18). Although the tasks they perform are diverse, their distinguishing feature is that each provides a single service rather than the array of services assigned to counties, villages, and towns.

NOTES

1. The temporary president of the state Senate and the speaker of the state Assembly follow the lieutenant governor in succession to the governorship.
2. The state departments are Executive, Audit and Control, Law, State, Agriculture and Markets, Banking, Civil Service, Commerce, Correctional Services, Education, Environmental Conservation, Health, Insurance, Labor, Mental Hygiene, Motor Vehicles, Public Service, Social Services, Taxation and Finance, and Transportation.
3. The current temporary president is Senate Majority Leader Warren Anderson, a Republican from Binghamton who has been in the Senate since his election in 1952. Anderson has served longer in these posts than anyone in New York State history.
4. Short V. Town of Orange, 1916 175 Appellate Division 260: 161 New York State 466.
5. Article I, Section 2, Town Law New York State Statute.

New York's Four Constitutions

by

Fred Bartle

Mr. Bartle is Associate Professor of Political Science
at the State University of New York at Oswego.
He is a former staff member of the 1967 Constitutional
Convention in Albany
working for the Committee on Local Government and Home Rule.

EDITORS' NOTE: *The basic governing document of any political system is its constitution. This chapter describes the four constitutions which have served New York's citizens since the first in 1777, revealing the changing priorities and values of the state.*

On July 3, 1776, there existed in a land area south of Canada, north of Florida, and between the Atlantic and the Mississippi, thirteen governments, each dependent upon the King of England. On July 4, there were none, for the immediate legal significance of the Declaration of Independence was to assert that British authority no longer existed. This claim had to be proved on the battlefield and at the conference table. In due time that did happen. But meanwhile, our revolutionary ancestors realized that the next order of business was to create new governments, to establish new legitimacy, and to replace the authority of the deposed King with some practical new authority.

The technical abolition of the King's thirteen charters did not lead to anarchy or even to confusion. In reality, the King's authority had been under considerable strain prior to 1776, and willful colonials were quite prepared to create new charters for their new country. Thomas Jefferson's next project after the Declaration of Independence was a draft for a new constitution for Virginia.

Twelve ex-colonies, including New York, moved expeditiously to write new constitutions for themselves in the months after independence was declared; only Connecticut felt that its charter—which had been drafted in Connecticut—was sufficient without change.

New York's First Constitution

New York's first constitution reflects throughout the search of revolutionaries for political legitimacy. A lengthy preamble, more like a propaganda pamphlet than a constitution, quotes entirely New York's own little declaration of independence of May 1776—a resolution passed by the "congress of the colony of New York" which itself quotes a resolution of the Continental Congress calling on the "states" to adopt new governments—and additionally quotes the entire national Declaration of Independence.

The first article of the new constitution addressed itself to the crucial issue of sovereignty. "No authority shall . . . be exercised over the people . . . but such as shall be derived from and granted by them." Exit King George. Enter the people of the sovereign state of New York.

It is mildly ironical, no doubt justified at the time by the presence of British troops on Long Island, in New York City, in Oswego, and in the Champlain and lower Hudson Valleys, that this first constitution was written at a convention not called by the people and was not submitted to the people for ratification. The convention itself was forced to meet at various locations, depending on where the scouts thought the British were. It was approved—if not drafted—at Kingston on April 20, 1777, at which time it simply and necessarily was deemed in effect. Exit the colony of New York. Enter the state of New York. The first New York constitution predates the nation-wide Articles of Confederation, and, of course, the federal constitution.

In 42 brief sections, the first constitution created a two-house legislature; provided for its initial apportionment and subsequent reapportionments as population should change; sketched legislative powers; established universal male suffrage subject to age and property qualifications; created the office of governor, but withheld from him independent appointment and veto power; authorized impeachment for gubernatorial misbehavior; established somewhat complex property qualifications for holding office depending on the office itself; established a statewide court system; provided for a variety of local office holders to be appointed by the state government; authorized the legislature to select delegates to future continental congresses; and, although not systematically or even in a single part of the document, began to itemize individual rights from land ownership to trial by jury to liberty of conscience to separation of church from state. The first constitution gave the state legislature authority to "naturalize . . .persons . . . born in parts beyond the sea, and out of the United States of America." This suggests that citizenship meant state citizenship; federal citizenship did not exist at that time. The constitution authorized an experiment in voting by ballot. The prevailing mode of conducting elections prior to that time was by voice vote at meetings held for that purpose.

The document is at once revolutionary and conservative. It is revolutionary because it announced its own existence in the name of the people who were not asked to consent to it. And it is revolutionary because it gave over all governmental power to the people. It is conservative because it guarded against two tyrannies: that of the executive and that of the majority of the people. The state's founding fathers took the rights of men with property seriously indeed. The men who owned the state could vote for those among them who had property because they alone could be trusted with office.

The state's first constitution established, not inconsistent with its own colonial past, the basic Western three divisions of government, complete with checks and balances, and that basic form has survived basically unchanged—save perhaps for the enhancement of judicial power—for two centuries. The office of governor and the legislature have been continuously elected, and a recent amendment to New York's fourth constitution has returned to the principle of the first one in providing for the appointment of the state's highest judges.

Changing Constitutions

Voters of New York State have ratified three newer constitutions—1821, 1846, and 1894. There have been twelve constitutional conventions in our state's history; two of those dealt with judicial matters only. The current (1894) document has been, and will continue to be, revised numerous times. Because each succeeding constitution has grown longer and much more specific than its predecessor, the need for revision inevitably grows greater. What seems appropriate for one decade becomes a restraint upon a future one. Attempts to purify government tend to muddy the future.

It is quite appropriate to ask why the federal constitution has endured with not even thirty amendments (and ten of those were really part of the original constitution) while state constitutions—New York is quite like other states in this regard—have had such short lifespans. The answer comes in two parts. During the pre-Civil War period, people in states paid much more attention to their state governments than they did to the relatively quiescent national government in far off Washington. Pressures for change were felt much more strongly in state capitals. The Jeffersonian and Jacksonian revolutions were nationwide in scope, but their characters were felt more keenly in Richmond and Nashville—and Albany—than in Washington. Hence, a need to change constitutions to keep abreast of political change.

Secondly, the new complexities of government in the post-Civil War period, attended by more demands for services and, alas, by corruption, burgeoned at the state level first. Almost every component part of big government as we know it in this century at the federal level had been advanced by the states as they wrestled with their problems. Hence, citizens who in a vague sort of way were pleased at the stability of the federal government were demanding simultaneously that state constitutions be changed to perfect government and to cure a broad variety of specific shortcomings. It is now commonplace to note that the federal constitution has in fact been amended hundreds of times by the Supreme Court's interpretive alchemy, but this is a twentieth-century observation. The people of New York State sought constitutional change to assuage their complaints and concerns. They sought—and got—those changes early and often.

New York's Second Constitution

It is significant that the presiding officer of the 1821 New York convention to write a new state constitution was Daniel Tompkins, the incumbent vice-president of the United States. His national duties were so inconsequential that he devoted his time (successfully) to writing a new state constitution and running (unsuccessfully) for Governor of New York, a position he had earlier held.

The 1821 constitution was approved by the state's voters. In a three-line preamble and nine articles, it detailed more precisely legislative powers and duties, gave the governor alone the veto power, and considerably scaled down property qualifications for voting (but did make it virtually impossible for blacks to vote, presumably correcting a 1777 oversight). The governor's term was reduced from three to two years. The governor's appointment power was clarified much to his advantage. Seven state-wide officials (secretary of state, comptroller, treasurer, attorney general, and others) were to be elected by the two houses of the state legislature meeting jointly, a procedure still in use today for electing the membership of the New York State Board of Regents. These officers were removable by a concurrent resolution of both houses. Justices of the peace were to be appointed by the governor only if local county boards of supervisors and county judges could not agree on a common list of candidates. And common councils, no longer the governor, appointed city mayors. Other powers of local governments were somewhat enhanced. This constitution recognized the importance of local governments more than did its predecessor.

The 1821 constitution devoted Article VII to a clear, detailed, and lengthy bill of rights for citizens. Some language from 1777 was retained. Much new language was added, including provisions for money for common schools ("a perpetual fund . . . inviolably appropriated and applied") and for inland navigation to be financed by a tax on salt as well as canal tolls. Land grants dating back to the King were continued in force. The rights of people were at least placed on a par with property rights; both were protected and enhanced.

The Third Constitution

By 1846, Jacksonian democracy had made its mark, and New York's third constitution clearly reflected new opportunities for the people to control their own affairs. With minimal residence requirements, all white males were enfranchised, black males who had been for three years citizens of New York and who owned freeholds worth $250 were also permitted to vote.

A thirty-two member Senate (two-year terms) and a 128-member Assembly (one-year terms) were to be elected from single-member districts. Earlier versions of the Senate utilized multi-member districts. Apportionment provisions were quite clear: districts were to be as equal in population as possible, except that each county was to have at least one assemblyman. The Legislature itself was to apportion assembly districts among the counties, but local boards of supervisors were to divide up large counties into individual districts. A special provision for Hamilton County was inserted in the constitution, and a version of it is still there; because of its very small population, Hamilton County was not permitted to have an assemblyman.

The powers of the governor were not substantially changed, and his term was still set for two years; during the 1840s and 1850s, the state had eight successive one-term governors. The greatest outburst of democracy in the constitution, however, is found in the list of other statewide officials to be elected: secretary of state, comptroller, treasurer, attorney general, state engineer and surveyor, canal commissioners, inspectors of state prisons, and four (of eight) judges of the state Court of Appeals. At no other time in the state's history have so many officials been so directly responsible to the state's voters.

Article VI gave the state's judiciary the general shape it still retains. There were to be supreme court judges elected from districts across the state, appellate division judges drawn from persons elected to the Supreme Court, and an eight-member Court of Appeals, half elected, the other half being designated from a panel of senior Supreme Court judges. All judges were made elective; the governor was given a power he still has of filling judicial vacancies.

The 1846 Constitution regulated state indebtedness for the first time. Provisions were made for paying for the Erie, Genesee, and Black River canals and for funding the debts incurred by state loans to railroad companies and other private corporations. The document assumed there would be an operating surplus from the state's canal system and placed this surplus into the state's general fund. However, the legislature was authorized sufficient taxing power in the absence of such a surplus.

Article X addressed matters of local government. Sheriffs and county clerks were to be elected by the people of each county but were removable, with cause, by the governor. The general principle of electing other local officials was inserted, again with provision for removal for "misconduct or malversation."

Our Present Constitution

Although there were many attempts to revise it, the 1846 document remained relatively unamended for almost fifty years. A new judicial article had been added during the 1860's, but it was not until 1894 that the people of the state wrote their fourth, and current, constitution. The 1890s were a particularly important decade in New York State's history. The fantastic growth of the population of the New York City area led to the creation in 1898 of the New York City of five boroughs (counties, actually) that exist today. It seemed in the 1890s that the population of this huge new city should certainly exceed the population of the rest of the state and perhaps alter power relations in the state very significantly. This never happened, but a new constitution seemed in order to prepare for the new century.

The 1894 constitution was new; it amended 45 sections of the 1846 constitution and also added 28 totally new sections. Eighteen sections of the older constitution were eliminated entirely.

Race disappeared from the suffrage requirements, but even though other states had already provided for women's suffrage, New York State did not. Secrecy was added to voting procedures and provisions were added for an orderly manner of registering voters.

The State Senate's membership was increased to fifty with provisions to increase that number to insure a more equitable apportionment. The Senate currently has sixty-one members. A 150-member Assembly was continued; again, every county except Hamilton was entitled to at least one member. It is not uncommon to find much negative language in state constitutions, and this especially in sections dealing with legislative behavior. New York's legislature had displeased honest citizens during the years before 1894, and the constitution revisers reflected progressive politics by placing restraints against potential abuses of legislative power.

The governor and the lieutenant governor continued to be elected separately, and their terms continued to be for two years. Not until 1938 was a governor elected to the first four-year term in the state's history. Only one governor of New York has died in office; six, however, have resigned, and one lamentable statesman was impeached and convicted. Thus, the second spot has statistical possibilities.

The Jacksonian melange of elected officials was trimmed in 1894, but not as significantly as might have been expected at a time when a shorter ballot was being touted by modern democrats. The comptroller, secretary of state, treasurer, attorney general and state engineer and surveyor were continued as elective offices, with terms increased to three years, and all Court of Appeals judges were made elective. By mid-century, though, only the governor/lieutenant governor ticket, the comptroller and the attorney general remained on a statewide ballot.

While judicial districts were changed to reflect new demographic facts more accurately and while the Court of Appeals was somewhat simplified, the basic court structure was continued. The Court of Appeals' jurisdiction was slightly limited from earlier times, and judicial removal was provided for with what one could reasonably call enthusiasm. Judges had not performed perfectly either.

The local government article was not greatly changed from 1846. The current Bill of Rights for Local Governments in the present amended constitution is the newest complete article in the present document. And in spite of its hyperbolic language, it materializes that local governments do not have very many rights. Again, as in 1846, the main themes were local election of local officials with removal authority, with cause, in the hands of the governor.

With the pending birth of greater New York in mind, the convention gave specific powers to the legislature to classify cities by size. It is a delicate lawyer's point that the legislature is forbidden to legislate specific controls over New York City without its own permission, but that it may legislate for all cities in the state with a population in excess of one million without New York City's permission. If that is logically and morally anomalous, the judiciary of the state has been quite solemn about its approval.

Since 1894

As if to emphasize Jefferson's assertion that the earth belongs to the living, the 1894 constitution continued the 1846 automatic referendum every twenty years at which the people would be asked if they wanted to convene a new constitutional convention to amend or perchance to rewrite the old one. And three conventions have been held since 1894, although their products have been either totally or partially rejected.

The constitution as it stands today is one of the longest in the nation, perhaps one of the more cumbersome, and contains much language subsequent conventions have sought to eliminate. Investigative journalists now perform what constitutional language could only try to do—save us from public scandal. Gubernatorial power has been enhanced by the reality of dealing with multitudinous problems, and virtually every governor since the 1920's has been a national leader in administration. The state's legislature is now one of the most professional of them all, with staffing adequate to deal with the complexities of modern administration and finance. If the constitution imposes checks that seem unreasonable to legislative and gubernatorial intent, an amendment is sure to follow. The current Court of Appeals is activist in character, somewhat in the mold of the late Chief Justice Earl Warren, and given the public attitudes of the incumbent governor who now appoints the court is quite likely to stay that way.

New York's Four Constitutions

New York's four constitutions, three of which were ratified by the people of the state, are important because they were and are the basic law by which we live our lives within the state, and also because they represent the best and the most powerful thinking of their respective times.

The Governorship in an Era of Limits and Changes

by

Gerald Benjamin

Mr. Benjamin is Professor of Political Science
at the State University of New York at New Paltz
and a Senior Fellow at the SUNY Rockefeller Institute.
He is co-author, with Robert Connery, of *Rockefeller of New York*
(Ithaca: Cornell University Press, 1979).

EDITORS' NOTE: *The focal point for political leadership in most political systems is the chief executive, and thus in New York the Governor. This essay details the legal, political, and institutional bases for the modern governorship and concludes with a discussion of the limits of the governor's power.*

GERALD BENJAMIN

Almost immediately after his election in November of 1982, New York's new governor, Mario Cuomo, began to be "mentioned" for high national office. This was not surprising. Since the civil war, almost a fifth of the persons nominated for the presidency by the major political parties have served as governor of New York. Three of these—Grover Cleveland, Theodore Roosevelt, and Franklin Delano Roosevelt—actually won the presidency. Five others—Horatio Seymour, Samuel J. Tilden, Charles Evans Hughes, Alfred E. Smith, and Thomas E. Dewey—failed of election. And most recently, of course, Governor Nelson A. Rockefeller was a serious presidential contender for almost all of this fifteen years in office, ultimately serving as vice president.

But the New York governorship would be notable even if it had not been such an effective springboard for attempts to gain the nation's highest office; many of its occupants achieved distinction among their peers for the way in which they did the governor's job itself. Thus, in an essay about the "ten outstanding governors of the twentieth century," George Weeks, former chief-of-staff to Governor William G. Milliken of Michigan, commented: "Based alone on the caliber of its governors, [New York] could have accounted for half the top ten if there had not been some attempt to recognize different times and circumstances." [1] Indeed, even after adjusting his analysis to avoid overemphasizing New York, Weeks included three of the state's governors—Smith, Dewey and Rockefeller—on his final list of the ten greatest.

If for no other reason, the level of distinction achieved by the office's incumbents makes the New York governorship worthy of study. What is it about this office that has attracted people of such quality, and what about New York's political system has allowed them to rise in it? In order to find answers to these questions, we need to understand a complex of factors: the presence in New York of social diversity and a political economy that demands and supports strong leadership, a constitutional design that provides the framework for such leadership, and a history of the use of executive power that creates the expectation that the governor will be the center of energy in the state political system.

The Framework

Commenting before New York's 1967 Constitutional Convention Committee on the Executive Branch, governor Nelson Rockefeller observed that "great men are not drawn to small office." Rockefeller noted further that the governor's powers "comprise a substantial grant of authority. And because our governors possess this authority, we have enjoyed leadership that has established New York as a pioneering, innovating, and eminently successful state." [2]

The governor's somewhat self-serving hyperbole notwithstanding, it is indeed true that over its history New York has been less chary of a strong executive than most of its sister states. During the revolution, when the norm was a one-year gubernatorial term, limited succession, and legislative selection of the governor, the New York constitution, drafted later and in a more conservative political milieu than prevalent in the other original states, provided for a three-year term, unlimited succession, and popular election. At a time when the veto power was anathema, identified as it was with royal authority, New York nevertheless allowed its governor first to share such a negative with others on a Council of Revision and then, in 1821, made it his alone. And, in that same year, the authority to make state appointments was taken from a Council of Appointment and given to the governor, subject to the approval of the State Senate.

Despite its early inclination to empower the executive, New York in the first half of the nineteenth century was subject to the same tides of Jacksonian democracy that swept the rest of the nation. In 1821 the governor's term was shortened to two years and in 1846 the number of statewide elected officials was increased to thirteen, with an impact on the power of the chief executive that one authority has called "devastating." [3] During the rest of the century, incremental advances of gubernatorial power—the addition of the item veto and a slight reduction in the number of statewide elected boards, for example—still failed to leave New York's governor in control of the administrative establishment.

Progressive reform reached its zenith in New York at the Constitutional Convention of 1915. At that convention, Elihu Root and others sought to re-empower the governorship by consolidating administrative agencies (there were 169, including 108 boards and commissions), by adopting a "short ballot" system to minimize the number of statewide elected officials and by giving the executive budgeting authority. Ironically, the state constitution that emerged from this convention, one that became a model for action in other states, failed of adoption by the people in New York when offered to them in a comprehensive package. It remained for Governor Al Smith, a Democrat and product of Tammany Hall, to push through piecemeal the progressive constitutional reforms implementing the short ballot (in 1925) and the executive budget (in 1927).

With the adoption of the four-year term the parameters of the modern New York governorship were in place. Contemporary comparative analysis of tenure, appointive, veto, and budget powers shows it to be one of the strongest in the nation.[4] Only in his authority to independently reorganize state government is New York's governor significantly less strong than the governors of many other states. Here, despite efforts at constitutional revision in 1967 and 1968, the legislature has remained predominant.[5]

Though the New York governorship cannot be understood without a review of its formal powers and duties, neither can it be known only by reading the state constitution and statutes. As in any American state, the governor in New York is the most visible and widely known political figure after the U.S. president.[6] Constitutionally required to "communicate by message to the legislature at every session the condition of the state, and recommend such matters to it as he shall judge expedient,"[7] he is expected by the people and other principal political actors of the state, even those elected statewide, to provide leadership. Regardless of the actual locus of formal authority, the governor is praised if things go well and blamed if they go wrong.

The expectation that the governor lead is most evident in times of crisis. In 1975, the New York State Urban Development Corporation (UDC) defaulted on its bonds and New York City and state tottered on the brink of fiscal chaos. Though only in office a few months, Governor Hugh Carey responded. His ability to organize public and private resources to avoid the fiscal collapse of the state, its public authorities, and its local governments won him wide praise; it proved to be his finest hour.

The power-enhancing qualities of crisis are well known to governors and their advisors, and at times leads them to cultivate atmosphere in the state. In their first years in office, governors Harriman, Rockefeller, Carey, and Cuomo did this in their budget messages. By emphasizing the severe, even unique, crisis in the fiscal situation he found upon assuming office, each of these governors sought informally to gain the upper hand in political bargaining with legislators and interest groups, and to emerge with the resources that he needed to begin to fund the new programs he sought over his entire four-year term.

But there is also danger in crisis. Nelson Rockefeller's handling of one crisis, the 1971 Attica prison uprising in which forty-three persons died, subjected him to the most severe criticism of his fifteen-year governorship. And a similar uprising at Ossining in January 1983 threatened to abort the promising Cuomo administration almost before it began. The successful resolution of the crisis at Ossining without death or any major concessions by the state, especially with Attica still a vivid reality in the memories of key New York state decision makers, illustrates another point about gubernatorial power. Success for a governor, however obtained, breeds later success by creating a political environment in which others not only expect him to lead, but to prevail.

William Ronan, Secretary to the governor during the Rockefeller years, remarked: "New York is a big, dynamic, high-powered state, and it wants a big, dynamic, high-powered man for its governor." [8] Indeed, formal gubernatorial powers do tend to be enhanced in those American states, such as New York, that are large in size with heterogeneous populations and great social and economic diversity. It is as if a center of substantial political power is needed so as to offset, balance, and broker the diversity of interests and concerns within these states.[9]

It is not insignificant, too, for gubernatorial power in New York that the state's principal city is a national and international media center. In all states, as in the nation, the chief executive—a single person, representative of and known to a broad constitutency—tends to be the focal point of media attention, and therefore is advantaged over others in the political arena. In New York this advantage is enhanced because state politics is the "local story" for media outlets of national and international importance. Governor Mario Cuomo, for example, received kudos around the nation for the State-of-the-State address he delivered in January of 1983, in which he established for his administration the theme of "the family of New York." In that same month forty-nine other governors, many of them new to the office, gave State-of-the-State addresses, but none were printed in full in the *New York Times.*

New York's importance in the nation and the world attracts to it an array of enormously talented people, providing for the governor a source of staff assistance and advice from outside government that is unsurpassed in its range and depth. During the fiscal crisis, for example, Governor Carey called not only upon the expertise available within the state and city governments, but also upon such New Yorkers as investment banker Felix Rohatyn. In New York, too, working with or for the governor gains added attractiveness because of his presidential prospects. An aide or advisor who does good work in Albany can hope, more realistically than those who work in most other state capitals, to later find himself or herself at a desk in the White House. Gubernatorial power is thus subtly served by the ambitions of others, those who wish to hitch their wagons to a rising political star.

As New York's "Chief of State," the governor serves in a ceremonial role that puts him in touch with the many worlds of the state, providing contacts that can be used across the lines that usually separate these worlds. Every invitation to give a speech, greet a visiting notable, or cut a ribbon creates an opportunity to do a favor, provide recognition and acknowledgement, develop a well-spring of later support.

As party leader, too, the governor has the opportunity to create support that can be useful later. The weakening of parties and the growth of personalized, media-based campaigning have diminished the importance of this role. Nevertheless, the use for party purposes of some of the remaining state patronage, even non-paying, largely ceremonial positions on boards and commissions, may give the governor an extra degree of influence over state legislators when he really needs it, through county party leaders.

Finally, to this array of formal and informal powers governors of New York have brought singular backgrounds and unique personal qualities, personal resources that defy easy generalization. All, however, shared the ability to succeed politically in a polyglot state, one that in its diversity and complexity is a mirror of the nation.

The Institutional Governorship

The governor is assisted in the exercise of his powers, both formal and informal, by a substantial staff. In recent years, New York's executive chamber offices have been budgeted at over $9 million, and more than two hundred people, about a third of them professional, have been employed on "the second floor" of the state capitol in the chief executive's service. In addition, a number of "control agencies" in the executive office of the governor are used by him for key policy making and implementation tasks, the most important of which is the division of the budget. Staffed almost entirely by career professionals, the division, one of the most powerful agencies of its kind in the United States, is responsible for both the development of the governor's financial plan and its detailed implementation through the year in response to changing events and circumstances.

Traditionally in modern New York government, the three top aides to the governor have been the counsel, the secretary and the budget director. In addition, in recent years the press secretary (elevated by Governor Rockefeller to "Director of Communications") has taken on a substantial role. From time to time, other positions have emerged as important in the governors office, for example, the director of planning services in the late 1960s. These, however, have not had the staying power of the four key positions or roles.

Any discussion of the roles of top staff in New York is necessarily artificial; it tends to obscure the degree to which the responsibilities of the governor's key aides overlap and thus understate the extent to which, as Governor Dewey liked to observe, theirs is a team effort.[10]

Nevertheless, it is fair to say that the counsel and his assistants take principal responsibility for developing the legislative program and shepherding it through the legislature, the budget director oversees preparation and administration of the budget and fiscal plan and the secretary is the governor's person for overall policy development and implementation. The secretary is assisted by the director of state operations, who handles day-to-day policy implementation, and by a group of program associates, responsible for monitoring the activities of groups of departments in specific areas and developing proposals for the governor in these areas.

In addition to these more institutionalized sources of advice, most recent governors have appointed special assistants for particular purposes or for the overall value of their counsel. Governor Cuomo's son, Andrew Cuomo, for example, has had a very significant role on his father's "second floor" staff, including a major voice in political liaison and the distribution of patronage, a task performed in previous administrations by an appointments secretary to the governor.

Upon coming into office, most governors have expressed concern about concentrating too much power in the hands of one staff assistant and, in explicit contrast with their predecessors, have insisted that they would organize their offices in a non-hierarchical manner, giving direct access to several key aides. Over time, however, one aide has always seemed to emerge as first among equals. Each of these men developed a special relationship with the governor they served and, as a consequence, wielded enormous power in state government, so much power that some called them surrogate governors.

In retrospectively describing his role as "Chief of Cabinet" while secretary to Rockefeller, William Ronan said:

> "The Secretary acts on behalf of the Governor and, in his name, deals with the departments and agencies of state government in liaison, also with the legislature in many matters, and . . . with various individuals and public groups who have business with the chief executive of the state. . . ."[11]

And of working with his Secretary, Governor Rockefeller commented:

> I know him. I trust his judgment. I know his background. We have worked together. I get the feel of the thing and I can make that decision very fast if he feels that he should ask me about it. Or he will inform me of decisions he has made. I just have not the time to hear these people. If a department feels very strongly that they have been shortchanged on a decision and it was wrong they will come to me and I will listen to them. But he is a fair minded man and they have confidence in him.[12]

National surveys of state commissioners have systematically shown that the New York governorship is one of the strongest in directing administration in the nation.[13] Those few departments that are not headed by gubernatorial appointees are still subject to the governor's influence through the executive budget process. But, New York governors rarely immerse themselves over long periods in day-to-day administration. As interest in a policy area is aroused a governor may get intensely involved with it, only to move on to another area after a tone or direction has been established. As on the national level, cabinet meetings in New York are rarely the locus of policy making. Commissioners act relatively autonomously, within each administration's broad policy parameters, calling upon the governor and his staff for support or direction as needed.

Several recent developments may attenuate the governor's administrative authority in New York. The first is the proliferation of public authorities. These agencies, many developed to finance capital projects on a fast tract in the go-go Rockefeller years, now number thirty-one. They have long-term debt of almost $25 billion and annual operating budgets of close to $8 billion (more than a quarter of that of the state itself, even after federal funds are included).[14] Though firmly controlled by Rockefeller, the governor who created them and made the initial appointments, the boards of some of these agencies, the members of which serve for fixed terms, have been less responsive to more recent governors. Indeed, the proliferation of quasi-independent agencies in New York is beginning to be reminiscent of the organizational disorder that confronted reformers at the 1915 Constitutional Convention!

The courts, both national and state, provide a second source of constraint on the governor's administrative powers. In 1975 the Willowbrook Consent Decree was signed by Governor Carey after scandalous conditions revealed in a state mental hospital led to litigation in federal courts. Negotiated between the state and civil liberties and mental health groups and supervised by Orin Judd, a federal judge, the decree established detailed criteria and timetables for the improvement of the delivery of a state service that was formerly entirely within the control of the governor.[15] In another limitation on executive discretion, the state's high court, the Court of Appeals, ruled that local assistance funds (more than 60% of the state budget) could not be impounded by the governor once appropriated by the legislature.[16] And finally, in another area heretofore little noticed, rules on the standing of a taxpayer to sue state officials on constitutional grounds were eased considerably by the courts and the legislature in the mid-1970s, potentially opening a wide range of official gubernatorial actions to challenge in the courts.[17]

Dependence on federal dollars and policies also makes the governor less autonomous in the administrative sphere. By 1982, almost a quarter of New York state's receipts from all sources came from the national government, much of it with strings attached. This enormous federal fiscal role requires the governor of New York, acting individually and in concert with this colleagues in the Northeast and the National Governor's Association, to be a lobbyist for the state in Washington. Acting through an office in the nation's capitol, the governor seeks to organize New York's senators and congressmen and women on a bipartisan basis in support of maximizing the resources made available for the state.

Relations with the Legisature

Nowhere are the demands upon the governor for leadership as prominently on display as in the annual legislative process. Each year the governor systematically canvasses the state bureaucracy and his network of advisors, both within and outside government, and then sets the political agenda in his State of the State and Budget messages. Department chiefs and interest groups alike struggle to have their priorities included in these messages, so as to marshall the clout of the executive chamber behind them. Often, parts of the governor's messages are leaked piecemeal to the press over a week's time, so as to maximize their political impact.

As the counsel's office puts programs in bill form, lines up key committee chairmen and other leaders in both houses (and parties) for sponsorship and support, and tracks the progress of program bills, the governor may augment his program with Special Messages. In addition, there is the authority of the governor to veto bills or items of appropriation (within ten days if the legislature is in session or thirty days if it has adjourned), subject to override by two-thirds of the elected membership of both houses, and to call the legislature into special sessions for a specific purpose, if he feels the need to do so.

Traditionally, New York has had a highly disciplined legislature. In fact, both Charles Breitel, when he was counsel to Governor Dewey, and William Ronan likened executive-legislative relationships in the state during the 1940s, '50s and early '60s to those in a parliamentary system.[18] During that simpler time, in order to put his program through, the governor bargained with the speaker of the Assembly and the majority leader of the Senate, and when a deal was struck the leaders delivered the necessary legislative majorities. Things went more smoothly, of course, when the governor's party controlled both houses, but, with some modifications, the system still operated when the legislature was of a different partisan stripe than the governor, or even when control was divided.

Things began to change in the mid-1960s, however, as reapportionment altered the composition of the legislature, party decline diminished the ability of the governor to discipline legislators through home-county partisan channels and the availability of professional staff to individual members, committees and the legislature as a whole gave legislators countervailing sources of information and expertise.

During the eight years of the Carey administration, tensions between the governor and the legislature grew as legislators continued to reassert themselves. The state constitution was amended so as to allow special sessions without gubernatorial initiative and the leaders took to recessing rather than adjourning their bodies, so that they could be called back at any time. In the context of fiscal austerity, in part dictated by economic circumstances and in part the result of conscious policy choices, state politicians became less distributive and more redistributive. With less to go around, executive-legislative confrontation became more and more common.

Matters were further exacerbated by bad personal chemistry between the governor and legislative leaders, Warren Anderson in the Senate and Stanley Steingut and Stanley Fink in the Assembly, and by Governor Carey's ill-concealed dislike for the legislature, which he more than once publicly characterized as "a zoo." The results were constantly missed budget deadlines, precedent setting Senate rejection of gubernatorial appointees for major posts, a successful lawsuit that, for the first time, gave the legislature a role in distributing federal funds in New York, and renewed use by the governor of the long dormant item veto as he fought to retain fiscal control.[19]

Over the last half century, New York governors have regularly vetoed between a fifth and a quarter of bills passed by the legislature, a far larger percentage than in most states.[20] This practice, and the fact that there had not been a successful veto override since 1870, made the veto threat (or "pre-veto," as Governor Dewey called it) a powerful tool in legislative negotiations, and led to regular legislative cooperation in the recall of measures from the governor's desk for changes to avoid veto.

The politics of the veto can be complex. Sometimes, as Governor Rockefeller once explained, legislators "went along" with bills to please individual members as a "courtesy" on local matters, only because they were confident that there would be a gubernatorial veto. "I'll be the guy who vetoes the bill," the governor said. "This is all part of the act."[21]

Despite the fact that Governor Carey used his veto far less than his predecessors, during his tenure the gubernatorial negative was overridden for the first time in a hundred years in 1976. With the psychological barrier to the veto override smashed, such actions became relatively common in the Carey years.[22]

An Era of Limits and Change

The governor of New York is powerful, but not all powerful. His challenge is to marshall the array of constitutional authority and political and governmental resources that are temporarily his, in pursuit of his personal vision for the state and its people. The paradox for the last decades of the twentieth century is that gubernatorial leadership has become more difficult just as it has become more necessary. In a corrosive political environment of resource scarcity, there is less slack: priorities must be more closely defined and vigorously pursued. But increasingly, administrative discretion is constrained by the courts and the national government. Increasingly too, the legislature insists on a greater role in policy making and implementation. Now a $100 million institution, it has girded itself well to share power.

In sum, as New York seeks to do "more with less" its political and governmental processes are open to more actors, legitimately on the stage. And the arithmetic increase in the number of participants may, or so it seems at times, result in an exponential explosion in the difficulties of reaching solutions "for the good of the state, rather than for the good of those who have the loudest voice in Albany." [23]

Historian Donald Roper has written that New York's most successful governors in this century, both Democratic and Republican, were all guided by a philosophy of "positive liberalism," a belief that the state could be an affirmative force in meeting the needs of its people.[24] In contrast, in the 1970s (well before the Reagan presidency), after a frightening fiscal crisis and in response to the cumulative effect of decisions taken in the Rockefeller years, state government came to be regarded not as an engine for progress but as a source of mischief and problems. It was seen, in short, as a danger against which New Yorkers had to be protected.[25]

Governor Cuomo signaled early in his administration that he believed that austerity, though a fact of life for the indefinite future, did not necessarily mean the end of "positive liberalism" in New York. Reconciling the state's great governmental tradition with current economic realities will be the test of his governorship, and of those that follow for the remainder of this century.

GERALD BENJAMIN

Afterword: A Governorship with Fewer Limits and Little Change

Politically, the first half decade of Mario Cuomo's governorship of New York was a triumphal march. Less than two years after his election, Cuomo's keynote speech at the Democratic National Convention confirmed him as a star in the firmament of a party on its way to electoral disaster. Two years later, as the most popular chief executive in the state since scientific polling began, Cuomo won reelection by the largest margin ever recorded in New York's history. And as another presidential election approached in 1988, Doonesbury cartoons devoted to the theme "Waiting for Mario" were just one indicator of the hope within his party that the governor would seek the presidency, despite his repeated denials of any intention of doing so. If nothing else, the Cuomo governorship confirmed that the Empire State is still a mother of potential presidents.

Trading upon his burgeoning reputation, Mario Cuomo proved an effective advocate for New York in Washington. The great victory of his first term in this area was preservation of the deductibility of state and local taxes in the 1986 federal tax reforms, an achievement that seemed impossible when the governor first took up the fight. Across the nation and in New York, Cuomo was often but not always a great communicator. There were gaffes, like the denial of the existence of "the Mafia"; unnecessary confrontations with reporters; and the questioning of critics' motives rather than responding to their arguments. But his ability to see possibilities in situations others thought impossible and to articulate simply yet eloquently new terms of political discourse quickly made Mario Cuomo the dominant presence in New York.

In stark and deliberate contrast with his predecessor, Hugh Carey, Governor Cuomo struck a conciliatory note with the state legislature. He recognized the contribution of leaders in both houses, Democrat and Republican, and shared the credit. The result was a lowering of voices, and budgets passed on time in the early years. Critics feared that the governor was not confrontational enough, and that to gain visible short-run achievements he would incur long-run costs—for example, through the erosion of executive budget authority. But toward the end of the first term and the beginning of the second, Cuomo showed himself more and more willing to take on the Senate and Assembly to gain his ends. Symbolic of this was his winning battle for meaningful ethics legislation, as scandal over the political use of public resources swept through the capitol's halls in 1987. The institutionalized governorship showed little change during the Cuomo years, despite the governor's much heralded "hands-on" management style. One apparent innovation was the creation of "czars" to coordinate and oversee selected policy areas. The role of one, Vincent Tese, in Economic Development was especially notable.

Tese was simultaneously made head of a state agency, the Commerce Department, and a public authority, the Urban Development Corporation, permanently putting to rest the myth that New York's burgeoning authorities were somehow separate from and independent of the rest of state government.

A master politician and an extraordinary communicator, Mario Cuomo still cannot be ranked a great New York governor. In substantive terms, his administration has been distributive. Very good times in New York have allowed simultaneous tax cuts and yearly advances in spending faster than the rate of inflation. Almost every area of state government has grown, with some—Corrections, Mental Health, local aid for social services, and recently aid for education—growing faster than others. In an era of fewer limits, there have been few hard choices, and still no one area has emerged upon which the governor has permanently put his personal mark. Unless he runs for president and wins, this challenge of greatness in the governorship is the principal challenge that history defines for Mario Cuomo in the years ahead.

NOTES

1. George Weeks, "A Statehouse Hall of Fame," *State Government* Vol. 55, #3 (Fall, 1982), p. 69. This issue hereafter cited as (*SG,* 1982).

2. Nelson Rockefeller, *Public Papers of the Governor,* Albany: Office of the Governor, 1967, pp. 208-211, at 209.

3. Thomas Schick, *The New York State Constitutional Convention of 1915 and the Modern State Government,* New York: National Municipal League, 1978, p. 8.

4. Joseph A. Schlesinger, "The Politics of the Executive," in Herbert Jacob and Kenneth Vines, *Politics in the American States,* 2nd ed., Boston: Little Brown, 1971, p. 232.

5. Thad Beyles, "The Governor's Power of Organization," in *SG,* 1982, pp. 79-87.

6. Larry Sabato, *Goodbye to Goodtime Charley,* revised ed., Washington: CQ Press, 1982, p. 8.

7. New York State Constitution, article IV, section 3.

8. Robert Connery and Gerald Benjamin, *Rockefeller of New York: Executive Power in the Statehouse,* Ithaca: Cornell University Press, 1979, p. 418.

9. See Schlesinger (1971) p. 233.

10. Richard Norton Smith, *Thomas Dewey and His Times,* New York: Simon and Schuster, 1982, Chapter 11.

11. Connery and Benjamin (1979) p. 117.

12. James E. Underwood and William Daniels, *Governor Rockefeller in New York: The Apex of Pragmatic Liberalism in the United States,* Westport, Ct.: Greenwood Press, 1982, p. 110.

13. Deil S. Wright, "Executive Leadership in State Administration," *Midwest Journal of Political Science,* Volume 11, Fall, 1967, pp. 1-26; and Glen Abney and Thomas Lauth. "The Executive as Chief Administrator," *Public Administration Review,* Vol. 43, #1, Jan/Feb 1983, pp. 40-49.

14. New York State Division of the Budget, *New York State Budget 1983-84* (Albany, The Division, 1983) pp. 655-667. See generally, Annamarie Hauck Walsh, *The Public's Business,* Cambridge: MIT Press, 1978.

15. Barbara Grumet, "Willowbrook Reforms: A Pandora's Box?," *Empire State Report,* Volume 1, #12, Dec. 1975, pp. 459-463.

16. *Counrty of Oneida v. Berle* 49 N.Y. 2nd 515 (1980).

17. *Boryszewski v. Bridges* 37 N.U. 2nd 361 (1975).

18. Connery and Benjamin (1979), p. 91, and remarks of William Ronan in Gerald Benjamin, ed. *Rockefeller in Retrospect,* forthcoming, 1984.

19. Janice Prindle, "Assessing the Legislature's Saratoga Session," *Empire State Report,* Volume 2, #8, September 1976, pp. 296-302; *Anderson v. Regan* 53 N.Y. 2d367 (1982); and Joseph Zimmerman. "Rebirth of the Item Veto in the Empire State," *State Government* Volume 54 (1981) pp. 51-52.

20. On the veto, see generally Frank Prescott and Joseph F. Zimmerman. *The Politics of the Veto of Legislation in New York,* Baltimore: University Press of America, 1980, 2 volumes.

21. *New York Times,* December 3, 1972, p. 41.

22. Humphrey Tyler, "The Legislature, Profile in Rancor," *Empire State Report,* Volume 2, #4 May, 1976, p. 131 ff.

23. Tyler (1976), p. 158.

24. "The Governorship in History," in Robert Connery and Gerald Benjamin, eds., *Governing the Empire State,* New York: Academy of Political Science, 1974, p. 16. Underwood and Daniels (1982) strike a similar theme, using the term "pragmatic liberalism."

25. See, for example, Peter D. McClelland and Alan L. Magdovitz. *Crisis in the Making: The Political Economy of New York State Since 1945,* New York: Cambridge University Press, 1981.

The Role of the Lieutenant Governor

by

Stan Lundine

Stan Lundine was elected lieutenant governor in 1986, as Governor Mario Cuomo's running mate. He served in Congress from 1976 to 1987, representing southwestern New York. He was mayor of Jamestown from 1970 to 1976.

EDITORS' NOTE: *This article presents a highly personal viewpoint on the position of lieutenant governor in the Cuomo administration. Of particular interest are the three proposals for change presented near the end of the article.*

Stan Lundine

The job of lieutenant governor—like that of vice-president of the United States— has long been a source of political humor. Jokes about the post portray its occupant as "standby equipment" given little to do, simply waiting to take over if the governor should leave office.

I wouldn't want a job like that—and I don't have one. When Governor Mario Cuomo asked me to be his running mate in 1986, he outlined a very different role for the lieutenant governor. The governor said he wanted a junior partner to help him run state government, someone who could function as a deputy and top adviser, and who could tackle the most challenging assignments.

Just as every corporation president needs and relies on a first vice-president, Mario Cuomo said he wanted to be able to rely on a strong lieutenant governor to help him run a state government that is larger and more complex than many of the nation's biggest corporations.

Knowing Mario Cuomo to be a man of his word, and finding myself in full agreement with his vision of a role of the lieutenant governor, I gave up a secure seat I had held in Congress since 1976 and accepted his offer to run for the state's second highest office.

Since becoming lieutenant governor in January 1987, I've found the job to be even better than I had expected. Unlike Congress, where you spend a great deal of time talking about and debating issues, the lieutenant governorship is at the action level of government. The job gives me a chance for some hands-on management of government, something I enjoyed at the start of my career in elected office when I served as mayor of Jamestown.

The role of the lieutenant governor in the second Cuomo administration is a full and varied one.

I attend senior staff meetings with the governor, and confer with him regularly, helping him reach decisions on how to best run the government, on what programs to propose to the state Legislature, and on how to respond to the many challenges that face New York.

I take on special assignments for the governor, such as working to attract major economic development projects to the state.

I attend negotiating sessions with the governor and legislative leaders, helping to work out agreements on key measures facing the Legislature.

I travel around the state to give speeches and to attend a broad range of events. I use these appearances to explain administration policies to the people of the state, to generate public support for Cuomo administration initiatives, and to gather information for the governor about the views and ideas of New Yorkers on major issues of the day.

I help guide the governor's program bills through the Legislature, meeting frequently with legislators and representatives of many groups to discuss pending legislation.

I serve as presiding officer of the state Senate, involving me directly in the legislative process.

One of the best aspects of being lieutenant governor is the opportunity it gives me to work in close partnership with Governor Cuomo. His hard work, intelligence, effectiveness, and determination to improve conditions in New York have made him known and respected nationally and abroad.

I also enjoy the chance to work closely with Gerry Crotty, the governor's chief of staff. We work together to help the governor serve the people of New York. Gerry Crotty is not well-known to the public, but plays a key role in working with administration officials and the Legislature to carry out the Cuomo program and keep government operating smoothly. As an elected official, I take a more public role. We are proving to be good partners.

While I have a small personal staff, I have the resources of state agencies and the governor's staff at my disposal. The Cuomo-Lundine administration functions as a team, with all members working toward the same goal. The assistance I have received from within the administration has been invaluable to me in carrying out my duties.

The role I have been given by Governor Cuomo gives me the broadest responsibility of any lieutenant governor since Malcolm Wilson occupied the office under Governor Nelson Rockefeller from 1959 to 1973.

Before taking office, I discussed the job of lieutenant governor with Governor Wilson, and I benefitted from his insights on how to make the job an important and effective one.

One reason I believe things have worked out as well as they have for me in my role of lieutenant governor is the way Mario Cuomo and I came together. In 1986, the governor enjoyed overwhelming popularity and could have been reelected with some other running mate. I'm confident that I could have won reelection to the job in Congress I so enjoyed. We formed our partnership because we respected each other and thought we could work well together. We felt that our different backgrounds and styles could complement one another, increasing our success as a team.

While my hopes and expectations about the job of lieutenant governor have been more than fulfilled, Governor Cuomo and I believe that the office could be improved further with several structural changes. These can only be carried out by changing state law or amending the State Constitution.

Here is a summary of the changes we are seeking:

- We would like to see the candidates for governor and lieutenant governor paired as a team on the primary election ballot, as is done in some other states. A candidate for governor should be allowed to choose his or her running mate, to ensure that the two have confidence in each other and have the ability and desire to work as a team. Candidates for these offices already run as a team in the general election. A "shotgun marriage" that forces a candidate for governor to accept a possibly unwanted running mate makes it much harder for the lieutenant governor to play a major role in government. It is in no one's best interest.

- We would like to change the outdated provision of the State Constitution that makes the lieutenant governor the acting governor whenever the governor leaves the state. This provision made sense in the age before modern communication and travel. In the 1800s, a governor riding out of the state on a stagecoach, steam locomotive or ship could be out of touch for days, and could require days or even weeks of travel to return to the state. Today, regular and mobile telephones make it possible for the governor to stay in touch with state officials no matter where he goes. And jet travel can speed the governor back to New York from anywhere in the world. It no longer makes sense to strip the governor of power at the state line.
- We would like to give the governor the power to appoint someone to the office of lieutenant governor if the office becomes vacant between elections. The office is simply too important to go unfilled. Currently, when the post is vacant, the State Senate majority leader is next-in-line to succeed the governor should the governorship become vacant. In addition, if there is no lieutenant governor, the majority leader becomes acting governor when the governor leaves the state.

With these changes, we can make the office of lieutenant governor even more useful to the governor and to the people of New York.

As a former lieutenant governor, Mario Cuomo knows the important role the second highest elected official in the state can play. By setting out from the beginning of my term to make the office an integral part of his administration, and by seeking changes to further improve the office, Governor Cuomo has set up a model for a productive relationship between the governor and lieutenant governor.

Many lieutenant governors have served before me and many more will serve after me. If future governors follow Governor Cuomo's blueprint for the lieutenant governorship, the office will continue to function as an important and valuable part of state government.

The Renewed Legislature

by

Alan Hevesi

Mr. Hevesi is a member of the Assembly of the State of New York.
He is also Assistant Professor of Political Science
at City University of New York at Queens College
and is author of *Legislative Politics in New York.*

EDITORS' NOTE: *This chapter describes the many changes in the state Legislature in New York, and demonstrates how the system of centralized leadership and party discipline which characterize the State Senate and Assembly have enabled the legislature to balance the power of the governor.*

ALAN HEVESI

Though of low prestige and low visibility, American state legislatures are incredibly important. While two centuries of court decisions, political changes, civil conflict, economic crises, and world war have led to an enormous expansion of the Federal government's responsibilities and power, one should not conclude that the role of state governments or state legislatures has in any manner diminished. Reverence for government "close to the people" remains a crucial American ideological tenet.

The Constitutional Context

The Federal Constitution, at least theoretically, is a charter of restraints. It declares that the powers granted to the Federal government are only those that are specifically listed and itemized in the document. Obviously, history and decisions of the Supreme Court have minimized the significance of many of the restraints, but the charter retains its essential character as a document of limitations.

State constitutions operate under the opposite presumption. The institutions, particularly legislatures, which they create are empowered to do anything they choose to do unless specifically limited by the state constitutions themselves. As a result of this constitutional circumstance, the New York Legislature has wide authority granted by the New York Constitution to regulate the lives of its residents in a most comprehensive manner. Few citizens recognize that the Legislature regulates the lives of New Yorkers from well before each of them has been born until sometime after they have died. The Legislature can determine the character of the relationship between a pregnant woman and her unborn fetus (although the Supreme Court in 1973 coopted part of the field in its Roe v. Wade and Doe v. Bolton abortion decisions), as well as the establishment of criteria under which a convicted murderer can be executed. The Legislature decides who will be present at the birth of a new-born baby, what tests and medical procedures will be performed, and who will perform them. The Legislature decides who will be buried in which cemetery and what taxes will be imposed in the process and a great deal in between. Elected lawmakers also make thousands of other decisions each year affecting jobs, education, family relations, professional life, economic well-being, and physical and mental health.

In addition, the Legislature grants vast amounts of resources from state revenues for thousands of programs providing services to people. Close to half the money going to educate our children comes from state aid. Millions more are spent on institutions of higher education both public and private. Assistance to local governments directly and indirectly is on the agenda of every legislative session. Dollars for capital construction and rehabilitation of transportation facilities, buildings, highways, roads and bridges are provided each year.

The Legislature creates and can regulate each of the thousands of local government units (cities, counties, towns, villages, sewer districts, school districts, public authorities, and the like) functioning in the State. Thus, localities are "creatures of the state." What goes on in local governments can be revised, reformed, prohibited or mandated as the legislature sees fit. The lawmakers may intrude on decisions affecting police, firefighters, sanitation workers, fishermen, salesmen, builders, farmers, consumers, as the lawmakers determine is appropriate.

Thus, the method by which our elected lawmakers interact, evaluate issues and arrive at decisions is of critical importance to millions of residents of the state. The Legislature is also a fascinating institution, chock full of human drama, brilliance, courage, stupidity, venality, and virtue. It is the subject of too much criticism and too little analysis. To understand how the Legislature works is to understand why things are as bad—or as good—as they are.

Reapportionment and Majorities

As is the case in 49 of the other 50 state legislatures, the New York legislature is a bicameral institution. Since 1974, the two Houses in New York have been controlled by opposite parties, the Senate under Republican control and the Assembly with a Democratic majority. While this split appears now to have some semi-permanence to it, it breaks a pattern of Republican control of both houses of the Legislature that has been a key characteristic of legislative life in New York State since the beginning of the Twentieth Century.

The most significant variable in determining who will control a legislature is the method and character of the reapportionment and redistricting system implemented under constitutional rules by act of the legislature. Redistricting is the redrawing of legislative district boundaries. Reapportionment is the determination of the number of people who will reside in such districts. Legislative district maps must be revised at least once a decade, after completion of the federal census, and the population of all legislative districts in a state must be equal in population. While voters may make independent judgments as between clearly identifiable candidates for the presidency, United States senate, governor and other state-wide positions, they rarely do so when it comes to state legislative contests. Instead, most citizens will generally vote for local and state legislative candidates on the basis of party identification and affiliation. Redistricting experts in the employ of political parties have for generations absorbed the detailed statistical information available on voting patterns in every town, hamlet, and precinct in a state and have developed some very sophisticated methods for predicting how voters will vote in subsequent elections. Therefore, the persons involved in drafting legislation redrawing district maps are able to create carefully designed districts that enhance the potential for a political party or faction to maintain or improve its control of its house of the Legislature.

In New York, no expense or effort is spared by the majority parties at a time redistricting is required in drawing maps which enhance the dominant party's potential for control. As many opposition blocks of voters as possible are carefully concentrated in a few opposition districts while others are dispersed among loyal voter strongholds in order to minimize or eliminate their impact. The result is that throughout the first two-thirds of the twentieth century, with Republicans in control of both legislative houses almost all the time, each succeeding Republican majority was careful to maintain or re-draw district lines minimizing or eliminating the impact of large blocks of Democratic voters and thereby maintaining Republican control. Prior to 1964, there were no requirements that the districts for Senate or Assembly had to be equal or nearly equal in population, so the opportunities for gerrymandering were dramatically enhanced. There were periods of time in which it took 230,000 to 250,000 voters in Brooklyn district to elect one Democratic member of the Assembly and fewer than 20,000 in individual rural counties to elect an upstate Republican. In other words, the voting power of rural (Republican) voters greatly exceeded that of their Democratic counterparts in the big cities. Although Democratic voter enrollments throughout the 1930s, 1940s and 1950s substantially exceeded Republican enrollments on a statewide basis and even though Democratic candidates could often win statewide office, control of the state Legislature was retained by the Republicans regularly and consistently. Governor Al Smith dubbed this process "a constitutionally Republican Legislature."

The pattern was broken only when special political circumstances occurred. In 1934, the Democrats captured control of both houses of the legislature as a result of voter disenchantment with the Republican performance during the Depression. That Democratic majority lasted for only one year (at the time a legislator was elected for a one year term). The Republican majorities were maintained in both houses for the next three decades until 1964, when, as a result of the landslide victory of President Lyndon Johnson over Barry Goldwater, the Democrats to their great surprise awakened the morning after to discover that they had won control of both houses of the legislature. They were so stunned by this development that they divided into bitterly competing political factions and failed to elect party leaders for five weeks. The impasse over which faction of the Democratic party would control the Legislature was broken only by the intervention and votes of Republican minority lawmakers on behalf of one of the competing factions. Because of new court orders involving redistricting issues, a special election was called one year later and the Demoracts lost control of the state Senate while retaining their majority in the Assembly. That Assembly majority lasted until the 1968 election. Beginning in 1969 and through 1974, Republicans were once again in control of both houses.

In 1974, the national reaction to the Watergate scandal presented New York Democrats with a new opportunity. Assembly Democrats were prepared. The candidates that they had chosen to run in traditional upstate and suburban Republican districts were generally very able, young, aggressive and sophisticated, and with the help of Watergate, a number of them were elected and the Democrats took control of the Assembly. These new Democratic members were given immediate recognition and influence in order to assure their reelection, and ten years later many of them were still in the legislature and in positions of substantial significance and power.

In 1981 and 1982 the Legislature again began the process of redistricting to meet constitutional requirements for a decennial reapportionment reflecting the changes in the 1980 census. With a split legislature there were, at one point in the process, four separate reapportionment plans. One was drafted by Senate Republicans and favored the Republican majority in the upper House while injuring Assembly Democrats. A second written by the Assembly majority, increased the number of Democrats likely to be elected in the lower house, while hurting Senate Republicans. A third was partially drafted by a special master appointed by the federal courts to implement the civil rights law and insure minority representation in both houses. A fourth plan, ultimately adopted, contained elements of the special master plan to deal with minority representation, the most partisan Democratic proposal to assure Democratic control of the Assembly and the most effective Republican plan to maintain Republican control of the upper house. In other words, the people with power got together and, in time-honored tradition, compromised in a manner designed, within court mandated restrictions, to strengthen their opportunities to maintain power.

In the election immediately following the deal, the Republicans maintained dominion over the senate by a 36 to 25 margin, a net gain of one seat. This was not a marginal victory. Since the Republican senators had been drawing district lines to their own advantage for decades and since there are more Democratic voters than Republican voters in the state (by a registration margin of nearly one million), most of the partisan advantage that could have been taken had been taken in prior reapportionment plans drafted by the GOP. Therefore, the one seat increase was a notable success.

The Democrats in the Assembly, on the other hand, had much more fertile ground upon which to plant the seeds of their majority. Since they had not drawn prior reapportionment plans and had won the majority in 1974 only through the historical fluke of Watergate, they had plenty of opportunities to increase their numbers by carving up Republican districts. Democratic Speaker Stanley Fink suggested that the Democrats were simply "rectifying the errors of the past." The end result was that the Democratic majority, which had been substantial at 88 to 62 in 1981, was increased to an enormous 98 to 52 in 1982.

Partisanship and Groupings

New York has one the most partisan legislatures, if not the most partisan, in the country. The legislative system reinforces a basic attutide brought to Albany by most newly elected lawmakers that the political party in the Legislature (as distinct from the state-wide, regional, county or other local party organizations) will provide the basis for many of the decisions made each session. Democrats automatically will oppose a Republican initiative (and Republicans will vote against a Democratic proposal) unless there is some good reason not to. The legislative party, especially if in the minority, views its role as not only keeping the majority honest—but of embarassing it at every possible opportunity.

Partisanship is institutionalized through the regular meetings of the four party conferences (Senate Republicans, Senate Democratic, Assembly Democratic, Assembly Republican). At these sessions full discussion and debate over the merits and politics of major issues occur and final decisions are made. Here final vote tallies are taken as leaders prepare to go the floor on issues with the results already assured.

Lawmakers, however, are not just members of their legislative political parties. They are also members of a variety of informal groupings, primarily in the Assembly, that meet to pursue the interests of those groups. For example, there is a Black and Puerto Rican Caucus made up both of senators and assemblymen who are members of those two ethnic groups. While it is generally marked, as is typical with political organizations, by factional and personal divisions, it is nevertheless highly cohesive on issues of particular interest to the substantial Black and Hispanic populations of the State. A newly organized group is the

Women's Caucus composed of the 18 women members of the Assembly, established in 1983. Less formally organized around a specific legislative agenda and more oriented toward research is the Democratic Study Group. This is a well-organized operation aimed at providing legislative services to its generally younger and more progressive members in the form of a review of specific legislation and issues.

In addition to membership in these kinds of special groupings, lawmakers are also members of their county delegations when those delegations have more than one or two members. County delegations have developed cohesive programs and they regularly meet with the leadership or with the chairmen of the relevant fiscal committees during budget time in order to push for county interests.

Members and Staff

One of the most significant developments over the past decade has been the substantial improvement in quality and ability of the people elected to legislative office and of the staff. Those who were interested in legislative office in New York because the Legislature was simply a steping stone for some other office or a comfortable sinecure with a decent salary, high prestige, and slim workload have almost disappeared because, while salaries and conditions have improved, the workload has grown enormously. A legislator is now a full-time public official even though the Legislature in New York meets in actual session only 6 or 7 months a year. Each member maintains an Albany office and a district office. Members put in long hours in dealing both with legislative issues (including casting about 2,000 votes on bills each year) and with a continuing series of constituent and community demands.

Fewer and fewer hold down second full-time jobs or careers. Where nearly two-thirds of the lawmakers were attorneys in the early 1960s, less than one half of the senators and only about one third of the assemblymen were attorneys in the early 1980s. The members elected during the turmoil of the 70s and early 80s were younger, more aggressive, better educated, more highly motivated, and definitely more productive and serious than their predecessors. The Legislature which met from January to the end of April in the early 1960s was meeting from the beginning of January into early July by the early 1980s, with fall sessions every year. Members have to sacrifice outside careers and their privacy in order to keep up with the workload.

That is not to suggest that being a legislator is a life of continuing sacrifice; there are enormous satisfactions involved including knowing one is participating in a process that directly affects people's lives. Through constituent work and through legislation, lawmakers can help both individuals and large numbers of people. They are in the public eye, and their minds are constantly challenged. But the work is long and hard, the remuneration meager, and the stress and pressure continuous. It is not a job for the laid-back.

Equally significant has been the deep commitment on the part of legislative leaders over the past decade to improve the quality of the legislature's staff. While there continues to be, and probably always will be, a partisan or political component to the selection of individual staff members, there has also been a clear-headed and calculating attempt to develop the kind of professional staff that will allow the legislature to compete with the governor and his resources. For generations, governors in New York and elsewhere have had a monopoly on knowledge through the development of large and sophisticated staffs that were able to dominate the legislative process. That has now changed. For 104 years prior to term of Governor Hugh Carey, no gubernatorial veto was overridden. Carey was overridden on a number of occasions, despite the fact that for his entire two terms (eight years), the Democratic Carey had a Democratic majority in the Assembly.

Similarly, prior to 1974, almost all of the budget decisions made by the governor and the division of the budget were adopted by the Legislature. In each session there would be a few controversial items that had to be negotiated and compromised and (rarely) a rebellion might occur over a prospective tax increase. Since 1974, however, the Legislature has played an increasingly prominent role in the development of the state budget and the financial plan, even rewriting substantial portions of the entire budget.

To a large extent this is a result of the recruitment and hiring of substantial numbers of professional economists, statisticians, social scientists and the like, primarily young, ambitious mobile and hardworking people who know that the intense experience of working for the Legislature will give them an extraordinary opportunity to become most expert in their assigned areas. While the pay is not particularly high and the hours are often impossible, these young staffers know that the experience will open doors for them. For example, both Governor Carey and Governor Mario Cuomo, hired former Assembly ways and means staff aides as their chief assistants (secreatary to the governor). This new professional staff has rendered the New York Legislature capable of competing on an equal footing with the governor's office and has forced recent governors to adjust their presumptions about the Legislature's response to their initiatives.

Rules and Committees

The most significant operating documents in both houses of the Legislature are the rules adopted by majority vote in each house at the beginning of each session. The rules define the structure, operation and division of power within the institution. They establish the authority of party leaders, the creation of committees, and the method by which bills will be introduced, processed through the legislative labyrinth, and finally adopted.

Command of the rules of a legislative body is an enormous source of power. Generally, the legislative leaders not only have an intimate knowledge of the rules themselves and the precedents for action and decision-making that have been established in the context of those rules, but also the power to change the rules to their own advantage. The individual member who knows and understands the rules can greatly improve his or her own position in the legislature, not only by taking advantage of an opportunity to impress colleagues regarding command of such a subject area (always a good strategy for a legislator on the make) but also because knowledge of the rules can give him or her a weapon in a tight parliamentary struggle that will improve the opportunity for a tactical victory.

In New York State, the rules in both houses of the Legislature provide for the operation of a standing committee system. Each committee has jurisdiction over a subject area and bills on these subjects are referred to the relevant committee for review. No bill can become law without the affirmative vote of the majority members of the standing committee since no bill will be brought to the floor of either house without committee affirmation.

Each committee's chairman and members are appointed to the committee not through seniority, or through a conference, caucus, or steering committee process as is the case in other legislatures, but simply by appointment of the speaker in the Assembly and the Senate majority leader in the Senate. Minority party members are also appointed by these leaders on recommendation of the minority party leaders elected in each house. Committees review bills referred to them, hold hearings, investigate, review executive decisions made by administrative agencies in the context of legislation already adopted, do research projects, and function as do committees in other legislatures. The distinction resides primarily with the greater control that New York legislative leaders can exert over their operations if those party leaders choose to.

The Legislative Leaders

No understanding of legislative power is possible without acknowledging that, in the New York State Legislature, to a degree surpassing that of any other legislature in America, the elected heads of the majority parties hold enormous power to control the destiny of legislative decisions made in their respective houses. A combination of factors, mutually reinforcing, grant the Senate majority leader and the speaker of the Assembly great power.

Under the Rules, formal power is vested in the speaker of the Assembly in his house and the Senate majority leader in his, to control not only the flow of legislation but also the destinies and careers of individual members. For example, New York's leaders have the formal authority to appoint all other legislative party leaders and committee chairmen and to make all committee assignments. Thus, an individual lawmaker wishing promotion to the chairmanship of a committee or to a position in the leadership (such positions as majority leader in the Assembly, deputy majority leader, assistant speaker, party whip) needs the good will of the legislative leader. A rural representative wishing to be on the agriculture committee must request such an assignment from the relevant legislative leader.

Likewise each majority party leader has the power to appoint all staff personnel, even those staff persons hired by individual members. That is not to say that leaders will do the hiring for other lawmakers but that they have ultimate personnel control and can remove from the payroll any individual they choose.

The leaders also control the flow of legislation through their respective chairmanships of the rules committees in each house. In the Senate, the rules committee takes over for all other standing committees in the latter few weeks of a legislative session. Therefore all bills that come to the floor are reported from that panel. Thus any bill opposed by the Senate majority leader dies in his committee, a committee that he completely controls and that rarely meets.

Additionally the Senate majority leader has the power to remove a bill from the calendar or to star the measure (starring a bill means taking it off the calendar of the day and putting it on a special starred calendar where the bill remains until the star is removed).

In the Assembly, as a result of rules adopted after the Democrats captured control in 1974, the power to star was removed from the speaker and is vested solely in the sponsor of legislation. Nevertheless, the speaker can determine which bills come to the floor of the Assembly, particularly at the end of the session when all bills reported from standing committees are reported to the rules committee which operates similarly to its Senate counterpart. Additionally the speaker, through his "special" relationship with appointed committee chairmen can affect if he choose to, what measures are reported out of committee. It is not rare for the leader to pass the word to a committee to hold or kill a bill in committee for whatever motive or reason he might have and it is very rare that a committee chairman will not respond.

The rules also grant the leaders the power to control the $67 million joint budget of the Senate and Assembly and therefore requires each of them to administer a large operation. They hire and oversee personnel, cleanup staff, computer experts, mail clerks, bill drafters, counsels, researchers, writers, regional office managers, and clerical people. They are political leaders, legislative leaders, administrators, and managers.

The vast array of formal powers granted to the leaders would have less significance if the informal understandings and psychological atmosphere of the Legislature created presumptions on the part of the 209 other members of both houses (61 senators and 150 Assembly members in all) that the utilization of the power vested in the leaders would be used in precisely expected ways.

Such informal restraints frequently apply in legislatures; nevertheless the tradition in New York State has *not* been one of restrained leadership discretion but quite the reverse. As a result of history, tradition, and the nature of the political organizations in the Democratic and Republican parties over the decades, the expectation of most New York lawmakers has been that elected legislative leaders will use the power that has been granted to them at maximum effectiveness to pursue the goals of the party itself and of the leader. Thus the membership expectation in the New York State Legislature for the assertion of strong leadership reinforces the vast array of formal powers that are granted to leaders by the rules.

Another critical variable in the effective use of power by the leaders are the individual skills that leaders bring to their jobs. In a classical case twenty years ago, Walter Mahoney used his position as Senate majority leader to save the career of a Suffolk County colleague. Mahoney mobilized the Republican Senate Conference to take a position opposing the entire governor's budget and opposing any legislation that would work to the advantage of Suffolk County unless the leadership in that county was induced to change its collective mind and its decision to deny Senator Mahoney's colleague the nomination for his senate seat. The Suffolk officials judiciously retreated and Senator Mahoney's colleague was reelected.

While an extreme case, the Suffolk incident indicated how the character of the relationship between leaders and their members affects the leader's ability to rally his troops. Mahoney was a grand master at developing atmosphere that said to each member of the Senate majority, "We are a club. We must stand together against the rest. We must stay loyal to each other and protect each other." He had his colleagues' respect, affection and loyalty because he was committed to using his power for their individual and collective well-being. In that atmosphere, the team became very important when either the team or its leadership was threatened by the opposition party, by action taken in the other house, by the Governor, by the press, or even by the public.

As true as this conclusion was two decades ago, so it is also true today. But times change and with greater coverage by the media of the Legislature, with younger, more skeptical members being elected to the Legislature, the character of the leader's style has changed. Senator Warren Anderson (Republican, Binghamton) has been the Senate majority leader since 1973. He is a courtly, refined gentleman, an upstate lawyer who is highly respected and unfailingly courteous. Yet power still is centralized in the hands of the Senate majority leader and his staff. On major issues involving grand policy questions, he must operate within the restraint of the consensus of the Republican Party Conference. That is the case in any collegial body. But with respect to the wide range of middling important and parochial or local bills, his discretion, and that of his staff, is absolute.

The Senate Republican majority, operating under these basic ground rules, and feeling totally secure in terms of command of the house, was startled in 1983 by a very effective rebellion organized by the Senate Democratic minority. The rebellion came in the form of an attack on Senate operations in which the Democrats rose in a carefully staged manner over a period of several weeks to debate every resolution, parliamentary notion, and minor issue at great length in order to slow down the proceedings of the Senate.

The Democrats had been angered by Republican actions that were perceived to be threats to the minority's prerogatives. Despite being in the minority, Democrats long had often had their local bills passed by the commanding Republican majority. They also were permitted to obtain appropriations in a special supplemental budget adopted each year that provided grants to programs in their local districts. In the 1982 elections, however, the Democrats had launched a very serious effort to take the majority away from the Republicans. That effort had not succeeded but the threat was clear. The effort was so intense that many senior Republican senators decided that teaching the Democrats a lesson was appropriate. Democratic bills were not reported out with the same frequency during the early period of the 1983 session and seven Democratic senators were informed that none of their local appropriation items would be adopted. Thus the Democratic rebellion.

The Republicans were caught short. They were not used to a rebellious minority; and after a great deal of anger, friction, and hostility, and with little business being transacted, the Republicans gave in. They restored the old, unwritten rules of the prior relationship, agreeing to appropriate the supplemental budget items desired by the Democrats and passing local bills. The rebellion was a victory for the Democrats who exploited the Republican desire to maintain a smooth and efficient operation. The Republicans preferred to give some concessions rather than to be perceived as having lost command of the operation of the Senate.

Through all this, however, the basic power of Senator Anderson as majority leader to guide the destiny of legislation was never challenged. The rebellion meant slow down, it did not mean a loss of command on the part of the Republican majority or its elected leader.

The Assembly in the early 1980's was a different story. Its elected speaker, Stanley Fink of Brooklyn, had a completely different style and temperament than his Senate counterpart. Fink is an extremely bright, gruff, outspoken, tough political leader. A veteran of the political wars in Brooklyn, he succeeded Stanley Steingut to the speakership when the first Democratic speaker in a generation was defeated for reelection to the assembly in 1977. Fink recognized that knowing what a piece of legislation said and what its ramifications were, in as much detail as was humanly possible, would give him enormous advantages in convincing his own colleagues to go along with the measure. Additionally, he was never shy, almost in violation of one of the cardinal rules of politics, to tell off a member, to cut him down with a sharp remark and to bluntly say, "No!" This could be a liability in a different personality but Fink was perceived by his members as being extremely fair. He was also a most supportive ally who fought hard for his colleagues when he thought they were right or that they had a legitimate problem. So the combination in Stanley Fink of fairness, knowledgeability, and toughness and the willingness of the Assembly's Democratic members to believe in him were factors that reinforced the formal powers granted to him by the rules, to render him a commanding legislative leader.

Conclusion

For most of the twentieth century, gubernatorial control over state legislatures was a key characteristic in almost every one of the fifty states. The part-time, amateur, understaffed and under-financed state legislatures could not compete with the substantial resources of chief executives.

This is no longer the case in many states, and certainly not in New York. The legislature has awakened. It has recognized its constitutional power and the need to provide itself with sufficient resources to assert that power. It has come to realize that its system of centralized leadership is appropriate to maintaining a balance with the governor. And it has become an attractive arena for ambitious politicians.

As one assemblyman said, when asked after his freshman year why he didn't run for a local post that paid a higher salary with greater security and a four year term (as opposed to a two year legislative term), "I'm staying here because here is where the action is."

Despite the passage of time, the conclusions about the nature of power in the New York Legislature have not changed in any essential manner. There have been important changes in leadership personnel and management practices in the Legislature, but the essential power of the Assembly Speaker and Senate Majority Leader remain the same. The rules of each house continue to grant those leaders enormous power over appointments (of members to leadership positions and committees), expenditures and the scheduling of legislation. These formal powers continue to be augmented by the unwritten tradition that New York legislative leaders forcefully utilize such formal powers on behalf of themselves and their respective party majorities. The traditional restraints against assertion of leadership prerogative that might exist elsewhere do not apply in New York.

This remains true despite the campaign for and election of a new Speaker in 1986, a brutal fight between both legislative leaders and the governor over ethics legislation, and the indictment of several lawmakers, including the Senate Minority Leader.

With the announcement in the spring of 1986 by Assembly Speaker Stanley Fink of his retirement, a number of senior members began a six-month campaign to replace him. Half a dozen candidates emerged, the strongest acknowledged to be Arthur J. Kremer of Nassau County, this writer from Queens, and the eventual victor, Melvin Miller of Brooklyn. Despite the stress of such a conflict, it was resolved fairly quietly with the withdrawal of all opponents when it became clear that Miller had the majority of votes required. He was unanimously elected by the Democratic Conference in 1987.

Declaring his intention to maintain the Assembly as an independent institution, Speaker Miller openly disagreed with Governor Mario Cuomo on a number of important issues, such as tax cuts, as the 1987 session opened. On these issues, Miller forged a bipartisan alliance with Senator Warren Anderson, the long-term Republican leader of the Senate.

When a series of scandals involving New York City officials spilled over into the legislative arena with accusations of unethical practices being made against some Albany lawmakers by a couple of investigative reporters, Miller and Anderson continued to stand apart from Governor Cuomo. The Assembly had in the past championed legislation requiring full disclosure of lawmaker financial interest, public financing of elections, and prohibitions on legislator representation of clients before state agencies. Periodically, bills reflecting these ideas had passed the Assembly—the first as early as 1975—but had never been considered by the Senate.

In the atmosphere of accusation and indictment in early 1987, the Senate finally hinted that it would pass something in the way of ethics legislation. The Assembly leadership was willing to compromise, and an ethics bill with provisions relating to full disclosure and state agency prohibitions passed both houses.

The governor, declaring the compromises to be loopholes, denounced both the bill and the legislature and vetoed the measure. The Legislature, in turn, refused to pass legislation creating an Ethics Commission to review the scandal, objecting to its proposed chairman, former Cabinet Secretary Joseph Califano. Newspapers across the state attacked the Legislature in a drumbeat of denunciation. It was a low point for the state's lawmakers.

Eventually, an acceptable ethics bill was passed and signed into law, and an Ethics Commission (without Califano) was created. But a great deal of damage had been done both to the reputation of the Legislature and to its relationship with the governor.

That reputation was not enhanced later in 1987 with the indictment of Senate Minority Leader Manfred Ohrenstein (D-Manhattan) and three other current or former senators on charges of misuse of public funds in the hiring of election campaign workers.

Despite these tribulations, a great deal of beneficial legislation was passed in 1987 including substantial tax cuts, refinancing of the state's mass transportation system, and meaningful improvement in a wide range of services. Additionally, the Legislature's own operations were enhanced with additional computer systems, more staff, and the prospect of management improvements.

Significantly, as wounded as the leaders might have been vis-à-vis the governor and the public over the ethics issue, their ability to govern internally had not been shaken as 1988 approached. The formal powers granted by the rules to the leaders, the expectations of the members, the obligation members generally feel towards their leaders and basic institutional loyalty, have all served to maintain a system of very strong leadership that has, for the most part, strengthened the Legislature as an independent and successful institution. Whether that independence and success can be sustained in the future if there are more accusations, indictments, and convictions of lawmakers remains to be seen.

The Policy Process and the Bureaucracy

by

**Michael E. Lynch
and Dennis R. Delong**

Mr. Lynch is Associate Professor and Chairman of Political Science at the State University of New York College at Oneonta.

Mr. Delong is Director of the Public Affairs Center at Empire State College, State University of New York.

EDITORS' NOTE: *This paper describes the "fourth branch" of New York government, the bureaucracy, and explains its extensive role in the public policy process.*

The term "bureaucracy" is one of the most misused, misunderstood, abused, and maligned in our society. The idea of governmental bureaucracy conjures up dreadful images of red tape, inefficiency, waste, corruption, indifference, and confusion. Such negative images are not particularly surprising in view of the social and intellectual history of this nation. The United States was founded upon a distrust of the ruling regime and its colonial governors. Thus, we have a long tradition of distrust of centralized authority, large government and government regulation. To most Americans, bureaucrats are the personification of all these negative images of government. For, after all, it is the bureaucrat who represents "the government" in transactions affecting citizens (see Figure 8). To the bureaucracy falls the task of refusing to issue the building building permit, denying the unemployment benefits, delivering the summons, or closing the unsanitary restaurant. When the average New Yorker confronts a particular government action which she or he dislikes, it is the bureaucrat, the enforcer of the law as it applies to individuals, who normally takes the heat. The legislature which passed the bill authorizing the action usually is not blamed, neither is the governor who signed the bill into law.

In New York State, as in other states, the bureaucracy is deeply involved in the process by which public policy is initiated, formulated, and implemented to bring governmental action to bear on the State's problems. The process is complex, and disjointed, involving the legislature, the governor, political parties, interest groups, the courts, municipal governments, and the Federal government, along with the public bureaucracy.

The State Bureaucracy

The government of the State of New York has developed a large bureaucracy consisting of a number of diverse and complex agencies. State employees are by no means exclusively found in the capitol city of Albany (see Figure 9). The State Constitution limits the State government to twenty cabinet agencies. This restriction has been circumvented, however, by the creation of a catch-all executive department which contains over thirty separate subdivisions, many of which exceed several of the nineteen cabinet agencies in number of personnel and budget. Table 13 lists the thirty-five state agencies with the largest operating budgets, whether each is cabinet or executive in nature, the number of positions, the operating budget, and the amount of said budget which is allocated

Figure 8

Distribution of New York State Government Employees By Function 1982

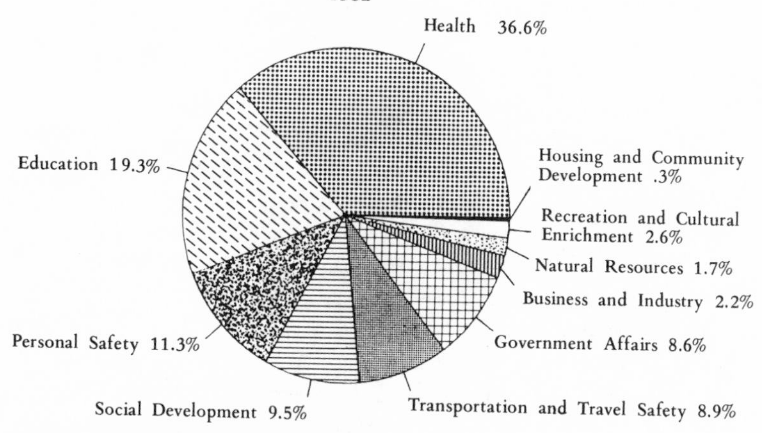

Note: These percentages represent 206,586 filled positions of which 162,000 are under the direct jurisdiction of the Department of Civil Service. Also included are filled positions in the State Police (4,059), the Division of Military and Naval Affairs (776), SUNY (35,562), Commissions and Authorities (3,589), and the Unclassified Service (600). Legislative and Judicial employees are not included.

SOURCE: New York State Department of Civil Service.

to local assistance. (A complete organization chart of New York State's bureaucracy may be found on p. 102.)

State agencies vary from the huge Department of Mental Hygiene, which actually operates as four separate entities (Office of Mental Retardation and Developmental Disabilities, Office of Mental Health, Division of Alcoholism and Alcohol Abuse and Division of Substance Abuse Services) to the Office of Parks, Recreation and Historic Preservation. Except for the Division of the Budget and the Office of General Services, which are staff units,[1] the agencies in Table 13 administer a vast variety of programs. Some programs provide direct services to citizens, such as the State University's educational offering and the Department of Mental Hygiene's facilities for the mentally ill. Other programs are primarily regulatory, e.g., the Public Service Department's regulation of utilities and the Department of Environmental Conservation's control over toxic waste. Several agencies provide assistance directly to local governments, for programs operated by these governments. Funding for these programs is by the local assistance portions of agency budgets.

All state programs are authorized by state legislative statute, the governor's executive order or action of the federal government. Many state agencies are utilized by the federal government to carry out its programs. (See the federal component of agency budgets in Table 19.)

Figure 9. New York State Government Employees[1] in Counties and Major Cities 1982

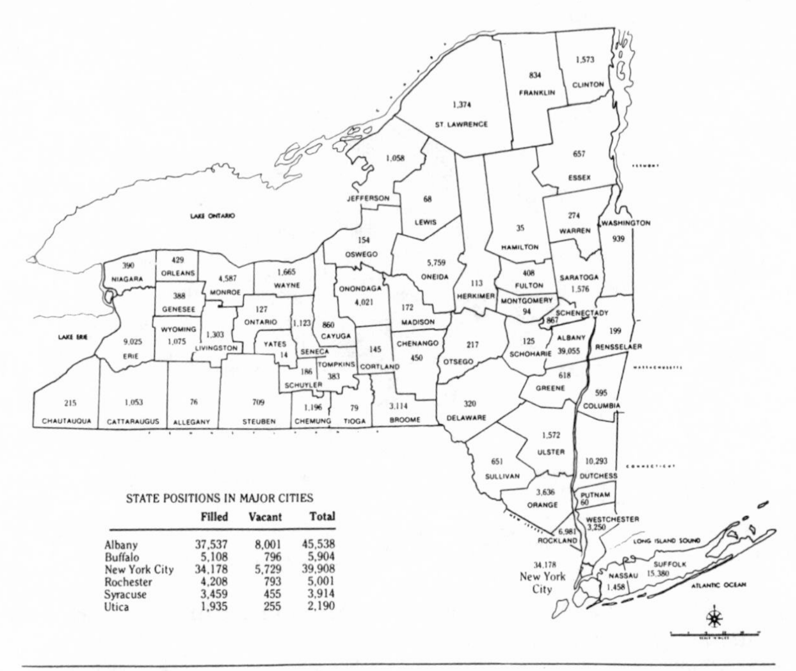

STATE POSITIONS IN MAJOR CITIES

	Filled	Vacant	Total
Albany	37,537	8,001	45,538
Buffalo	5,108	796	5,904
New York City	34,178	5,729	39,908
Rochester	4,208	793	5,001
Syracuse	3,459	455	3,914
Utica	1,935	255	2,190

[1]Total = 167,439 which includes 57 out-of-state filled positions and 226 filled positions for which county location was not recorded. Included are all filled positions in all departments of the Executive Branch except the State University of New York. Excludes commissions, authorities and other agencies which are not part of the Executive Branch. Also excludes the Legislature and Judiciary.

SOURCE: New York State Department of Civil Service.

The Bureaucracy and Public Policy

According to traditional organization theory, the head of any government bureaucracy is the chief executive. Thus, the president of the United States heads the federal bureaucracy, the governor heads the New York State bureaucracy, and the mayor is at the apex of New York City's executive bureaucracy. It would be misleading, however, to assume that a chief executive is in complete control of the bureaucracy; rather she or he has *influence* over the bureaucracy.

In our pluralistic political system, influence is also exercised by the legislature, the judiciary, the media, public opinion, interest groups, clienteles, and political parties.[2] These institutions often compete with the chief executive for influence over bureaucratic policy formulation and implementation. In fact, well into the twentieth century this nation had a tradition of weak governors, with limited authority to lead the bureaucracy. The government reorganization movement, which grew out of the Progressive reform proposals, increased the authority of New

Table 19

BUDGETARY AND POSITION DATA FOR THE THIRTY-FIVE LARGEST NEW YORK STATE AGENCIES

Agency	# of Positions	Operating Budget	Local Assistance	Total
Office for the Aging +	32	4.26 (2.90)	86.54 (69.46)	90.80 (72.36)
Dept. of Agriculture & Markets *	609	52.51 (1.53)	0.00 (0.00)	52.51 (1.53)
Council on the Arts +	88	3.79 (0.48)	32.60 (0.60)	36.39 (1.08)
Dept. of Audit and Control *	1,415	61.32 (0.00)	5.64 (0.00)	66.96 (0.00)
Dept. of Banking *	475	21.66 (0.00)	0.00 (0.00)	21.66 (0.00)
Division of the Budget *	302	13.61 (0.00)	0.00 (0.00)	13.61 (0.00)
Dept of Civil Service *	726	25.50 (0.00)	0.00 (0.00)	25.50 (0.00)
Dept. of Commerce *	301	25.03 (0.63)	3.35 (0.00)	28.38 (0.63)
Dept. of Correctional Services *	15,934	546.01 (0.13)	0.00 (0.00)	546.01 (0.13)
Div. of Criminal Justice Services +	607	18.12 (1.38)	65.54 (1.92)	83.66 (3.30)
Dept. of Education *	1,583	178.23 (39.76)	5,524.49 (601.23)	5,702.72 (640.99)
Dept. of Environmental Conservation *	1,430	147.01 (63.69)	39.54 (0.00)	186.55 (63.69)
Division of Equalization & Assessment +	532	19.49 (0.00)	0.08 (0.00)	19.57 (0.00)
Office of General Services +	2,447	347.12 (0.75)	0.01 (0.00)	347.13 (0.75)
Dept. of Health *	4,082	231.86 (29.96)	232.27 (151.14)	464.13 (180.20)
Higher Education Services Corp. (Independent agency under purview of Board of Regents)	252	26.79 (0.00)	370.68 (6.45)	397.47 (6.45)

Table 19—Continued

Div. of Housing & Community Renewal +	402	18.13 (0.57)	127.84 (0.40)	145.97 (0.97)
(Local assistance includes community development funds)				
Dept. of Insurance *	677	30.08 (0.00)	0.00 (0.00)	30.08 (0.00)
Dept. of Labor *	595	416.61 (400.14)	1,730.75 (1,720.00)	2,147.36 (2,120.14)
Dept. of Law *	1,368	59.27 (11.90)	0.00 (0.00)	59.27 (11.90)
Dept. of Mental Hygiene *	63,625	1,681.60 (10.95)	516.95 (41.58)	2,198.55 (53.53)
(Includes Office of Mental Health, Office of Mental Retardation & Developmental Disabilities, Division of Alcoholism & Alcohol Abuse and Division of Substance Abuse Services)				
Div. of Military & Naval Affairs +	690	30.82 (9.88)	4.53 (3.41)	35.35 (13.29)
Dept. of Motor Vehicles *	2,629	79.27 (0.00)	0.00 (0.00)	79.27 (0.00)
Div. of Parks, Recreation and Historical Preservation +	1,695	73.32 (1.54)	2.59 (2.17)	75.91 (3.71)
Division of Parole +	1,268	35.34 (0.00)	0.00 (0.00)	35.34 (0.00)
Division of Probation +	73	2.72 (0.00)	34.28 (0.00)	37.00 (0.00)
Dept.of Public Service *	649	32.87 (0.28)	0.00 (0.00)	32.87 (0.28)
Dept. of Social Services *	2,488	1,100.73 (920.46)	7,766.09 (4,854.53)	8,866.82 (5,774.99)
Dept. of State *	612	18.61 (2.66)	56.52 (46.29)	75.13 (48.95)
Division of State Police +	3,754	135.17 (0.00)	0.00 (0.00)	135.17 (0.00)
State University Of New York	32,545	1,524.59 (64.71)	157.14 (0.00)	1,681.73 (64.71)
(Independent agency under purview of Board of Regents)				
Dept. of Taxation	4,954	140.19 (0.00)	801.36 (0.00)	941.54 (0.00)

Table 19—Continued

Dept. of Transportation *	10,789	393.34 (24.87)	862.54 (5.39)	1,255.88 (30.26)
Workman's Compensation Board (Part of Department of Labor)	1,415	44.79 (0.18)	0.00 (0.00)	44.79 (0.18)
Division of Youth +	2,989	107.33 (0.00)	66.82 (0.00)	174.15 (0.00

* cabinet
+ executive dept.

FIGURE NOTE: Budgetary figures are drawn from New York State Legislature, *Report of the Fiscal Committees on the Executive Budget, Fiscal Year April 1, 1983 to March 31, 1984.* Figures are legislative appropriations for fiscal 1983-84 for State purposes and aid to localities, i.e., State funds provided to local governments and school districts. Not included are capital construction funds, (for facilities, highways, rail improvements, etc.), which are substantial in the case of several agencies. Position figures are drawn from the State of New York, *Executive Budget* for fiscal year 1983-84, and in the case of several agencies, the figures do not include positions funded from other than State sources. The thirty-five agencies are those with appropriations from general funds exceeding 13 million for fiscal year 1983-84.

All budgetary figures are expressed in millions of dollars. Figures within parenthesis represent the amount of the department's budget derived from federal funds.

York State's governor. The creation of an executive budgeting system and increasing gubernatorial powers of appointment did much to strengthen the governor's hand in dealing with the bureaucracy. However, the governor is still limited by the existence of two constitutionally elected department heads (attorney general-Department of Law, and comptroller-Department of Audit and Control), the accountability of the commissioner of education to the Board of Regents, and the existence of a number of semi-independent public authorities.[3]

Earlier in the twentieth century it was fashionable for students and practitioners of public administration to adhere to the "politics/administration dichotomy" theory, sometimes referred to as the "policy/administration dichotomy." Under this theory, bureaucrats were supposed to have no role in policy-making and, thus, no part in the political process. Rather, bureaucrats were supposed to be neutral implementors of policies made by the political branches of government—the legislature and the elected chief executive. The proponents of this dichotomy theory believed that it would strike a blow against the patronage-ridden bureaucracies of the political machines and provide a rationalization for a permanent career civil service able to serve a chief executive from any political party.[4] In fact, the public bureaucracy has never been completely divorced from politics and the bureaucracy has become increasingly involved in the policy-making process since the New Deal.

Bureaucratic involvement in the political/policy process has been largely at the invitation or insistence of other components of our pluralistic political system. Interest groups urged the original creation of agencies. Once created, agencies' policy roles, budgets, and personnel are openly and actively supported by agency clienteles. The clientele of an agency is the segment of the public most directly affected by, and therefore most interested in, agency policies. Agency clienteles include organized interest groups which lobby both the Legislature and the executive on behalf of the agency because they perceive a close connection between the fate of the agency and their own interests. For instance, environmental organizations are generally supportive of the New York State Department of Environmental Conservation, the tourism industry supports the Commerce Department's "I Love New York" campaign, and agricultural interest groups support the Department of Agriculture and Markets' programs to promote produce "grown in New York State."

The state Legislature has also supported increased bureaucratic involvement in the policy process. The bureaucracy is a depository of very considerable expertise. The executive bureaucracy is much larger than the legislative bureaucracy. Consequently, in a highly complex, technological society, the Legislature has come to rely on the expertise of the bureaucracy in the policy-making process. This reliance has taken two forms. First, the majority of the legislative bills effecting agency policies originate within the bureaucracy. The bureaucracy is the source of ideas for new legislation. This is not surprising, for it is the bureaucracy which is charged with implementing existing laws. Bureaucrats frequently are in the best position, because of their experience and expertise, to point out the inadequacies of existing laws and proffer remedial legislation. Secondly, the Legislature has delegated policy-making discretion to the bureaucracy. This discretion is shown as the "rule-making authority."

Under our separation of powers system, the law-making authority resides in the legislative branch, not the executive. In the twentieth century, however, legislatures discovered that they lacked both the time and expertise necessary to pass detailed, technical legislation in a wide variety of policy areas. In a sense, big government had outgrown the legislatures' ability to legislate in detail. In the face of this, legislatures turned to the practice of passing broad, general policy statutes. These general statutes delegated rulemaking discretion for the bureaucracy to formulate the specific "rules and regulations" necessary to achieve the intent of the statute. Bureaucratic policies made pursuant to "rule-making authority" have the same force and effect as statutory laws passed by legislatures.[5]

Controlling the Bureaucracy

There has long been justifiable concern over possible abuse of the rule-making authority by the bureaucracy. This concern has heightened in the post-Watergate and post-Viet Nam era. Consequently, legislatures have taken the following actions:

1. tightened authorizing legislation so as to leave less discretion to the agencies;
2. increased legislative over-sight in an attempt to insure that the bureaucracy is adhering to legislative intent;
3. increased their staff assistance; and
4. passed more detailed procedural legislation governing the methods whereby the bureaucracy exercises its rule-making authority.

For instance, the New York State Legislature has been staffing up over the past decade. Both houses have developed large, sophisticated central program and fiscal staffs. Furthermore, the legislature has created staff units specifically charged with responsibility for overseeing the bureaucracy. It has created the Legislative Commission on Expenditure Review, the Assembly Committee on Legislative Oversight, Analysis and Investigation, and the Administrative Regulations Review Commission. These organizations, along with the New York State Administrative Procedure Act, all are designed to help maintain the Legislature's constitutional role in the policy-making process. Further explanation of these developments is necessary.

The Administrative Regulations Review Commission (ARRC) was created in 1978, the outgrowth of a Joint Legislative Commission. Article 5-B of the Legislative Law gives ARRC the mandate to:

> exercise continuous oversight of the process of rule-making and examine rules . . . adopted or proposed by each agency with respect to (i) statuatory authority, (ii) compliance with legislative intent, (iii) impact on the economy and on the local governments, and (iv) impact upon affected parties. . . .

The intent of the statute establishing ARRC was clearly to guard against potential abuses of the rule-making authority by establishing an organization to provide continuous legislative oversight of agency rules and rule-making procedures. ARRC does this by examining rules on a regular basis, developing remedial rules, holding public hearings in order to obtain some reaction to both proposed and existing rules, and informing the public of its existence. methods, and objectives. Some critics claim that ARRC has been charged with an unrealistically broad mandate.

In 1976, the New York State Administrative Procedure Act went into effect. It was modeled after the Federal Administrative Procedure Act. Both are broad statutes which set forth the methods and procedures to be followed by all bureaucratic agencies in the exercise of their rule-making authority. With limited exceptions, the New York State Administrative Procedure Act (APA) requires public notice of all proposed rules and regulations. These are published biweekly in the *State Bulletin,* prepared by the Department of State. Rules and regulations must be published at least twenty-one days prior to their going into effect. Once effective, they are printed in *State of New York: Official Compilation of Codes, Rules, and Regulations.*

Another attempt to improve legislative oversight of the bureaucracy is illustrated by the New York State Assembly's creation of the standing Committee on Oversight, Analysis and Investigation. The committee investigates agency actions at the request of the speaker, the committee chairman or constituents. It can recommend legislation to correct agency wrongdoing. However, the committee does not meet with great regularity (e.g., three meetings in 1981). Furthermore, its highly partisan nature and the fact that its jurisdiction conflicts with other legislative committees serve to limit its effectiveness as a vehicle for the oversight of bureaucratic policy-making.

A major effort to improve legislative control of the state's bureaucracy was initiated in 1969. In that year, the Legislature Commission on Expenditure Review (LCER) was created as the first legislative oversight commission in the United States. The Legislature Commission on Expenditure Review serves as an "independent" source of continuous review of agency programs.[6] The commission not only review agency expenditures, but also oversees agency policies. It performs three types of audits: (1) a compliance audit to determine if legislative intent is being adhered to; (2) an operation audit to verify that agencies are operating efficiently; and (3) a program audit to ascertain whether or not the agency is accomplishing its goals. The first of these, the compliance audit, has direct relevance to agency policy-making. In practice, LCER's work has been confined to policy recommendations, as opposed to suggestions to improve administrative economy and efficiency. After concluding an audit, LCER submits its report to the agency, which has 180 days to respond. The final report is distributed to every member of the legislature, and to the press as well. Thus, the potential adverse effects of a negative report are very real in the eyes of agency administrators.

Conclusion

It seems appropriate to conclude that the bureaucracy has been enticed and commanded to enter the political realm of policy formulation by clienteles, interest groups, legislatures, and chief executives. The all too common perception that bureaucrats have usurped political power in the face of unanimous opposition from other participants in the policy-making process simply is not accurate. As has been indicated,the legislature has strengthened its ability to scrutinize and question bureaucratic involvement in the policy process. Nevertheless, the enormously complex bureaucracy in New York State seems likely to continue to retain significant autonomy and to continue performing a crucial role in the policy process of the Empire State.

NOTES

1. The distinction between line and staff is basic to the study of any bureaucracy. Line units make direct contributions to the purpose or objective of the organization; they provide governmental services or exercise governmental regulations. Staff units, on the other hand, provide the supporting services which the line needs to carry out its responsibilities, e.g., personnel, budget, purchasing, central stores, research, and a variety of advisory functions. For a discussion of the line/staff distinction see: William L. Morrow, *Public Administration: Politics and the Political System,* New York: Random House, 1975, pp. 104-109.

2. For a detailed discussion of the pluralistic power centers which influence public bureaucracies see: Robert C. Fried, *Performance in American Bureaucracy,* Boston: Little, Brown, 1976, especially Chapters 4, 5, and 8-15.

3. A synopsis of the strong executive movement is to be found in: William O. Winter, *State and Local Government in a Decentralized Republic,* New York: Macmillan, pp. 187-197. Note: Public authorities are discussed in a separate chapter herein.

4. Samuel J. Bernstein and Patrick O'Hara, *Public Administration: Organizations, People and Public Policy,* New York: Harper & Row, 1979, pp. 214-215 and Lewis Mainzer, *Political Bureaucracy,* Glenview, Ill.: Scott, Foresman, 1973, pp. 69-72.

5. All texts on public policy or public administration discuss the role of the public bureaucracy in policy formulation. For instance see the following texts: William L. Morrow, pp. 2-5; John Pfiffner and Robert Presthus, *Public Administration,* 5th edition, New York: Ronald, 1967, pp. 46-54; or Charles E. Jacob,

Policy and Bureaucracy, Princeton, N.J.: Van Nostrand, 1966, especially pp. 77-81. For classic treatments of the topic see either: Paul H. Appleby, *Policy and Administration,* University of Alabama Press, 1949; or Peter Woll, *American Bureaucracy,* New York: Norton, 1963.

6. The Commission is bi-partisan, comprised of the following ex-officio members: President Pro Tem of the Senate, Assembly Speaker, Assembly Majority Leader, Assembly Minority Leader, Senate Minority Leader, Chairmen of both the Senate Finance and the Assembly Ways and Means Committee, Ranking majority and minority members of both the Senate Finance and the Assembly Ways and Means Committee, and one non-legislative member appointed by each house.

For One Zealous Judge, Hard Bargaining Pushes Cases Through the Courts

by

Sam Roberts

Sam Roberts is urban affairs columnist for the *New York Times.*

EDITORS' NOTE: *While the specifics of this report focus on one judge in New York City, the issues raised concerning plea bargaining, bail, society's needs versus rights of the accused, and rehabilitation are central to the criminal justice process throughout the state and nation. This article originally appeared in longer form in the* New York Times, 29 April 1985.

"It's really enraging to me," the judge tells the prosecutor assigned to his courtroom in State Superior Court in Manhattan. "I don't know why the assistants can't get the vacation schedules of the police officers. I have three prisoners and three defense attorneys ready to go and trial parts available and I can't send this case out."

Charging off the bench, he grabs a wall phone to berate the assistant district attorney assigned to the case: "It drives me to the wall that I found out the officer is on vacation in Mexico." Then the judge hangs up.

"Let's go," he barks, and the next case is called: a man accused of criminal possession of seven-eighths of an ounce of heroin and a quarter of an ounce of cocaine.

"I'd give him a year on each count, concurrent, if he takes it today, one to three consecutive, if he doesn't," Justice Harold Rothwax tells the defense lawyer.

Expediting Court Business

The defendant is ambivalent, the lawyer says. He asks the judge to keep the lower offer open until the defendant's next court appearance. "Why," the judge asks, "so he can consult with his buddies on Riker's Island for better legal advice? He's always free to go to trial. If he's ever going to plead, he's better pleading sooner than later."

As one of six judges assigned to the six so-called calendar parts in the criminal section of State Supreme Court in Manhattan, Justice Rothwax's job, as he describes it, is "to push everyone, kicking and screaming, ahead on each case."

"That means," he said, "every time a case is on the calendar it must be moving forward, either to disposition or to trial."

In processing arraignments and motions, calendar judges either extract guilty pleas from defendants or speed the case to other judges who preside at trials.

How he does his job assumes a special significance now as state court officials reorganize the way judges are assigned criminal and civil cases.

Changing the System

Currently, judges usually handle only certain aspects of a case, such as motions or trials. Under the individual assignment system, to be phased in selectively before the end of the year [1985], judges generally would handle cases from start to finish.

The role of middlemen like calendar judges could be reduced and eliminated under the new system, proposed by Chief Judge Sol Wachtler, although it would be preserved in some form under at least one version being considered by court officials.

In any event, what occurs in the calendar parts over which Justice Rothwax and his colleagues preside illustrates the skills that will be required of virtually all judges, who, under the new system, will be responsible for managing large and diverse caseloads—though far fewer cases than each of the calendar judges now confronts.

"It's partly an act but it's partly real," Justice Rothwax said of his style. "I know that unless I put on that act, nothing happens."

Last year, plenty happened.

Justice Rothwax arraigned 1,094 defendants, disposed of 1,535 cases—including 1,338 when defendants pleaded guilty—and imposed 1,457 sentences.

Each case is handled in a matter of minutes, often under the premise that a negotiated plea, with swift and certain punishment, is preferable to the vagaries of a trial.

Of the 30,279 felony cases resolved last year [1984] in the State Supreme Courts in New York City, 19,008 were settled by plea or dismissal before trial by judges assigned to the calendar parts.

Justice Rothwax expressed concern that the new individual calendar system, which court officials say they will impose cautiously and flexibly, "overlooks the fact that individual judges are different."

"Many of them simply cannot handle the volume," he said. "It says that all judges are equal and can be expected to do whatever they're assigned. That simply isn't true."

"The master calendar arranges people according to their strengths," he said of the present system. "Now you can say, 'We have a lazy judge, let's not assign him complex cases, let's not give him matters he'll mess up.' An argument for individual calendaring is you'll isolate responsibility, that we'll be able to know the judges who are good and who aren't. We know that now."

Indeed, the calendar judges handling criminal cases in Manhattan draw their assignments because they have demonstrated an ability to speed dozens of cases through the system daily.

A Model of Efficiency

They are all acting Supreme Court justices, elevated from the Criminal Court bench, and like the elected Supreme Court justices, their salary is $82,000 a year.

Justice Rothwax, who is fifty-four years old, was appointed to the

Criminal Court by Mayor John V. Lindsay in 1971. He is now a senior acting Supreme Court justice. By his choice, and by the designation of court officials, he has been a calendar judge for two and a half years—longer than any of his colleagues in Manhattan, who usually are rotated every six months or so. For that reason and others, he is rated by court officials as the most productive judge in his courthouse.

Before 10 A.M., an hour after he has arrived at the courthouse on a three-speed bicycle from his Upper West Side apartment, Justice Rothwax is on the bench dealing a stack of five-by-seven inch cards as if preparing for a game of solitaire.

Each card bears his synopsis of the cases on the day's calendar: the charge, the defendant's name, whether he is in jail or out on bail, the names of the assistant district attorney and the defense lawyer assigned to the case, and a brief record of prior court appearances. He places the cards in four piles: those cases that are ready for sentencing, those for trial, those for pretrial motions, and the "unusuals."

His props in place, Justice Rothwax awaits the other players: the private defense lawyers, the Legal Aid lawyer assigned to handle all Legal Aid cases in his courtroom for the day, and his counterpart from the prosecutor's office, who arrives to find a shopping cart bulging with folders for each of the day's cases.

When Conrad Martin, the court clerk, mellifluously calls the first case, the bargaining begins. Nearly all of it takes place off the record in conferences among the lawyers and the judge.

Out of earshot are the fifty or so spectators and other lawyers who, on a typical day, wait for their cases to be called, chat, telephone their offices, and intermittently shout out the name of a defendant who they may be meeting for the first time. Occasionally the judge raps his gavel to silence them.

For each case, the prosecutor hands over a "pink sheet" listing a plea offer and the recommended bail, and a handwritten page from a yellow legal pad, which recounts the salient details of the crime.

From these sources, Justice Rothwax draws most of his conclusions about a case—even to the point of noticing that on one pink sheet, a supervisor had downgraded the plea offer, which indicated, the judge said, that "they're saying anything that would get rid of this case they'd be happy with."

On the average, each case takes two to ten minutes. Then the next court appearance—for defense motions, the District Attorney's response, sentencing or trial—is scheduled, usually for several weeks hence.

The process is subject to myriad pressures: a court stenographer who appeals to the judge to finish for the day by 5 P.M. so he can keep a doctor's appointment in New Jersey; a defense lawyer unable to return to court that afternoon because she is getting her hair cut (but she sends her law partner); a disruptive spectator who, after ignoring one warning from the judge, is hustled off to a detention pen for several hours.

Rhythms of a Courtroom

The specific cases differed on several days earlier this month [April 1985], but the rhythm remained the same.

Case Number 20, April 11: a seventeen-year-old upper Manhattan youth accused of sexually abusing a five-year-old boy who lives in the same apartment building.

"We're willing to do anything that will hold out a nonjail possibility," said the defense attorney—including pleading guilty if Justice Rothwax agrees to classify the teenager a youthful offender instead of prosecuting him as an adult.

The judge summoned Linda A. Fairstein, the chief of the District Attorney's Sex Crimes Unit, who was skeptical about a solution that relied solely on psychiatric treatment without confinement. However, the judge decided on carefully monitored counseling, while warning the defendant that he would send him to jail if he fails to comply.

Another case involved two repeat felons charged with burglary. One of them had no lawyer, but rather than adjourn the case, the judge appointed a lawyer from among those waiting in the front row. The District Attorney's offer: two to four years.

"After today, it's three to six, after that, it's four to eight," the judge said. "If they're ever going to plead, today is the time to do it."

When the defendants reject the offer, the judge declared: "We'll make it very easy. It's four to eight after today. Let's play hardball." The defense was instructed to submit motions in four weeks.

Getting Results

"You see," the judge said, "if I'm mean and intractable, I get all sorts of results that would otherwise not have been contemplated."

Sometimes, the speed with which justice is dispensed raises questions.

For one thing, are suspects receiving adequate defense from lawyers they may never have met before?

"Defense attorneys sometimes say they don't know if a defendant is guilty or not," Justice Rothwax said. "I say, 'You don't but he does.'" He recalled that as a Legal Aid lawyer, he was asked by his mother why he would represent a suspect in the robbery of an elderly man returning home with a container of milk. The defendant said he was innocent, Justice Rothwax replied. His mother's rejoinder: "If he can rob, he can lie."

Does the system presume defendants innocent until proven guilty?

Only when a judge is instructing a jury, Justice Rothwax said, and not, for instance, when he is considering bail. When a lawyer requests reasonable bail for a defendant with a history of bail-jumping, Justice Rothwax replied: "Reasonable bail is the only kind I set. But no defendant should be offered a constitutional right to jump bail on more than one occasion. Enough already! You get one chance to jump per case."

Sixty-Five Cases for the Day

At 5:38 P.M., Mr. Martin, the clerk, called the last case—sixty-five in all this day. The score: twelve sentences, nine pleas, three dismissals, one case sent for trial, and the rest adjourned.

Justice Rothwax said, "If you want a speedy trial you'll find a friend in me." Yet he also recognized the advantages of letting a defendant plead guilty to reduced charges.

"Plea bargaining provides certain things that trials don't: promptness, certainty, finality," the judge said. "Isn't it better to have a prompt, certain, final result, even if the punishment is a little less—that certainty is better than severity?

"You can't have plea bargaining unless the defendant seeks it out, if he says, 'Judge, what will you offer me?' Anybody who says he wants a trial gets a trial."

Justice Rothwax rejected criticism by some defense lawyers that he places too much pressure on defendants to plead guilty by steadily raising the stakes.

"I say I'm going to give you my best offer at the outset," he said. "If you're going to litigate, then the value of plea bargaining diminishes. You have to work out a system where the incentive is to plead early. I don't view it as coercion. I feel it's straightforward, it's fair."

The judge said he gave young first offenders more time for the initial threat of a jail sentence to sink in.

Justice Rothwax warned that a state panel's proposal to limit judicial discretion in sentencing could result in many more trials, because the range will narrow between the plea a judge could offer and the worst the defendant would receive after conviction.

"Retribution Is In"

"We used to have definite sentences," he recalled. "At the turn of the century, indeterminate sentencing with rehabilitative philosophy was the reform." Now, he said: "Rehabilitation is out. Retribution is in."

If managing the calendar becomes the job of every judge under the new assignment system, Justice Rothwax's daily experience would be instructive.

The basic rules, he said, are simple. "Something has got to happen each time; you have to control the courtroom; the process must be both fair and efficient, and those two are always in conflict.

"Basically," Justice Rothwax continued, "there has to be an orientation that I will not allow things to drift. If judges tolerate shoddiness, they get shoddiness. If they don't tolerate shoddiness, they may not get excellence, but they'll get less shoddiness."

"Leaving force of personality aside," Justice Rothwax said, "to be a calendar judge you have to believe in it. Then you've got to begin with some appetite for it. It's got to upset you that the system doesn't operate the way it's supposed to."

Our Other Governments: The Public Authorities

by

Keith M. Henderson

Mr. Henderson is Professor and Chairman of the Political Science Department at State University College at Buffalo, New York.

EDITORS' NOTE: *The least known units of New York State government are the thirty-odd public benefit corporations and authorities which perform specified missions in areas such as transportation, commerce and development, and finance. This chapter reveals the structure of these agencies and their advantages and disadvantages as a form of government.*

Keith M. Henderson

The Port Authority of New York and New Jersey, the New York State Thruway Authority, the State Power Authority, the Housing Finance Agency, the Dormitory Authority, and the Metropolitan Transportation Authority are among the most important public agencies in New York State, yet their structure and financing is little understood by the public. Only when a crisis is imminent (the threatened bankruptcy of New York City which led to the creation of the Municipal Assistance Corporation for the City of New York; the default in 1975 of the Urban Development Corporation) does widespread attention befall this unusual form of government.

In New York State there are over thirty major public authorities (technically: public benefit corporations and authorities) with billions of dollars worth of assets and debt. They are separate, largely autonomous corporations and are not operating departments of the State.

Generally, most share certain common characteristics in their legal structure (they are created by special act of the New York State Legislature), their broad administrative autonomy, and their concern with financing, constructing, or operating revenue-producing facilities or providing public services outside the normal restrictions of state government. Often, their activities span several local government jurisdictions enabling them to deliver area-wide services on an area-wide basis without recourse to the other jurisdictions. Since they have no authority to levy taxes, they must finance themselves through user charges, fees, tolls, and revenue bonds. Additional funding may be provided by general purpose governments. Most authorities have the following features:

1. They are administered by boards or commissions whose members are typically appointed by the governor.
2. They borrow outside governmental debt limits.
3. They are exempt from taxation for both bonds and property, although in the latter instance, payments may be in lieu of taxes.
4. They have the power of eminent domain.
5. They have discretion in establishing rates and charges.
6. Their employees are independent of the civil service system.
7. They can pay higher salaries to their employees than the State proper.
8. Their decision-making is isolated from the political process.

To begin to understand these agencies, it is useful to look at them as three functional groups.[1] The Transportation Group includes the

Thruway Authority and the Metropolitan Transportation Authority and subsidiaries together with other authorities which provide transportation services including mass transit, highway, bridge, and port services. The Commerce and Development group includes the Power Authority and other organizations whose principal function is the development and promotion of New York's commercial environment. The Finance group includes the Urban Development Corporation, Housing Finance Agency, Dormitory Authority, and other entities engaged in providing low-cost financing and other services to both public and private concerns.

The Transportation Group

The Transportation Group includes the Thruway Authority—well known to all motorists in New York State—and the Metropolitan Transportation Authority—well known to commuters in the New York City area. Although created by an Interstate Compact as a bi-state agency and, hence, operating under different legal authority, the Port Authority of New York and New Jersey (originally called the Port of New York Authority) is among the largest such agencies in the world. It operates LaGuardia, Kennedy, and Newark Airports, as well as Teterboro Airport in New Jersey and two heliports; the Port Authority Bus Terminal in New York City; six bridges and tunnels in the New York City area; the World Trade Center; the Trans-Hudson (PATH) system; one Motor Truck Terminal; and, as its name suggests, various marine terminals. By any standard—even the scale we are used to in New York State and New York City—it is a gargantuan operation.

Few who use the Thruway in New York State, the Long Island Railroad, or facilities of the Port Authority will realize how profitable or unprofitable that operation is. Some transportation operations, in fact, are quite profitable; others require large subsidies from state or local governments or from both levels. An example of the former, an agency that makes a profit from its revenues, is the Port Authority. (It is sufficiently affluent that other governments—such as the City of New York—occasionally seek ways to tap its revenues). A task force appointed by then Governor Carey in 1980 had recommended that the Authority sell its World Trade Center and use the profits for other state projects. In December, 1982, a panel of experts appointed by Carey and Governor Kean of New Jersey proposed creation of a Regional Development Bank, among other recommendations.[2] Generally, the Authority has gone its own way, occasionally using differences between New York and New Jersey—whose Governors jointly control it—to its advantage. It has been criticized frequently for avoiding risky projects and from time to time is even subject to suggestions that it be dismantled.

Examples of unprofitable agencies, whose revenues do not cover their expenses, are much more numerous than the profitable ones. Some, such as the subways in New York City which are under the Transit Authority, a subsidiary of the Metropolitan Transportation Authority (MTA), seem to be in nearly constant financial difficulty.

Another important Authority in New York City, also a subsidiary of the MTA, is the Triborough Bridge and Tunnel Authority which now operates the Triborough, Bronx-Whitestone, Throgs Neck, Henry Hudson, Marine Parkway, Cross Bay Veterans Memorial, and Verrazano-Narrows Bridges; and the Queens Mid-town and Brooklyn-Battery Tunnels. Tolls are charged at each of these facilities. The spectacular Triborough Bridge, originally planned by New York City in 1929 with municipal bond financing, could not be built when the stock market collapse rendered municipal credit useless.

One man, Robert Moses, whose name recurs again and again when Authorities are discussed, was able to arrange for the financing and construction of the bridge by establishing a public authority. The legendary Moses, whose career spans over 40 years, had been effective in New York State government as an aide to Governor Al Smith and has already established a popular base of support by the time he began to spearhead the Triborough to completion. The obstacles he faced were considerable, including a personal grudge against him by the President of the United States, Franklin D. Roosevelt, who—through his Secretary of the Interior and Administrator of the Public Works Administration (PWA), Harold Ickes—vowed to withhold Federal PWA funding unless Moses was removed from the Triborough Board. The measure of Moses' aggressive political skill is that he outmaneuvered the president with carefully timed press releases that made it appear FDR was "playing politics," ultimately forcing the president to relent.[3] When completed—FDR reluctantly participated in the opening ceremonies—the Triborough Bridge began almost immediately to generate more traffic and revenue than even Moses had anticipated and became a model PWA project.

In later years, the Authority was expanded, also under Moses' vigorous manipulating, to include other bridges and tunnels. In a revealing statement Robert Moses described the significant governmental role which public authorities play:

> The nearest thing to business in government is the public authority, which is business with private capital under public auspices, established only when both private enterprise and routine government have failed to meet an

> urgent need, and this device is often attacked because it is too independent of daily pressures, too unreachable by the boys and therefore essentially undemocratic.[4]

The bonds, notes, and other commitments of the numerous transportation authorities amount to a staggering sum. In virtually every corner of the state there are bridge authorities, port authorities, or other transportation authorities. A partial listing follows:

Niagara Frontier Transportation Authority
Rochester-Genesee Regional Transportation Authority
Capital District Transportation Authority
Central New York Regional Transportation Authority
New York State Bridge Authority
Ogdensburg Bridge and Port Authority
Buffalo and Fort Erie Public Bridge Authority
Port of Oswego Authority

The Commerce and Development Group

Some public authorities are primarily concerned with commerce and development rather than transportation or finance. For example, the Central New York Regional Market Authority and the Genesee Valley Regional Market Authority were established to operate market facilities for the buying and selling of agricultural products. Warehouses, frozen food lockers, truck garages, sheds for wholesale dealers, stalls for farmers, and other facilities are maintained. In a very different field of activity, the New York State Energy Research and Development Authority was created in 1975 as a response to the energy crisis. The former Atomic and Space Development Authority was transformed into the new agency and given a mandate to accelerate the development and use of energy technologies consistent with the State's economic growth and protection of its environmental values. Although, at the present time, new energy sources seem less urgent (there is an oil glut), this was a high priority after the oil crisis of 1973–74.

By far the largest authority concerned with commerce and development is the Power Authority of New York State, which provides electric power through its various facilities including nuclear power plants. Under the leadership of Robert Moses, who served as Chairman for 1954 until 1962, the Authority expanded its role, completing the St. Lawrence Power Project and the Niagara Power Project. The final generating unit of the latter was placed on line on November 11, 1962. It is now part of an impressive complex which tourists on the Niagara Frontier may visit. The Power Vista, a public observation building, crowns the south buttress, some 350 feet above the river, and provides a view of the 1840-foot plant which houses thirteen hydro-generators. In the background are the twelve units of the Lewiston Pump Generating Plant.

The Authority also operates other plants including Indian Point 3 (nuclear) in Westchester County. Recently, the Nuclear Regulatory Commission, a Federal agency, has held hearings regarding the required emergency evacuation plans for areas surrounding nuclear plants. "The low level of risk with or without prompt evacuation offers compelling justification for continued operation of Indian Point 3," according to the Authority's current head, Leroy Sinclair.[5]

Finance Group

The word "development" also occurs in the names of public authorities whose primary purpose is providing financing and undertaking construction projects. One of the most controversial of the finance authorities is the Urban Development Corporation, which not only can raise its own funds but can override local building and zoning codes. One expert has maintained that the U.D.C. was created in order to build at top speed and, "was rammed through the legislature (by Governor Rockefeller) on a 'message of necessity' following the assassination of Martin Luther King."[6]

Officially, the U.D.C. was created to provide or obtain the capital resources necessary to acquire, construct, rehabilitate or improve industrial, manufacturing, commercial, public, educational, recreational and cultural facilities, and housing accommodations for persons and families of low income, and to carry out the clearance, replanning, reconstruction, and rehabilitation of substandard and insanitary areas."[7] Its primary focus has been to provide financial aid for construction of low income housing, industrial parks, shopping malls, sports facilities, schools, hotels, and new communities (Audubon, near Buffalo; Radisson, near Syracuse; and Roosevelt Island, in New York City). The U.D.C. has been involved in various ways, from partial funding to lending of technical help, in the New York Convention and Exposition Center, the 42nd Street redevelopment (New York City), the Carrier Dome stadium in Syracuse, the Grand Hyatt Hotel (New York City), the Albee Square shopping mall in Brooklyn, the Sheraton Motor Inn in Utica, and other projects.

The U.D.C. has been through stormy times, particularly in 1975 when its inability to make payment on some of its debt brought about a restructuring of the agency.

At the present time, it is reducing the emphasis upon financing large-scale construction projects and turning to support of emerging industries such as those in high-technology. The agency will be renamed the New York State Development Corporation, dropping "urban" from the title, to reflect a widened scope of activity. For example, in rural upstate areas it might help provide facilities, research and development capacities, or venture capital for existing or emerging businesses. In January, 1983, Governor Cuomo's former campaign treasurer, William J. Stern, assumed the role of Chairman and President of the U.D.C.—the first head to have both titles and the first not to have a background in construction (Stern was a highly successful business entrepreneur in computer software). In carrying out his mandate to redirect the agency towards emerging high-tech industry without abandoning its traditional role, he has reduced the heavy reliance on outside consultants and lawyers—for which the agency had been criticized—and has made top-level personnel changes. A related part of Stern's task is to improve the image of the agency and open it to public scrutiny.[8]

Other finance authorities include the New York State Housing Finance Agency, New York Dormitory Authority, State of New York Mortgage Agency (recently brought back from the brink of obscurity), and New York State Medical Care Facilities Finance Agency.

In 1975—a fateful year for New York State and New York City—the Municipal Assistance Corporation for the City of New York (quickly nicknamed Big Mac) was created and, in conjunction with it the New York State Emergency Financial Control Board for the City of New York, to rescue the finances of the City. A public benefit corporation was the instrument for aiding the nation's largest city!

Problems and Prospects

The importance of New York State's other governments should be obvious. The various authorities discussed here (plus those not mentioned) provide valuable services and advantages which would not otherwise be available. More so than most states, New York has used the device of the public benefit authority and corporation to extend the function of state and local government beyond the usual realms. Through issuance of tax-free bonds and notes and exemption from restrictions applicable to general-purpose governments, the authorities have made possible a wide variety of transportation, developmental, and financial activities.

Critics of some aspects of the authorities' scope and operations have pointed to their separation and lack of direct public control, as well as their legal powers to override local government desires. From time to time, careful studies have called for greater accountability, access by the public to records and proceedings, and better co-ordination with the general-purpose governments.[9] Some are worried about the credit-worthiness of agencies whose combined debt exceeds that of state government proper by several times.

The flexibility and business-like structure of the authorities, however, suggests that they will continue to be a critical aspect of government and politics in New York State.

NOTES

1. These are the categories used in the 1982 *Annual Report of the Comptroller, State of New York,* p. 32. The Port Authority is classified separately as a Joint Venture, p. 33.

2. Annmarie Walsh and James Leigland, "The Only Planning Game in Town," *Empire State Report,* May 1983, pp. 6-10.

3. See Robert A. Caro, *The Power Broker, Robert Moses and the Fall of New York,* New York: Alfred A. Knopf, 1974, a 1200 page study of Moses. Moses is also discussed in detail in Eugene Lewis, *Public Entrepreneurship, Toward a Theory of Bureaucratic Political Power,* Bloomington, Indiana: Indiana University Press, 1980, and Jeanne R. Lowe, *Cities in a Race with Time,* New York: Random House, 1967.

4. Editors of Fortune, *The Exploding Metropolis,* New York: Doubleday, 1958, p. 81.

5. "Indian Point Unit Says Risk Doesn't Justify Closing," *New York Times,* May 27, 1983, p. B1.

.6 Charles R. Morris, *The Cost of Good Intentions, New York City and the Liberal Experiment, 1960-1975,* New York: McGraw-Hill, 1980, p. 37.

7. *Manual for the use of the Legislature of the State of New York, 1980-81,* Albany: Department of State, p. 705 (this is known as the "Blue Book").

8. See, "U.D.C. Chief Steering Agency Into New Area," *New York Times,* April 13, 1983, p. B1; and Arthur Greenspan, "U.D.C. Goes High Tech," *Empire State Report,* March 1983, pp. 28-31.

9. See, for example, Report of the Temporary State Commission on the Powers of Local Government, *Strengthening Local Government in New York,* Part 2, 1973, pp. 83-88.

The State of the Executive Budget

by

Robert P. Kerker

Mr. Kerker is Deputy Chief Budget Examiner,
State of New York Executive Department, Division of the Budget.
He is the principal author of a history of the executive budget system
in New York State.

EDITORS' NOTE: *The action in New York government often revolves around the preparation and administration of the annual state budget. The changing nature of the process throughout the twentieth century since the adoption of the executive budget system is described here, with emphasis on recent developments and the future of the budget process. Portions of this essay originally appeared in the June-July 1979 issue of* Empire State Report.

There is no mystery about the awakening of interest in budgeting in the early twentieth century. Although New York State comptrollers were alarmed by the increase in costs resulting from the "new and vast undertakings on the part of the State along new lines," advocates of an expanding government often found a sympathetic ear in both the executive chamber and in the legislature. "There is not the slightest ground," Governor Charles Evans Hughes told the legislature in 1910, "for the expectation that the people of the State will permit any substantial reduction of our activities."

The initial impact of this burst of activity on the tax payers was in some ways screened. "Indirect" sources of revenue, such as licenses, fees and business taxes, had masked the immediate cost of new institutions and regulatory programs, and the most visible source of revenue, the "direct" State tax on real and personal property, was even dispensed with altogether from 1906 to 1910. But the acceleration in state expenditure was rapidly using up the hidden dividend, as Governor Martin H. Glynn noted in a perceptive message in 1914:

> From 1893 to 1906 receipts of the State mounted rapidly, due to the constant addition of new sources of indirect revenue. During the same period expenditures increased slowly. . . . From 1906 to 1913, this condition of affairs has been reversed. Receipts have increased slowly and expenditures have risen with lightning speed. . . .

Both the concern for the common welfare and alarm about the rising cost of government seemed ultimately to point to the same conclusion: New York needed a more efficient government. And, in the eyes of most observers, this meant increasing the responsibilities of the State's chief executive. Although New York's governor had been given responsibility for many of the new activities added between 1880 and 1910, he was still just one of many elected executives, and even aggressive governors, such as Theodore Roosevelt or Hughes, lacked the tools or the authority to "manage" the system in any modern sense of the term. Leading the parade of proposed reforms was the introduction of a "budget system" which would provide some mechanism for systematically relating proposed expenditures to anticipated revenues. Such a system would function most efficiently, it was agreed, if the chief executives were charged with responsibility for preparing a comprehensive budget and presenting it to the legislature for consideration in its entirety. The case for reform was persuasive elsewhere as well, and twenty-four states adopted some form of executive budget between 1911 and 1919.

Attempts to Reform the Budget

New York State was not among the twenty-four, although it experimented briefly with a form of budget presentation in 1913. More important, a state constitutional convention in 1915 under the leadership of Elihu Root, Henry L. Stimson, and Alfred E. Smith had produced a plan of government which was almost the prototype of the Progressive Ideal (a short ballot, consolidation, the executive budget). The proposed constitution lost at the polls, however, and for a decade the state struggled with a system that assigned preparation of an annual budget to the legislative fiscal committees.

The defeat of the constitution in 1915, nevertheless, did little to dampen interest in the executive budget. Governments had continued to grow both in size and in cost as they expanded highway construction, the regulation of business, institutional care for dependent populations, and aid and services to education. By forcing legislative consideration of a complete plan of expenditures, prepared and defended by a governor who would be responsible for its administration, the executive budget could in theory help increasingly complex and interventionist governments make conscious, if not necessarily better, choices among competing claimants for public support. More subtly, in view of the new tendency of chief executives to seek election on the basis of what they could accomplish, rather than what extravagances they could prevent, it would enable the governor to develop a coherent plan for carrying out his campaign commitments.

Elected governor in 1918, Smith established a commission that once again made the case for a both active and responsive government and for changes in organization and financial management. And, by the time Governor Smith began his third term in January, 1925, he had not only kept up the pressure for structural reform, including the executive budget system, but had successfully sponsored bond referenda totaling $465 million which authorized the first substantial funding for the construction of state institutions and capital facilities, the development of the state's park and parkway system, and railroad grade-crossing elimination. In addition, he campaigned successfully for a constitutional amendment which would require reorganizing the executive branch along the lines laid down by a special commission in 1919.

Even before the amendment was approved by the voters in November 1925, Smith and the reform coalition had agreed to place responsibility for proposing a reorganization plan in the hands of an independent commission headed by former Republican Governor Charles Evans Hughes, and the commission's recommendations faithfully reflected Smith's views. As anticipated, the report of the Hughes Commission became the agenda for action at the 1926 session, and in accepting the reorganization program, the legislature created a new agency, the Division of the Budget, whose head would be appointed by and be directly responsible to the governor. In addition, the legislature passed for the first time with the constitutional amendment charging the governor with responsibility for preparing a "complete plan" of proposed expenditures and available revenues—an amendment overwhelmingly adopted by the electorate in November 1927.

"The executive budget," Al Smith argued, was "probably . . . the biggest reform in the manner and method of the state doing business of all that has been so far suggested." It was not self-executing, however, and Smith lost little time in making sure that the system functioned, instructing his department heads in meeting after meeting on their new responsibilities. The integrity of the new system was at stake, he reminded them, and it would be "kind of a black eye" if the legislature still found itself able to make substantial reductions.

The Early Tests

The real test of an institution's strength is the degree to which it retains its energy and sense of purpose when an administration changes hands. It was fortunate that Smith's successors shared his commitment to the executive budget system, because they faced problems which sorely tested its viability.

Critical trials came early, as the Great Depression upended the state's economy. Although the state managed to close fiscal year 1930 with an accumulated surplus of nearly $100 million, the reversal from 1931 to 1933 was appalling. In two short years, the depression converted the surplus into a deficit of $100 million. At the same time it threatened the very functioning of municipal government within the state, put the state into the largely uncharted waters of relief administration, and sharply cut capital development—despite the increasing demand for space in state mental hospitals and the need to modernize the highway system. In retrospect, it was fortunate that both the executive budget system and the reorganized government were in place. They gave the state the ability to allocate its constricted resources to critical priorities, launch the nation's most ambitious state relief effort, assist distressed local governments, and maintain for a time fairly high standards in institutions despite over-crowding and a deteriorating capital plant.

Completing the Puzzle

With the election of Thomas E. Dewey in 1942, the budget division entered the modern era. Dewey's first budget director, John E. Burton, not only built a staff commensurate with the responsibilities being assumed by state government, but revolutionized state financial management and the administration of the executive budget system:

- Responsibility for estimating revenue, formerly carried out by independent consultants, was transferred to the division: the director was now responsible for preparing a complete financial plan not simply the necessary expenditure estimates.
- A new per capita local assistance program was developed to replace a system of shared taxes which had proved unreliable during economic downturns.
- Research and administrative management units were established in recognition of the administration's need for a continuous flow of policy, funding and operational analyses.
- Most important, perhaps, the budget division in 1947 was given formal responsibility for managing the capital construction program.

Burton's efforts attracted nationwide attention, thanks in part to the interest in "the men around Dewey" as prospective members of a new presidential administration, and the revitalization and structural improvement of the Division continued under his successors. The distinguishing feature of the New York executive budget system, it was observed in the early 1950s, was the support of the governor—"the general impression that the governor will 'back up' his budget director in case of dispute." [1] In a sense, wrote a later observer, the Dewey administration "became the national model of what an extremely strong-minded governor with a reorganized administration could do." [2]

The 1960s: Budgeting for Growth

For American governments everywhere, the 1960s were explosive years for growth. There was a sense of confidence about government's ability to bring about change and a widely shared assumption that all barriers would give way if enough money, energy and knowledge could be brought to bear in a systematic way.

Few people reflected this mood or articulated it more forcefully in the early 1960s than New York's governor, Nelson A. Rockefeller. In messages to the legislature, in the executive budget, and at other times and places the new governor outlined his concept of "the responsible state." And in program after program—housing, transportation, higher and secondary education, pollution control, mental health and retardation, the rehabilitation of drug abusers—his administration began to translate its theory into practice. By any measure the price tag was high. State debt soared and total expenditures, which had risen by 99 percent between 1950 and 1960, climbed 212 percent between 1960 and 1970. Although a major share of this growth during the 1960s reflected increased aid to schools and localities, the cost of state operations was increasing at an unprecedented rate.

Such periods can be challenging and stimulating for those who work in government, but they are also difficult for budget agencies. The role of the budget officer is to reduce uncertainty, try to anticipate contingencies, seek precision, assure an orderly evaluation of priorities, question costs. Not surprisingly, the Division of the Budget often appeared to be blocking traffic during the early years of the Rockefeller administration. Its procedures and values and its stress on balancing expenditure commitments against available resources inevitably seemed obstructionist or nitpicking to those committed to rapid change.

Moreover, the Rockefeller administration was by no means as dependent on the budget division for research and program development as its immediate predecessors had been. A sizable staff emerged in the executive chamber. The governor himself leaned toward the use of task forces and commissions. For an agency accustomed to being consulted well in advance of any contemplated action, the experience was disappointing and even alarming.

Communication between the budget division and the executive chamber, tense in the early 1960s, improved dramatically as the decade wore on. Even though the administration continued to seek advice from a broad spectrum of outside advisers, the division did much of the work required to establish new agencies, reorganize old ones, and get new programs and facilities started and operating. It prepared legislation, regulated the scope and pace of funding, helped recruit staff, stimulated the introduction of data processing and analyzed management issues. Even the case of authorities—funded and largely controlled outside the normal budget process—the division often played an important role in coordinating funding from multiple sources and helping to move an enormous range of projects through the different stages of development from a prospective site to an occupied building.

More expeditious development, funding, and construction unquestionably enabled the administration to carry on a program without parallel in the history of New York or, for that matter, any other state. And there is much to show for this effort in the celebrated if controversial Empire State Plaza, in improved facilities generally, and in broadly expanded programs in such areas as higher education, middle-income housing, environmental control, and public transportation. Moreover, the state's innovative funding devices became the prototype for similar efforts throughout the United States. At the same time, however, the effort to do so much in so little time strained the resources of state government, for it assumed a level of sustained economic growth that simply did not materialize.

A Watershed: The Crisis of the 1970s

More than a change in the calendar took place at the end of the 1960s. Revenue growth slowed markedly and, as the new decade began, it led to tighter budgets, with sharp cutbacks in programs started only a few years earlier with an almost crusading spirit. The state enjoyed only a modest recovery before it sensed the preliminary tremors of the recession of 1974–1975. Indeed, New York's economy performed so poorly during the early and mid-1970s that it was apparent that at least some of the causes must be either peculiar to the state or so pronounced in New York as to be virtually unique.

Critical as it was, the condition of the state economy was by no means the only issue of concern. No single event in the last half century has had a more dramatic impact on the state's financial system than the fiscal crisis that gripped New York City in the mid-1970s. It challenged fundamental assumptions about the relations of city and state and highlighted their interdependence. It forced the state's leaders to probe the limits of governmental action as governor and legislature sought to contain the city's crisis and prevent it from undermining the foundations of a state financial structure that was itself dangerously overburdened. Facing the crisis became the preoccupation of Hugh L. Carey's first administration, just as the Great Depression had dominated the Roosevelt and Lehman administrations in the early 1930s. Overtly or tacitly it became a factor in every significant programmatic, managerial, budgetary, or financial decision.

Fiscal crisis was by no means unknown to New York City, but as the 1960s drew to a close warnings that the city's financial situation was perilous were increasingly urgent. The impact of recessions—once less severe in the city than in the rest of the country—was now more serious. The city, moreover, had dangerously overextended its social and economic commitments. Its range of municipal services, for example, was without parallel. Not only did New York City, in common with New York State counties, bear a significant portion of the state's welfare costs, but it also operated hospitals, schools, and a university, and subsidized health care and mass transportation. The combination of a deteriorating economic structure, an increasingly dependent population, an unusual range of public services, low productivity and high fixed costs brought an annual budget deficit that ultimately produced the powder keg of the fiscal crisis, the extraordinary increase in the city's short-term debt which had mushroomed from $747 million in 1969 to almost $6 billion by 1975. "The existence of this large short-term debt and the magnitude of the current deficit," observed the Congressional Budget Office, meant "that New York must borrow every month or so regardless of how unattractive market conditions may be. . . ." The default of the state's Urban Development Corporation in February, 1975, had a devastating impact on the municipal money market, and by April the city could find no one interested in its offerings. With more than $6 billion in short term debt coming due within twelve months, default seemed inevitable.

There was neither precedent nor groundwork to guide Governor Carey and the legislative leaders as they hammered together a rescue plan designed to:

— Refinance the city's short-term debt and convert it to long-term debt;
— Develop interim credit sources until the city regained normal access to the credit markets;
— Hold the line on the accumulations of new obligations through reduced operating deficits and curtailed capital expenditures.

Refinancing the short-term debt required the creation of a new state entity—the Municipal Assistance Corporation for the City of New York (MAC)—designed to serve as an interim borrowing agency for the city. Chaired by financier Felix Rohatyn, it would sell state bonds and lend the proceeds to the city to enable it to convert its short-term debt into long-term obligations.

The second element in the plan, closely related to the first, was to develop interim sources of credit until the city's paper was once again marketable through conventional channels. Among these were short-term federal loans and state advances to enable the city to service the loans as payments came due and to meet basic payroll and operating requirements. The union trustees of the city employee pension funds and the heads of several of the most important banks located in New York City, in a surprisingly productive alliance, underwrote many of the refinancing agreements by purchasing both MAC bonds and city securities. By June 30, 1978, all of the city's former short-term debt had been converted to long-term bonds, achieving a result that was by no means a foregone conclusion when the rescue effort had been launched more than three years earlier.

The third component of the rescue plan was in some ways the most critical: the demonstration that the city could in fact hold the line on expenditures and avoid running new deficits. The instrument devised to help achieve a balanced budget was the Emergency Financial Control Board, created in September, 1975, and chaired by Governor Carey.

The interdependence of the credit structures of the state, its political subdivisions, and its debt-incurring agencies was becoming startlingly apparent. "What the whole fiscal crisis of the past eighteen months has done," remarked Budget Director Peter Goldmark in October, 1976, "has really ripped off the covering that lay over the skeleton of fiscal interrelationships in this state." The creation of MAC tied city and state debt together. State advances bound it to the city crisis at a time when chances of a full-scale default seemed better than even, an unprecedented commitment that adversely affected the ratings of all state agencies. And a failure to maintain balance in the state budget could unravel the rescue package.

In the end, the keystone of the rescue effort, the state budget, stayed firmly in place, kept in balance in the two perilous fiscal years of 1976 and 1977 through the extraordinary efforts of the governor and the legislative leaders and an ingeniously executed if fragile "build-out" plan. Developed and coordinated by the budget division, the plan capped the state's capital requirements, arranged funding to permit essential construction to continue, and enabled the state to protect the access to the money markets on which the success of the city rescue effort depended.

New York State Budgeting in the 1980's: More Players on the Field

As the 1980s unfold, the institutions of state government are changing— or being changed— in significant ways. And one of those institutions on which the pressure for change will be greatest over the next decade and a half is the state's budgeting system. Some changes, such as the introduction of a new accounting system, are highly technical. Others, however, reflect a more complex relationship with the legislature, judicial pressure to recast budgets in favor of particular classes of persons, and increasingly critical ties to the financial community.

THE RESURGENT LEGISLATURE.

Howard F. Miller, who had come to the budget division during the Harriman years as a deputy director, and was later to serve as director under Governor Carey, noted in 1961 that its small staff had made the legislature excessively reliant on executive staff work, on an "executive crutch." And, as secretary to the Assembly Ways and Means Committee in 1965 he set out to remove the need for the crutch. The Johnson presidential landslide in 1964 had produced the first Democratic legislature in 30 years, and Miller seized the opportunity to build a staff which became "a focal point for intelligent opposition to executive fiscal initiatives."

The Senate, too, added staff, and by the early 1970s neither the governor nor the legislative leaders were in a position to ignore the claims of the other parties in the annual battle over the executive budget. "Success" in the years ahead will probably be measurd by the aptitude of the chief executive and the leaders of both houses of the legislature to play a difficult three-cornered game, avoiding prolonged deadlocks whose results can only damage the state's credibility with the rating services and the money market.

THE ACTIVE JUDICIARY.

Another phenomenon of the last third of the twentieth century, with enormous potential for changing the environment of public budgeting, has been the emergence of the judiciary as an active and aggressive participant in public spending decisions. Despite the unwillingness of New York State's highest court in 1982 to shift the problem of school finance from a legislative to a judicial arena, there is no clear national trend, at this writing, toward or away from judicial intervention. The role of the courts, therefore, continues to be of critical importance in the theory and practice of the executive budget system. It is particularly important in an era of tight budgets.

Among the most dramatic judicial interventions in public spending decisions was the Willowbrook Consent Judgment that dealt with the quality of care of the mentally retarded at a state institution in New York City. Sweeping in its scope, it covered virtually every facet of institutional operation, and required the state not only to make immediate and major revisions in staffing, space, and program, but to reduce the population of Willowbrook over the following six years from 5,000 to no more than 250 by developing a network of community facilities. Although New York State had to absorb the Willowbrook costs at a time when it faced a budget crisis of enormous dimensions, at Governor Carey's initiative it stretched its resources to meet not only the letter of the decree but its spirit as well.

Faced with any class action, the extent to which the courts will take into account the ability, or the willingness, of the state to meet its demands is unclear. As Nathan Glazer has observed:

> The judge will be bound by the case before him and will be unable to take into account the effect of his order on other state services. Nor may he consider taxpayer resistance and constitutional and market limitations on borrowing, which may all affect the balance of expenditures for a variety of state services as a result of his order requiring a rise in expenditure for the service he is considering. The case before him is not necessarily one in which needs are greatest or treatment is worst.[3]

However valid the case for the plaintiff, intervention by the court raises significant questions about the continued vitality of one of the central functions of the executive budget process—the balancing through political decisions of the public perception of need with the public's readiness to commit its resources.

CREDIT WHERE CREDIT IS DUE.

Continued access to the money market remains the great imperative of public finance. Nothing demonstrated so vividly the depth of New York City's crisis in the mid-1970s as the loss of its ability to borrow; nothing was more critical for the state than maintaining its own credit standing. The influence of the rating services has been unmistakable, and the financial community has been demanding and getting more and more data to support each sale of notes or bonds. The level of objectivity and comprehensiveness required by the financial community has admittedly had a salutary effect. It has required a candid explanation, for example, of the vulnerability of the projections which make up the state financial plan and a detailed assessment of pending litigation or administrative rulings.

Other aspects of the relationship with the credit rating services, however, have raised troubling questions for both the executive and legislature, and even for the rating services, as to the extent to which non-government entities now influence public policy. As Budget Director Michael Finnerty has argued, a bond rating has become not simply a judgment on the quality of an offering, but often, in the public's mind, a factor in judging "executive competence." Given the weight elected officials must now place on the response of the rating services, he observed, one may ask if the new relationships are not undermining the political decision-making processes.[4]

Working out the implications of the new and more critical relationships of government, its credit market and the rating services will, indeed, be one of the most challenging problems of the 1980s. The rating services themselves are disturbed by the extent to which they not infrequently become unintentional participants in the political decision process, and the degree to which the public may assign more weight or meaning to the rating placed on an offering than warranted by the scope or depth of the research underlying the judgment.

Conclusions

Nearly six decades have elapsed since New York State adopted its executive budget system as an integral part of the sweeping restructuring of state government orchestrated by Governor Alfred E. Smith. The system has served well, not least when the controls of the budget process and its credibility in the eyes of the money market provided the critical underpinning for the rescue efforts during the fiscal crisis of the mid-1970s.

Nevertheless, it is apparent at the beginning of the 1980s that the executive budget system is undergoing extensive changes. Budget systems cannot function independently of the forces which shape and reshape the government itself, and changes in that framework require adaptation in budgetary systems. The modern legislature is equipped to challenge the governor at every point. The judiciary has demonstrated in the recent past that it is ready to bypass the political process and reorder spending priorities in favor of particular classes of persons. The financial markets, albeit uneasily, are playing an increasingly crucial role as makeweights in the annual effort to balance needs against resources.

The outcome of this pressure to change both methods and ways cannot be forecast with any degree of confidence. Nevertheless, the key actors in New York's budgetary process will in the long run find it difficult to discard its fundamental assumptions:

- State budgeting continues to require a balancing of competing demands against a relatively fixed pool of resources. Nothing on the horizon suggests a marked increase in those resources.
- A budgetary process which cannot assume deficit financing, continues to demand accountability, particularly in its execution.
- The fragmentation of responsibility for state financial management cannot be tolerated — not least of all by an increasingly sophisticated financial community.

In sum, the essential goals of the reformers who plumped for the adoption of the executive budget—coherence, accountability, responsibility—will remain intact as the bedrock of the budgetary system.

The forces which for twenty years have been bringing about changes in the budgetary system are still in evidence in the late 1980s. The Legislature continues to play a forceful and challenging role. The courts continue to argue—in all parts of the United States—that inadequate services can constitute a denial of rights. The financial markets continue to hold public sector borrowers to high standards of "full disclosure." "Coherence," "accountability," and "responsibility" continue to be the bedrock of New York State's budgetary system, and current trends have only enhanced their importance.

At its best, a budgetary system is at bottom a disciplined process through which an entity chooses among competing priorities. The fiscal crisis of the mid-1970s aside, the need to make such choices has not been so urgent since the years of the Great Depression as it is today.

Needs remain unabated, dollars tight. Pressure to cut costs at the federal level continues to present the states with wrenching decisions on priorities at the same time that all states face the problem of deteriorating physical infrastructures and education systems that do not seem to measure up to the levels required by the demands of the modern economy. It seems clear that in some areas states will have to raise public investments to unprecedented levels. Homelessness, public health, and an aging population will lead to predictable demands whose long-run impact on public resources is only just beginning to be felt. All governments remain committed to holding the line on taxes. "Doing more with less" in American state government has thus become more than a slogan. It has become an imperative in government finance. For many, this means an annual "zero-sum game." If we want to expand this program, what are we going to give up?

Nearly half a century ago, V.O. Key observed that budgetary reform in the United States had tightened the system administratively—its mechanical foundations—but was still no closer than ever to the central issue of budgetary choice: "On what basis shall it be decided to allocate x dollars to activity A or activity B?"[5] In fact, by 1940, when Key's article appeared, states had often faced this problem—even if they had sidestepped theory. The depression of the 1930s had, for example, forced all levels of government to make stark choices as needs grew and revenues fell. Do you maintain levels of school aid and let highways go?

What Key was calling for, however, was a system of "'canalizing' decisions . . . to place alternatives in juxtaposition and compel consideration of relative values." For half a century Key's ideas seemed elusive, as such system developments as PPB and zero-based budgeting ran into a wall of conceptual confusion, pragmatic skepticism, and institutional indifference. But as governments try year after year to balance demand with a resource base whose boundaries are painfully evident, it may be argued that the era of "something for everyone" is behind us. Implicit in a zero-sum game is a choice among relative values. Whether or not these choices emerge from a process which systematically places them in juxtaposition, it seems apparent that we have reached a point where Key's question is once again relevant.

NOTES

1. Frederick C. Mosher, "Executive Budget, Empire State Style," *Public Administration Review,* 1, Spring, 1952, p. 53.
2. James T. Crown, "The Development of Democratic Government in the State of New York through the Growth of the Power of the Executive since 1920," unpublished Ph.D. dissertation, New York University, 1955, pp. 216-217.
3. Nathan Glazer, "Should Judges Administer Social Services?" *The Public Interest,* No. 50, Winter 1978, p. 70.
4. Budget director Finnerty's remarks were made at a panel on "Government and its Credit Market" at the National Conference on the American Society for Public Administration, New York City, April 18, 1983.
5. V.O. Key, Jr., "The Lack of a Budgetary Theory," *American Political Science Review,* 34, December 1940, pp. 1138-42.

The State-Local Service Delivery Structure

by

Paul D. Moore

Paul D. Moore is Executive Director of the New York State Legislative Commission on State-Local Relations.

EDITORS' NOTE: *This article provides a brief introduction to the extensive research conducted by the Legislative Commission of State-Local Relations into the nature of local government services actually provided in New York.*

Former New York State Assembly Speaker Stanley Fink often stated his belief that "the only reason for the existence of government at any level, whether it is a rural town or national government, or a small village or the State government, is to provide services to the people who live in those particular jurisdictions."[1] While this statement may seem obvious, only recently has research been conducted about the nature of services being provided in New York and how they are produced.

At the local level during 1985, there were 9,876 separate governmental entities providing services. The most important were 2,337 "municipal corporations" consisting of 57 counties, 62 cities, 932 towns, 536 villages and 730 school districts.[2] They interact—both with the State and with each other—through a complex web of functional responsibilities and financial arrangements to provide a vast and varied set of services to New Yorkers.

The State's role in service delivery is essentially two-fold. New York statutes and agency rules and regulations define the legal framework within which State and local service providers must operate. In addition, State government itself directly provides services in local communities. Most apparent, perhaps, are the highway and bridge services performed by the Department of Transportation and the law enforcement activities of the State Police.

Recent research on New York's service delivery system focused attention on nineteen separate areas specifically chosen to highlight the great breadth of services provided by New York's local governments.[3] That research constitutes the framework used in this chapter to describe the statutory division of responsibilities between the State and local governments, and the actual set of services being provided in New York.

Inherent Tension Between the State and Its Local Governments

The most important force driving the division of service responsibilities may not be money but different institutional interests. The State and its local governments are, of necessity, partners in providing services. There have been, however, periods of tension in that relationship. The State's interest in ensuring adequate and uniformly available services, for example, may be in conflict with local government's desire for self-governance without State intervention. Since this tension is inherent to the structure of our governmental system, an appropriate goal of State and local policy makers is to achieve and maintain the proper balance.

Article IX of the State Constitution, known as the Home Rule Article, contains grants of powers to local governments and the requirement that the Legislature enact a Statute of Local Governments (the resultant statute is known as the Municipal Home Rule Law). Generally, the legal framework established by these provisions give local governments the power to adopt and amend local laws which relate to their "property, affairs or government" and which are not inconsistent with provisions of the State Constitution or any general State statute. Bernard Evans Harvith, Professor of Law at Albany Law School, views the current balance between the State and local interests as follows:

> ... the best guarantee of home role in New York is not the State Constitution. It exists in State legislator's seasoned judgement and conscientious representation of constituents deeply concerned about local control. . . . The opposite side of this conclusion is that most alleged State infringements on home rule are not violations of the State Constitution. Often they are not even withdrawals of local powers, or failure to grant powers desired by localities.[4]

The issue that most clearly reflects the inherent tension between State and local interests is mandates. One widely used definition of mandate is a statutory directive which requires a local government to undertake a specified activity or to provide a service which meets a State minimum standard. Friction between State and local interests becomes most intense when local resources have to be used to carry out State policies. New York State currently does not directly reimburse local governments for the cost of complying with mandates.

> Probably the battle cry of home rule is most often hurled at State mandates, sometimes because the municipalities object to the tasks, but most usually because the full funds to pay for them do not accompany the mandates.[5]

State Responsibilities

Table 20 shows some examples of the responsibilities of New York State government in providing law enforcement services. In the area of police, for instance, the chart shows that the State Constitution grants local government the power to protect persons or property and to keep order. In addition, a Division of State Police has been created, and it may be utilized by certain local governments.

Local Responsibilities

Table 21 shows the division of responsibilities between each class of municipal corporation (i.e., counties, cities, towns, and villages) for pro-

Table 20

NEW YORK STATE GOVERNMENT'S STATUTORY ROLE IN SERVICE DELIVERY

Selected Examples

Service Area	Established Framework	Provide Service	Statutory Responsibilities
Law Enforcement:			
Police	X		The state grants local governments the power, except to the extent restricted by the legislature, to govern, protect, keep order, conduct, safety, health and well-being of persons or property therein [NYS Constitution, Article 9, §2(c)(10)]
	X		There shall be a division known as the "New York State Police," which is led by the superintendent of state police, who is appointed by the governor. [Executive Law, Article 11]
		X	State police may be employed by towns, villages, or police districts as contracted by the governing board with the superintendent of state police. The superintendent shall detail such number of state policemen for a period of one year. [Executive Law §226]
Jail	X	X	The legislature may provide for the maintenance and support of institutions for the detention of persons charged with or convicted of crime and for systems of probation and parole of persons convicted of crime. There shall be a state commission of correction, of which the head of the department of correction shall be the chairman, which shall visit and inspect, or cause to be visited and inspected by members of its staff, all institutions used for the detention of sane adults charged with or convicted of crime. [Article 17, NYS Constitution]

Table 21

NEW YORK LOCAL GOVERNMENTS' STATUTORY ROLE IN SERVICE DELIVERY

Counties	Cities	Towns	Villages
Law Enforcement—Police			
Sheriffs required. [NYS Constitution, Article 13, §13(a); County Law, §400(1)]	Cities authorized to "maintain order, enforce laws . . . " [General City Law, §20(13)]	Towns are authorized to establish a police department and a board of police commissioners and to employ policemen and constables. [Town Law, §§20(1), 150]	Villages are authorized to establish police departments and to employ such personnel as may be needed. [Village Law, §8-800]
		Authorized to contract with superintendent of state police for regular assignment of state policemen. [Executive Law, §226]	See towns.
		Some towns and villages may establish joint police department. [General Municipal Law, §121-a]	See towns.
Authorized to make or grant requests for police assistance to other municipalities. [General Municipal Law, §209-m]	See counties.	See counties.	See counties.
Law Enforcement—Jails			
Each county is required to maintain a county jail. [County Law, §217] County sheriff is responsible for jail operations. Corrections Law, §500-c] counties within City of New York—city	Cities are authorized to establish and maintain jails [General City Law, §20(15)]	Towns are authorized to establish a town lockup subject to local referendum [Town Law,] §§81(1)(c), 220(3)]	Villages are authorized to establish a village lockup. [Village Law, §4-412(1)]

Table 21
(*CONTINUED*)

Counties	Cities	Towns	Villages
commissioner. County of Westchester—county commissioner. County of Monroe—civil jail under commissioner of community corrections.			
Any two or more municipalities (including counties) may jointly provide a jail for their joint use. [General Municipal Law, Articles 14d, 5-G, and §119-o(1) and 431]	See counties.	See counties.	See counties.

viding law enforcement services. The parallel construction between Tables 20 and 21 should facilitate an understanding of the interaction between the State and local governments in providing these services. From just the limited examples highlighted, a central conclusion from the Government Law Center study about the extent of State mandates emerges.

> One of the more striking conclusions to emerge from the charts is how similar local governments are to each other in terms of legal authority for providing most types of services. Except in areas such as social services and jails (where counties alone are required to act), most functions described are authorized to be carried out by all types of local governments. Furthermore, many basic local government services are *not* mandatory, although State mandates may attach to the extent and the manner in which they are provided (if and when a decision is made to provide them). An example of this is public safety, where there is no requirement for local governments (except counties) to establish police departments. Once established, however, there are State requirements as to training and other matters which will affect the organization, management and cost of the function.[6]

Table 22

NEW YORK'S LOCALLY PROVIDED SERVICES

Counties	Cities	Towns	Villages
	Examples of Law Enforcement Services (Percentage Providing Service)		
Jail (96)	Radio dispatch full-time (100)	Constable services (59)	Telephone answering service full-time (52)
Civil law enforcement (subpoenas, garnishments, etc.) (96)	Patrol service full-time (car) (100)	Telephone answering service full-time (17)	Radio dispatch full-time (40)
Traffic law enforcement (patrol and accident investigation) (92)	Telephone answering service full-time (95)	Patrol service less than full-time (14)	Office open to public less than full-time (36)
Probation (92)	Office open to public full-time (24 hours per day, every day) (91)	Radio dispatch full-time (13)	Patrol service less than full-time (car) (36)
Criminal law enforcement (88)	Lockup (91)	Office open to public full-time (24 hours per day, every day) (11)	Patrol service full-time (car) (28)
Support services to other local governments communications center (84)	Community outreach to schools (73)	Patrol service full-time (11)	Office open to public full-time (24 hours per day, every day) (26)
Program and alternatives to incarceration (80)	Neighborhood watch units (64)	Office open to public less than full-time (10)	Community outreach to schools (25)
Jail counseling services (80)	Computerized information systems (64)	Officer friendly program (visitation to schools) (9)	Constable services (22)
Support services to other local governments: information system (64)	Regularly scheduled foot patrols in high density areas (64)	Specialized police services such as homicide and drug control (8)	Lockup (22)
Juvenile counseling services (64)	Meter maid service (59)	Radio dispatch less than full-time (7)	Regularly scheduled foot patrols in high density areas (18)
Juvenile detention home (60)	Specialized police services (for example, laboratory analysis or full-time, controlled substance investigators—not communications or records) (55)	Probation officer (7)	Radio dispatch less than full-time (17)
Support service to other local governments: training facilities (48)	Training facilities (55)	Park police (4)	Telephone answering service less than full-time (16)
Prisoner's release counseling (44)		Telephone answering service less than full-time (3)	Trained dogs for police work (10)
			Probation officer (10)

Table 22
(*CONTINUED*)

Counties	Cities	Towns	Villages
Support services to other local governments: laboratory service (32)	Park police (45)		Specialized police services (for example, laboratory analysis or full-time, controlled substance investigators—not communications or records) (9)
Penetentiary (8)	Trained dogs for police work (27)		Juvenile detention home (7)
	Laboratory services (19)		Meter maid service (7)
	Probation officer (9)		Park police (6)
	Office open to public less than full-time (9)		Community detention homes (5)
	Telephone answering service less than full-time (5)		Neighborhood watch units (4)

Locally Provided Services

An extensive survey conducted by Cornell University in 1985 of 240 of New York's local governments sought to identify the range of locally provided services, and to determine if there was any association between the level of service provided and the class of government. Table 22 shows the range of law enforcement services Cornell researchers were able to identify, and the percentage of the sampled communities that provided the services. Coupled with results from the other service areas studied, they concluded:

> It is clear from the results that the level of service provision varies substantially within each of the four local government types. Hence, it is not true that the level of services provided by one county, city, town, or village is virtually identical to the level of services provided in any other county, city, town, or village, respectively. The results indicate that no single clear service hierarchy exists either in an absolute sense or on average between counties, cities, towns, and villages. The absence of such a hierarchy means in effect that counties, cities, towns, and villages as separate classes *do not* provide substantially different levels of service as classes.[7]

NOTES

1. Remarks of the Honorable Stanley Fink, Speaker of the New York State Assembly, *Summary of Proceedings from the Conference on New York's Fiscal System,* Legislative Commission on State-Local Relations, April 1982, p. 56.

2. Office of the New York State Comptroller, *1985 Special Report on Municipal Affairs,* Appendix B, pp. 454-55.

3. Michael R. Hattery, Christine K. Ranney, Lee M. Day, David J. Allee, and Duane E. Wilcox, *Services Provided by Local Governments in New York State,* a report prepared for the New York State Legislative Commission on State-Local Relations, by the Local Government Program, Department of Agricultural Economics, Cornell University, July 1986. *Selected Functions of New York State Local Governments,* a report prepared for the New York State Legislative Commission on State-Local Relations by the Government Law Center of Albany Law School of Union University, March 1983; as updated by the New York State Legislative Bill Drafting Commission, January 1987.

4. New York State Legislative Commission on State-Local Relations, *New York's Local Government Structure: The Division of Responsibilities,* p. 38.

5. *Ibid.*

6. *New York's Local Government Structure: The Division of Responsibilities,* an interim report of the New York State Legislative Commission on State-Local Relations, April 1983, p. S-2.

7. Hattery,Ranney, Day, Allee, and Wilcox: *op. cit.,* pp. x-xi.

Part III
Public Policy

Public Policy in New York State Today

by

Peter W. Colby and John K. White

EDITORS' NOTE: *Traditionally, New York State has been a leader among the states in developing new and innovative public policies. Since the 1970s, New York's vast and expensive array of government programs has come under increased public scrutiny. This introductory essay analyzes the ongoing debate about the role government ought to play in our lives, and provides a context for the policy-specific chapters that follow.*

There have been many eloquent descriptions of the goals that animate our form of government, but none more incisive or concise than the simple prose of Abraham Lincoln: "The legitimate object of government is to do for the people what needs to be done, but which they cannot, by individual effort, do at all, or do so well by themselves."[1] For much of the twentieth century, New York was the Empire State of public policy—a leader to be admired and emulated in the development and implementation of successful programs. Its governors, both Democratic and Republican, took credit for new policy initiatives; and some, such as Franklin Roosevelt, Thomas Dewey, and Nelson Rockefeller, made them the centerpieces of their campaigns for president. Although only Franklin Roosevelt made it to the White House, other states and even the federal government looked to New York for ideas and programs.

New York and American Federalism

Over the years, New York sent more than its share of innovative policy makers to the nation's capital. In 1964, one of them, then a young assistant secretary of labor in the Lyndon Johnson administration, told presidential chronicler Theodore H. White:

> Maybe we're entering a new phase of government. Maybe the old legislative politics is coming to an end, the time when you passed a new law which set up a new bureau with a new appropriation to run new machinery. What lies ahead may be problems not answerable by law or by government at all. But that's nothing you can discuss now in 1964—that's years ahead.[2]

The "new phase of government" forecast by Daniel Patrick Moynihan has come to pass. In 1987, Gallup surveys found that a whopping 75 percent declared that "the federal government should run only those things that cannot be run at the local level."[3]

Voters are asking the states—including New York—to do more. But during the 1970s and early 1980s, New York State was not poised to meet many of the needs of its citizens. For one thing, the population of the Empire State declined drastically during the 1970s (see Table 23). New York was one of just two states (the other was Rhode Island) to actually lose people during the decade. The loss was particularly dramatic in the state's largest communities. The thirteen cities and villages with more than 50,000 residents lost people, and all but three lost 10 percent or more of their residents. If anything, the difficulties of upstate New York were

Table 23
POPULATION OF THE STATE OF NEW YORK
1900–1980

CENSUS YEAR	POPULATION	INCREASE OR DECREASE OVER PRECEDING CENSUS NUMBER	PERCENT	PERCENT INCREASE OR DECREASE FOR U.S.
1980	17,557,288	−684,103	−3.8	11.4
1970	18,241,391	1,459,087	8.0	13.3
1960	16,782,304	1,952,112	13.2	18.5
1950	14,830,192	1,351,050	10.0	14.5
1940	13,479,142	891,076	7.1	7.3
1930	12,588,066	2,202,839	21.2	16.2
1920	10,385,227	1,271,613	14.0	15.0
1910	9,113,614	1,844,720	25.4	21.0
1900	7,268,894	1,265,720	21.1	21.0

more severe than those of New York City; eight of the nine large cities north of Westchester County lost a greater percentage of their population than New York City (see Table 24). Peter K. Francese, publisher of *American Demographics,* compares the drain to a steamroller that once in motion is "very hard to stop."[4] Only the suburbs and very small villages in the state gained population, and that was far from sufficient to offset losses elsewhere (see Table 25).

"Demography Is Destiny"

In 1970, Richard Scammon and Ben Wattenberg coined the phrase "demography is destiny."[5] In New York, changing demographics have led to an era of limits—economically and governmentally. As the population has shrunk, those who chose to stay behind tended to be older and economically downward-mobile. In New York City, the fastest growing segment of the populace are those aged seventy-five and older. Faced with this kind of demographic destiny, Janet S. Sainer of the city's Department of Aging pleads, "We're going to need more services, not less."

The new demography also meant fewer employment opportunities in the state. Those New Yorkers who migrated to southern and western states took their jobs with them. Several indicators illustrated New York's difficulties: from 1970 to 1975, unemployment doubled; real output fell by 2 percent; new business formation was sliced in half. Manufacturing and construction industries—once the backbone of New York's economy—were especially hard hit. From 1970 to 1975, manufacturing jobs declined by 19 percent; the number of construction workers fell by

Table 24

NEW YORK'S LARGEST CITIES AND VILLAGES
(OVER 50,000 POPULATION)

CITY	1980 POPULATION	CHANGE 1970-1980
New York City	7,071,639	(−10.4%)
Buffalo	357,780	(−22.7%)
Rochester	241,741	(−18.4%)
Yonkers	195,351	(− 4.4%)
Syracuse	170,105	(−13.7%)
Albany	101,727	(−12.1%)
Utica	75,632	(−17.4%)
Niagara Falls	71,384	(−16.6%)
New Rochelle	70,794	(− 6.1%)
Schenectady	67,972	(−12.7%)
Mount Vernon	66,713	(− 8.3%)
Troy	56,638	(−10.0%)
Binghamton	55,860	(−12.9%)

nearly 22 percent. In the five years that followed, manufacturing employment improved by 3 percent; but construction was off yet another 13 percent (see Table 26). Signs held by workers picketing the closing of several General Electric plants in upstate New York captured the prevailing mood: "Automate, Emigrate, or Evaporate."[7]

Ironically, government remained New York State's "growth industry." From 1970-1975, government jobs rose by 9.1 percent, and they held steady from 1975 to 1980 (see Table 26). As government grew larger, public dissatisfaction increased. Programs once thought of as innovative and forward looking were seen as over-budgeted and over-staffed. In fact, New York does have higher taxes, higher public spending, more government employees, and more regulations on economic activity than most states (see Table 27).

Table 25

WHERE DO NEW YORKERS LIVE?

	1980 POPULATION	CHANGE 1970-1980
Central Cities	8,345,808	(−10.4%)
Urban Fringe	5,446,567	(+ 9.9%)
Other Places of 10,000 or more	515,315	(−24.4%)
Other Places of 2,500 to 10,000	550,378	(−15.7%)
Other Places of 1,000 to 2,500	412,487	(+12.2%)
Other Rural	2,287,517	(+ 0.9%)
Total	17,558,072	(− 3.7%)

Table 26

EMPLOYMENT IN NEW YORK STATE, 1970, 1975, AND 1980
(IN THOUSANDS)

	1970	1975	1980	Percent Change 1970–75	Percent Change 1975–80
Manufacturing	1,760.5	1,421.9	1,463.9	−19.2	+3.0
Construction	270.5	211.7	184.9	−21.7	−12.7
Transportation & Public Utilities	500.6	434.0	433.0	−13.3	−0.2
Wholesale and Retail	1,445.7	1,402.3	1,456.1	−3.0	+3.8
Finance, Insurance, & Real Estate	592.1	577.3	611.7	−2.5	+6.0
Service and Miscellaneous	1,360.8	1,446.7	1,670.7	+6.3	+15.5
Government	1,218.1	1,318.7	1,323.9	+9.1	+0.4
TOTAL	7,148.4	6,822.6	7,144.2	−4.5	+4.7
Index of Output (1967 = 100)	106	104	116	...	...

Source: The New York State Economy in the 1980's: A Program for Economic Growth, a report to Governor Hugh Carey by the Governor's Office of Development Planning, Albany, New York, January 1981, p. 13.

Fewer jobs meant a shrinking tax base. In 1975, newly elected governor Hugh Carey declared, "The days of wine and roses are over." As if to punctuate Carey's remark, New York City hovered on the brink of bankruptcy. Although many factors led to New York's near financial collapse, an extensive and expensive government, high taxes and stiff regulations, loss of businesses and jobs, and a shrinking population were mostly to blame. These conditions were not only prevalent in the city, they were factors restructuring policy making in the state at large.

New York City was not alone in feeling the effects of reduced expenditures. Cuts in statewide unemployment benefits placed New York State in the lower tier of states in helping the jobless. Highway expenditures, symptomatic of what was called the "infrastructure problem," also fell dramatically, leaving New York far down the list of states in spending for road maintenance. Many of the state's roads, bridges, and water and sewer systems were falling apart.

New Yorkers, though skeptical of government, wanted it to do more. A $1.25 billion "Rebuild New York" bond issue was approved by voters to fix the state's crumbling roads. And as New York's economy improved along with much of the nation's beginning in 1983, state government was able to do more. Since 1982, nearly 350,000 jobs have been created in the

Table 27

HOW NEW YORK RANKS AMONG THE 50 STATES

ITEM	AMOUNT	RANK
Per Capita State and Local Taxes (1980)	$1404.87	2
State and Local Debt per Capita (1980)	$2648.00	6
State and Local Direct General Expenditures Per Capita (1980)	$2203.67	3
Expenditure per Pupil for Public Elementary and Secondary Day Schools (1980)	$3197.00	2
Per Capita Direct State and Local Expenditures for Libraries (1980)	$ 41.30	6
Per Capita State and Local Public Welfare Expenditures (1980)	$ 358.07	1
Per Capita State and Local Expenditures for Health and Hospitals (1980)	$ 197.02	3
Per Capita State and Local Expenditures for Police Protection (1980)	$ 86.79	2
Per Capita State and Local Expenditures for Corrections	$ 41.30	6
Per Capita State and Local Highway Expenditures (1980)	$ 123.02	41
Percentage Change in Population, 1970–1980	−3.8%	50

Source: David R. Morgan, *Handbook of State Policy Indicators*, 4th Ed. (University of Oklahoma Bureau of Government Research: Norman, Oklahoma, 1982).

Empire State, and unemployment has dropped below the 7 percent mark.

Pro and Con: Voter Attitudes Toward Government

But the improved economy did not translate into a "return to normalcy" as far as government was concerned. New Yorkers, like Americans in other states, continued to hold contradictory views about the role of government.

Karlyn H. Keene and Everett C. Ladd note that pollsters and politicians "keep trying to get the public to declare itself as pro- or anti-government. Americans keep responding that they are neither, or both—or, more precisely, that they just don't see why the issue must be cast in such terms."[8] New Yorkers do not want a reinflated state government akin to the Rockefeller era. But they do want their government to do more. According to a January 1988 Marist Institute for Public Opinion poll, 80 percent of all New Yorkers say they are more likely to vote for a candidate who "advocates increasing government programs for the poor and elderly."[9]

The public's disillusionment with government by the end of the 1970s has led to a tempered pragmatism at the end of the 1980s. Today, New Yorkers want their elected officials to maintain tight controls on spending. But they also want state government to take the lead in responding to new challenges. One of these is the plight of the homeless. According to Governor Cuomo, "The homeless are an example of a glaring, immediate need."[10] In 1983, the legislature created the Homeless Housing and Assistance Program (HHAP). HHAP has acquired and renovated 115 buildings sheltering 5,000 homeless persons. Governor Cuomo proposed spending $138 million for the homeless in 1987, of which $65 million would be available to local governments for public shelters and other emergency housing.[11]

But the plight of the homeless, desperate as it is, is not the most vexing dilemma facing policy makers. In the coming decade the state will face a daunting test in meeting the plague of AIDS in New York State. The cost to the state alone in hospital care of these patients is estimated at $1 billion.

In its approach to the homeless, to those suffering with AIDS, and the countless other needs of its large citizenry, New Yorkers will be neither pro- nor anti-government. The late New York Governor Thomas E. Dewey spoke for many when he pledged four decades ago, "It is our solemn duty to show that government can have both a head and a heart, that it can be both progressive and solvent."

Conclusion

Public policy in New York State today is driven by the twin objectives of holding the line on taxes and spending in order to attract and retain business, and meeting the needs of its citizens in as generous a manner as possible. Many believe that New York's high level of public services and facilities represent, potentially at least, a competitive advantage over rival states with warmer climates and less-unionized work forces. Thus, repair of the infrastructure and continued support for education are priority areas as well as part of the campaign to revive the state's economy.

NOTES

1. Quoted by Mario Cuomo in his Annual Budget Message to the Members of the Legislature of the State of New York, 22 January 1985.

2. Theodore H. White, *The Making of the President, 1964,* New York: New American Library, 1965, p. vii.

3. Survey by the Gallup Organization for Times Mirror Company, 25 April–10 May 1987.

4. "Ten Years of Population Changes,"*New York Times,* 19 April 1981.

5. Richard Scammon and Ben Wattenberg, *The Real Majority,* New York: Coward-McCann, Inc., 1970, p. 45.

6. Michael Goodwin, "More Stress in Economy is Predicted for the Northeast," *New York Times,* 7 June 1981, p. 42.

7. Morton Schoolman, "Reindustrializing New York State," *Empire State Report,* October 1983, 10.

8. Reported in Karlyn H. Keene and Everett C. Ladd, "Government as Villain: Has the Era Ended? What the Public Says," *Government Executive,* January 1988, p. 15.

9. Marist Institute for Public Opinion, survey, 4–6 January 1988.

10. Mario M. Cuomo, Annual Budget Message to the Members of the Legislature of the State of New York, 22 January 1985.

11. Mario M. Cuomo, Annual Budget Message to the Members of the Legislature of the State of New York, 15 January 1986.

Lobbying in the New York State Legislature

by

Alan S. Chartock

Alan Chartock is a Professor of Political Science
at SUNY New Paltz and a Professor of Communication
at SUNY Albany. Chartock teaches, among other subjects,
a graduate class in lobbying. He is Project Director
and Executive Publisher of the *Legislative Gazette,*
a weekly newspaper that covers the New York State Legislature.
He is also Executive Director and Board Chairman of
WAMC, WAMK, and WCAN, which are National Public
Radio stations serving five northeastern states.
He is a newspaper columnist and interviews
Governor Mario M. Cuomo each week on the syndicated
radio program, "The Capitol Connection." He appears nightly
as a political commentator on WRGB Channel 6,
the Capital District's CBS affiliate.

EDITORS' NOTE: *Alan Chartock is a well-known observer and critic of New York State government. Here he offers his views on interest group representation in Albany.*

New York State has thousands of lobbyists who work in and around the Capitol. Nearly every organized interest group has recognized that it has to find representation if it hopes to remain competitive. As a result, the New York governmental system is so politicized that any group that does not have a lobbyist in Albany is at great disadvantage with those of its competitors that do.

Lobbying has become a very sophisticated enterprise. Once primarily associated with the legislature, lobbyists have to be conversant with all three branches of government, especially the executive. They are expected to provide complex information quickly and to tell the truth always. A lobbyist who lies finds himself or herself branded and largely ineffective.

Money and Influence

The rising stature of lobbyists is the direct consequence of the role of money in politics. Lobbyists have been able to provide funds needed by legislators to win reelection and thereby extend their tenure at the capitol.

The growth of Political Action Committees (PACs)—the money arms of interest groups that support candidates for public office—has enhanced the effectiveness of lobbyists. In effect, the lobbyist has become the bird dog of PACs. The implicit message is: "If you cooperate with us, you'll get money from our Political Action Committee." While most lobbyists claim their PACs have little clout, their proliferation suggests otherwise.

All of this has guaranteed access to lobbyists. Access is a vital commodity to the lobbying enterprise. In Albany, access is defined as the ability to get a legislator's, commissioner's, or governor's ear. Some do this better than others. Recently, one close associate of the governor was approached by a lobbyist who asked to go into his office for a few minutes so the lobbyist could tell his clients he had met with the governor's man. While actual access is important, so is the perception of access. That perception often translates into political power, not to mention the ability to recruit clients for the lobbyist.

Ethics Legislation and Its Impact on Lobbying

With the advent of ethics legislation in 1987 prohibiting some of the glaring conflicts of interest in legislative politics, the entire lobbying process may be facing some changes.

The New York legislature has always been an insider's game. Most New Yorkers have little idea who represents them in Albany. Thus, there is almost no conception of legislative issues, even among the few with some knowledge about goings-on in the Capitol. Press coverage of the legislature has been pathetic. Even the *New York Times* usually relegates its reporting on state politics to the inside pages. That puts lobbyists with access to cash in an excellent position. State legislators often return favors with little fear of being held politically responsible.

Lawyer-Legislators

Under the new ethics law, it is illegal to pay a legislator or his partner to do legal work on a matter pending before an agency of state government. But the law specifically says it is not illegal to go to a legislator's law firm to get representation before a state agency. In other words, you can still hire the law partner of the legislator to lobby for you. And, of course, there are lobbyists who will advise their clients to hire a legislator's law firm to perform work unrelated to the client's interests before the legislature.

Compared to the code of ethics used by the United States Congress, New York is still in its "Dodge City" days. Legislators can practice before state courts, making it easy for special-interest groups to hire legislator-lawyers. These potential conflicts of interests led one wag to remark: "If you take a bribe in New York State, you are out of your mind. There are legal ways to do the same thing."

Some of these conflicts of interests may end under the new ethics legislation. One provision demands full disclosure by state office-holders, including legislators. Depending on how accessible that material is, there will be more information available to the press about what some have characterized as "informal bribery."

Categories of Lobbyists

There are three types of lobbyists in Albany: "white hats," (or good guys—also called goo-goos); "black hats," (also called heavy hitters or entrepreneurial lobbyists) including some who maintain stables of clients and other who are single-client lobbyists; and agency or governmental lobbyists.

Let's consider the agency lobbyists first. Every government agency is represented by a person who may have another title but is really a lobbyist. In the case of the various line agencies, their work is coordinated by the governor's office. But quasi-independent agencies—like the state Education Department, the State University, and the various authorities—are also represented. Several of the most prestigious lobbyists in Albany previously represented New York City.

The top commercial lobbyists, sometimes called "black hats" or "heavy hitters," are important messengers in the legislative process.They are communicators who shuttle among key players on both sides of the political aisle, cementing deals and acting as mediators. Black hats make it their business to get to know the key leadership and committee staff members, who often have more clout in Albany than the many legislators. Often they have influential friends in the press, and much of what they report is communicated by lobbyists. Frequently, they know more about decisions than some of the senior legislators do!

The rewards to this class of entrepreneurial lobbyist can be enormous and it is not difficult to understand why. The more successful the reputation of the lobbyist, the more likely he or she is to attract other clients. One of the most successful is Lester Shulklapper, who represents the New York City real estate industry, the commercial banks of the state, and other selected clients. Shulklapper can get into virtually every office in and around the legislature. With his flamboyant and identifying matching necktie and silk handkerchief, he patrols the halls of the Capitol. The best place to get to see him is not really in his office, but in the very halls for which his profession is named.

Far from being pariahs, lobbyists have become respected parts of the political process. In fact, most legislators maintain lists of lobbyists who receive copies of legislation with a cover letter asking for the lobbyists' reactions. Ironically, some would argue that lobbyists in Albany currently enjoy better reputations than many of the legislators themselves!

Good government lobbyists ("goo-goos") represent those who are theoretically attempting to keep the environment pure and the government responsive. Among the best known are Common Cause, dedicated to keeping the governmental process responsive; New York Public Interest Research Group, an offshoot of Ralph Nader's "Nader's Raiders" funded largely by student governments around the state; and the New York Citizen's Union, an umbrella of environmental lobbies including the Sierra Club.

These groups have very little money compared to the entrepreneurial lobbyists. But lobbyists and legislators frequently cite the power of "goo-goos" in Albany. Despite the formidable press coverage given them, "goo-goos" are usually little more than one person or a single office staffed with a part-time professional or volunteers. As a result, it is possible that they legitimize an imbalanced system, giving the impression that it is really more representative than it is.

Nevertheless, groups like the Mental Health Association and the Association for the Help of Retarded Children have been terribly important as whistle-blowers, prodding the legislature and governor to act.

Often they work closely with the major agencies, garnering resources in a way that a commissioner cannot.

Many "goo-goos" periodically release report cards giving grades to legislators for their work in education, mental health, or the environment. An official who receives a poor grade usually moves quickly to mend fences.

Despite their relative lack of money and resources, "goo-goos" work together and form convenient coalitions to pass key legislation. Examples include the bottle bill, which mandated deposits on bottles, and toxic tort legislation, which allowed those affected by dangerous drugs to sue years after they got a disease rather than immediately after taking the dangerous drug.

Despite these symbolic victories, entrepreneurial lobbyists have fought effective rear-guard actions to prevent such legislation from passing for years. When it does pass, it inevitably includes provisions inserted at the behest of "black hats" who are making the legislation more palatable to their clients. In Albany there is a saying: "No one walks away from the table empty handed, and it is against the rules to break the other guy's rice bowl."

While it is dangerous to generalize, almost everyone in and around the legislature understands that it is predictable in its orientation. The Republican Senate, for example, almost always opposes bills that will hurt business interests, while the Democratic Assembly tends to favor bills that will advance minority rights and help traditionally poorer segments of the society. That has led to the appellation "one house lobbyists," a name attached to those whose interests lie with one house or the other. There is a coalescence of business groups that tend to gravitate around the Senate, just as there are those who network on the other side around the Assembly. These can be both formal and informal.

In New York State, one of the most powerful lobbies is the New York State Business Council. In 1987 the council hired Daniel Walsh, the former Democratic Assembly Majority Leader. The move was considered a brilliant one, since businesses in the state had been associated with the Republican-controlled Senate. (Ray Shuler, Walsh's predecessor at the Business Council, also was a Democrat.) The Business Council was so intent on recruiting Walsh that they made him head of their affiliated research organization. The position allowed Walsh to lobby during the requisite two-year "cooling off" period that all legislators are required by law to undergo before they are allowed to return to lobby their former colleagues.

The Lobbying Commission

Following the failed presidency of Richard Nixon and the ensuing Watergate scandals, New York was besieged by calls for cleaner government. The legislature attempted to satisfy public demand by creating what is now called the Temporary State Commission on Lobbying.

True to the expectation of skeptics, the early years of the Commission were not distinguished. The agency slowly began to collect data, but little in the way of enforcement occurred. Lobbyists generally complied with the law, but there were so many loopholes that it was difficult to ascertain what lobbyists received in fees and how much they spent. Today, most lobbyists view the Commission as a pain which they endure. Few have major problems with it, and almost all indicate that information collected and disseminated by the Commission does not reflect what lobbyists do or how much they earn.

In any case, the Lobbying Commission publishes an annual list of money earned and clients represented. Ironically, that list is one of the hottest items in Albany. Legislators seeking money for their campaign coffers frequently use it as a "hit list"—inviting those appearing on it to come to fund-raisers where they will be "hit up" for contributions.

Lobbying the Governor

There is probably no player more important in the legislative process than the governor. Each has a different style. Mario Cuomo, for example, is less likely to allow his subordinates to make deals with lobbyists than his predecessor, Hugh Carey. Nevertheless the governor's office, like the legislature, is divided up into substantive areas with various counsels and subcounsels responsible for policy in their area. In 1987, anyone lobbying in the education area would have had to be aware of the important role of Cornelius "Neil" Foley. In environment, it was Frank Murray.

Perhaps because of the high visibility of the governor, lobbyists have found it difficult to make the same kinds of associations that they have made with the more accessible and invisible legislators who have more freedom of action. Mario Cuomo, who is quite accessible to the press, is distant to even the most important Albany lobbyists. Nevertheless, governors do exercise vetoes and sit at the bargaining tables when decisions are made. When the legislature and the governor fight, and we have seen much of that in the Cuomo administration, lobbyists frequently help mobilize support for one side or the other. Such a role can be crucial in policy outcome.

The Future

It is naive to expect lobbyists in Albany to change much. Legislators depend on them to supply information, carry messages, build support for legislation, and funnel cash to enhance their reelection prospects. In a town where friends count, many lobbyists are counted as best friends to many legislators. They jog, dine at the best restaurants, travel on trains, and have family gatherings. Some previously served in the legislature, where they still have many friends. Most of all, it is important to remember that lobbyists, despite the sinister connotation of their profession, are human beings who are liked.

Their influence cannot be underestimated. But the profession is changing. The days of the back-slapping "I'll take you to lunch" cigar smokers are being replaced by the men and women who run five miles every morning, lead clean lives, and depend on the most advanced methods of collecting information. They work hand in hand with attorneys who are likely to sue the government if mistakes are made.

For example, in 1987 the New York State Public Health Council was sued by a coalition of tobacco and business interests who objected to the "encroachment" by the Business Council on legislative prerogatives. The business interests hired B.J. Costello, one of the best lawyer-lobbyists in Albany, to sue the Public Health Council. The Business Council said the Public Health Council had no right to promulgate regulations banning smoking in some public places. Costello won each court case, including one decided by the New York Sate Court of Appeals, the state's highest court. Once again, lobbyists proved they can fight with a varied arsenal, including the law.

The message is clear: The access and clout of lobbyists may be limited by new ethics legislation and amendments to the law governing their activities—but lobbying works. There are unprecedented numbers of lobbyists competing for clients. There is more access to information about the legislative process than ever before. Magazines like *Empire State Report* and *The Legislative Gazette,* and programs such as public radio's "The Capitol Connection" and public television's "Inside Albany," are focusing more attention on the Capitol. Reporter Frederic Dicker of the *New York Post* has put lobbyists and legislators on guard against making deals that would have once been regarded as common.

Despite the changes, Albany still conducts business as usual, with lobbyists among the most essential of all those doing business. That is unlikely to change.

Educational Policy Making in New York State

by

Leonard P. Stavisky

Leonard P. Stavisky is a member of the New York State Senate
and former Chairman of the Assembly Education Committee.
He has also served as Chairman of the Education Committee of the
National Conference of State Legislatures
and as a Commissioner on the Education Commission of the States.
He holds the Ph.D. from Columbia University where he is Adjunct
Professor of Political Science
in the School of International and Public Affairs.

EDITORS' NOTE: *No area of policy in New York State is more significant than education. Here Leonard Stavisky utilizes both his scholarly training and his experience in the New York State Legislature to describe the legal authority and responsibility, political interests, and major current issues in state education policy.*

Under the federal system, education is a matter of national interest, state responsibility, and local control. While the United States Constitution is silent on the subject of education, over the years successive presidents, congresses and courts have expanded the boundaries of national involvement to include land grants, vocational training, civil rights, and concern for disadvantaged and handicapped pupils as well as financial assistance to students, researchers, and institutions. With the advent of the Reagan administration and its version of the New Federalism, further initiatives seemed unlikely and some existing programs were curtailed.[1]

At the state level, however, the obligation is clear. By virtue of constitutional provisions, statute law, departmental regulations, and court decisions, education remains a primary state function. State governments exercise plenary powers over elementary and secondary schools. Even in the delegation of responsibility to local education agencies, the states determine the ground rules under which school districts are founded, governed, financed, staffed, operated, audited, and abolished.

Education Policy in New York

Within New York State, educational policy making is a shared responsibility. All branches of government contribute to the process. The Constitution vests in the legislature the duty to provide for the maintenance and support of a system of free common schools wherein all of the children of the state may be educated. Furthermore, the Constitution declares that the regents—the statewide board of education—shall head the state education department and, at their pleasure, appoint and remove the chief administrative officer, the commissioner of education. By statute law, the sixteen members of the Board of Regents are elected by the two houses of the Legislature for staggered, seven-year terms. Twelve of the regents represent areas that are coterminous with the state's judicial districts; four members are chosen at large to compensate for population concentrations in metropolitan regions.

Unlike chief executives in many other states, the governor of New York plays no direct role in the selection of the state-wide board of education or the chief state school officer. The governor's educational influence is concentrated in fiscal and legislative affairs. The executive budget incorporates funding for the state education department and the local school districts. Indeed, the Constitution prohibits the Legislature from making any appropriation until all of the budget bills submitted by the Governor have been acted on by both houses. Obviously the governor's role in educational policy making is guaranteed by the right to submit program bills and to veto specific legislation with which he disagrees. The Constitution imposes upon all parties a clear prohibition against using public property, credit or funds for the support of religious instruction. The courts have consistently reviewed, and often rejected, executive and legislative attempts to provide financial assistance to parochial schools. The judiciary has also served as the arbiter for major constitutional disputes involving the adequacy and equity of the state's system of apportioning aid to public school districts.[2]

As a policy arena, education is preeminent in New York State. It consumes a substantial share of legislative resources and attention. State aid for elementary and secondary schools represents the largest area of appropriation in the budget. With $5 billion in state funds and $7 billion in local support, New York's taxpayers contribute more money for their schools than the United States government distributes in federal aid to all fifty states. The five volume Education Law, which encompasses more than 8,000 sections, has been amended more frequently than any other part of the Consolidated Laws of New York. Each year, 700 to 1,000 bills dealing with education are introduced in the New York State Legislature. The school aid negotiations preempt a large part of the lawmakers' agenda. The regents, the commissioner of education, the educational interest groups, the school districts and the media monitor the proposed changes in the formula amid weeks and months of continuing negotiations involving the governor, the legislative leaders, the standing committees and individual members of the Senate and Assembly. Even the selection of regents becomes a matter of public concern. Groups supporting proposed candidates submit nominations and lobby for support, while legislators from the affected districts regularly participate in the preliminary screenings and public hearings that are conducted by the standing committees prior to formal selection by joint session or concurrent resolution of the two houses.

In session after session, the Legislature has determined the parameters for education. Under the compulsory attendance law, minors between the ages of six and sixteen are required to attend school. Parents who fail to comply with the law may be charged with neglect. The Education Law provides for specific courses of study. It sets forth procedures for the establishment, annexation, merger and dissolution of school districts. It empowers boards of education to act as governing bodies with general responsibility for schools within their districts. The manner in which school board members are chosen—by election or appointment—is covered by law together with the terms of office and the powers and duties of each board. Statutes allow the boards to appoint superintendents of schools who are expected to possess certificates issued by the commissioner of education based upon approved course work and prior experience. Supervisors and teachers must receive state certification or, in New York City and Buffalo, licensure by a board of examiners in order to be eligible for appointment. The commissioner is authorized to waive these requirements, which he has done, or deny such requests, which has also happened. Other sections of the Education Law clarify probationary periods for school personnel, the granting of tenure and disciplinary proceedings as well as seniority, retention and displacement rights when positions are abolished. The law is generally silent on staff size, pupil population and the number of school buildings within a district.[3]

Notwithstanding the voluminous nature of statute law, the regents and the commissioner of education amplify legislative intent. The regents are empowered to adopt general Rules which have the full force of law. In implementing legislative mandates and regents policies, the commissioner exercises vast authority over New York State's educational network. He has the legal responsibility to supervise the operation of local education agencies, withhold the payment of state funds, conduct quasi-judicial hearings on appeals from aggrieved parties, and remove school officials for wilful neglect of duty or violations of law. In defining the mission, the state education department has identified certain functions—"planning, setting standards and monitoring, coordinating educational services, providing educational services directly to the public, assisting educational institutions, and cooperating with other government agencies to advance educational planning." The regents and the commissioner appear to be pursuing five priorities: 1) improving educational quality through demonstrations of pupil competency in certain skills as a condition for high school graduation; 2) extending educational services to special groups, such as low-income, minority, non-English speaking and handicapped children and adults; 3) serving out-of-school youths and unemployed young adults; 4) strengthening the allocation and management of educational resources; and 5) enlarging education's contribution to the economy by encouraging collaborative efforts with business and manpower training programs.

Apart from planning, coordination, oversight and technical assistance functions as well as statutory responsibility for state institutions for deaf and blind students, the state education department does not administer elementary and secondary schools. Direct service delivery exists below the statewide level in the form of a sprawling, decentralized network. In a recent year, forty-four Boards of Cooperative Educational Services provided special education for the handicapped and/or occupational training programs which otherwise would have proved too costly for small districts to handle. Throughout the state, there were 735 local districts, including six which contracted with neighboring systems to offer services for their students. Nearly 2,700,000 pupils were enrolled in the state's public elementary and secondary schools, with the numbers almost equally divided between grades K through 6 and 7 through 12. More than 193,000 professionals, including 167,000 classroom teachers, as well as 129,000 paraprofessionals and support staff members were responsible for educational activities in New York's 4,000 public schools.

Notwithstanding these statewide patterns, New Yorkers jealously guard the traditions of regional diversity and local control. The state's school districts vary markedly in size and complexity. The largest district, New York City, has over 900,000 pupils; by comparison, Fisher's Island, off the North Shore of Long Island, has slightly more than forty children, fewer than four per grade. The so-called "Big Five" Cities—New York, Buffalo, Rochester, Syracuse and Yonkers—enroll about two-fifths of the state's pupils; together, they account for 84% of the state's Black and Hispanic students, many of whom come from disadvantaged socioeconomic and educational backgrounds. The sixty-two city school districts are subject to constitutional tax limits which do not exist in neighboring suburban and rural districts where the voters participate in school budget elections. Every school district in the state, except for the Big Five, is fiscally independent of all other units of local government; the educational authorities raise their own money and receive direct state and federal aid. The five largest cities have fiscally dependent school systems in which educational appropriations pass through the municipal budgetary process. This has periodically given rise to allegations that certain big city mayors and local legislative bodies have funded education unfairly in comparison with other municipal services. Throughout the state, often in the same county, there are major discrepancies in wealth, per pupil expenditure, administrative overhead, local tax effort, staffing patterns, curricular offerings, educational facilities, support services, and extracurricular activities among different school districts. However, except for some dedicated school finance reformers, few officials appear willing to relinquish local autonomy as a trade-off for statewide uniformity.[4]

The Politics of Education

During much of the twentieth century, school advocacy groups have sought to erect walls of separation between education and politics. They have raised the spectre of unqualified applicants receiving appointments on the basis of political connections. Consequently, school board elections in New York State have usually been conducted on a nonpartisan basis, and professionalization has been the goal of educational administration. Separatism has been mirrored in academe. Rarely did teachers colleges in New York State focus on political decisions affecting the quality of education. Similarly, schools of government and politics routinely excised references to education from their own courses of study.

In recent years, revisionists have questioned basic assumptions about the apolitical nature of American education. Favoritism can be practiced by nonpartisan boards and professional administrators who squirrel away positions for preferred insiders. In addition, many academicians have come to acknowledge the political nature of significant school issues. In a pioneering work on *Schoolmen in Politics,* Stephen K. Bailey and his colleagues at Syracuse University frankly asserted that "education is one of the most thoroughly political enterprises in American life. . . . The future of public education will not be determined by public needs alone. It will be determined by those who can translate public need into public policy." [5]

Within the Empire State, organizations that have regularly resisted political involvement in education find no inconsistency in seeking solutions at the state capitol when they fail to achieve their objectives through normal channels. While prizing its own independence, the state education department lobbies for and against certain bills before the legislature. Even though it objects to mandates upon local school districts, the New York State School Boards Association staunchly supports state-wide provisions in the civil service law which penalize striking public employees with the loss of two days' pay for each day away from the job. Though professing to oppose interference with the collective bargaining process, the New York State United Teachers union regularly turns to the legislature for employee benefits which have not been achieved through contract negotiations. Similarly, NEA-New York repeatedly seeks teacher-center legislation, notwithstanding the fact that such programs could be established locally through employer-employee agreements. Even parents associations which have fought against legislative involvement in curricular matters perceive no inconsistency in pressing for statewide laws superseding a local school board's discretion in disciplining students.

There are multiple forces at work within the public education community—boards of education, chief school officers, administrators, supervisors, teachers, paraprofessionals, parents, youth advocates, students and teacher training institutions. These groups pursue divergent, and even contradictory, policy objectives. Nevertheless, each claims to be motivated by the best interests of children. One issue does unite them into a broadly-based common cause, the quest for additional funds. In New York State, the Educational Conference Board is an umbrella organization which espouses major increases in state aid to education. To achieve consensus, the member groups invariably endorse a "leveling up" concept so that no school district will lose money and all will gain.[6]

In the absence of such coalitions, deep divisions are likely to occur. Notwithstanding New York's vast commitment to education, funding is still finite and there are different ways to divide the pie. At times, competing interests and aspirations have been pitted against each other: upstaters and downstaters; rural, suburban and urban blocs; high and low wealth constituencies; spenders and tax savers; public and nonpublic school groups as well as advocates for gifted, disadvantaged, handicapped and even average students. Affluent suburban districts demand freedom to establish lighthouse programs of excellence without diminution of state funds. Some low-spending rural areas persist in reducing their already meager local contibutions whenever state aid is increased. High-tax, low-wealth districts pursue special forms of property tax relief outside the regular formula. City school systems seek help from the constraints of municipal overburden caused by the erosion of the local tax base and the concentrations of poverty-stricken families who require costly services. Declining enrollment areas clamor for "save harmless" guarantees that funding will not fall below prior levels. All districts appeal to their elected representatives to devise a system that will somehow solve their unique problems. From this educational Tower of Babel there has emerged a crazy-quilt of compromises designed to give each section of the state some discernible victories.

Equity in Financing Education

In frustration, school finance reformers have sought the intervention of blue ribbon panels and the courts, but the results have been discouraging. Both the Fleischmann Commission on the Quality, Cost and Financing of Elementary and Secondary Education, established by Governor Rockefeller in 1969, and the Rubin Task Force on Equity and Excellence in Education, created by Governor Carey in 1978, became justifications for delay pending the issuance of the final reports. In the end, the Fleischmann Commission's constructive suggestions were obscured by contentious disputes over a projected statewide property tax, school desegregation and aid to nonpublic schools. The Rubin Task Force's significant proposals for achieving equity contained the caveat that reconciliation of the diverse recommendations rested with the Governor and Legislature.[7] Probably the most significant reform effort was the *Levittown* v. *Nyquist* court challenge initiated in 1974. In opposing the state aid formula, the twenty-seven plaintiffs argued in state Supreme Court that discrepancies in resources between rich and poor districts violated the equal protection clause and the education article of the state constitution. Joining the original plaintiffs were four large city intervenors who contended that existing law ignored municipal overburden, and the excess cost of educating disadvantaged pupils. Although the lower court decided in favor of the plaintiffs and intervenors, no remedies were prescribed. As the case wended its way through the appeals process, influential state officials urged everyone to await the final verdict. In 1982, eight years after the suit had begun, the Court of Appeals reversed the lower court and held that New York's system of apportioning aid to education did not violate the Constitution. Inequities were the result of local demographic, economic and political factors and were not attributable to state action or inaction. The amounts, sources, and objectives of state support for the schools had to be resolved in legislative and executive arenas.[8]

Essentially, the courts and commissions have acknowledged what everyone already knew; major educational decisions are the preserve of elected officials who are expected to reconcile rival interests through the dynamics of the legislative process. While full equalization in school finance has not been realized in New York State, significant improvements have been achieved through incrementalism. In 1976, 99% of the state's school districts received funding under save harmless provisions; in subsequent years, the overwhelming majority of the districts earned their aid under a working formula. The introduction of new, more equalizing program elements directed substantial state aid toward hard-pressed urban and cash-poor rural districts without depriving others of existing funds. Over a recent four year period, increases exceeded a billion dollars. However, within its existing tax structure, the state did not have $5 to $7 billion in new money that the Levittown challenge, if successful, would have entailed.

Changing Federal Policy

Only the United States government has the resources to assume obligations of such magnitude, but the tide of support has been receding. Even at its zenith, federal funding rarely exceeded 8% of the cost of educating the nation's pupils. Still, national policies have exerted a direct impact upon the quality and cost of education in New York State. The federal government has prescribed programs for remedial services and improved access to education for disadvantaged, non-English speaking and handicapped students. During the 1960s and 1970s, the Elementary and Secondary Education Act, the Education for All Handicapped Children Act and initiatives undertaken by the Office of Civil Rights served as catalysts for change. In general, New York State's programs for targeted populations equalled or exceeded the national standards. Invariably, federal aid came in the form of categorical grants which sometimes failed to recognize programs already in place and imposed inflexible structures and procedures upon elected state and local officials who were responsible for raising most of the funds. In unveiling the New Federalism, the Reagan administration promised to decentralize decision making. Under Chapter 2 of the Education Consolidation and Improvement Act of 1981, approximately thirty categorical programs were merged into a single block grant to the state at reduced levels of funding. As they assessed the results, New Yorkers quickly realized that increased flexibility had its price. Within a two-year period, the state lost 58% of the money it had previously received through separate categorical grants.[9]

Under ECIA, block grant benefits had to be extended to nonpublic school pupils. In New York, there are approximately 575,000 parochial and private school students who represent about 18% of the state's total enrollment. The parents of these children argue that closing their schools would impose vast burdens upon taxpayers. They have sought public funds which could withstand constitutional challenges. Nonpublic school pupils already receive transportation, textbook loans, school feeding, health care, and diagnostic and therapeutic services as well as opportunities for dual enrollment. Each year the state provides a quarter of a billion dollars in services to these pupils. The constitutional test stops at the classroom door. Any activity that might foster religious instruction or sectarian values can't be supported with taxpayer dollars. A New York law permitting reimbursement to parochial schools for state-mandated record keeping was struck down by the United States Supreme Court on the ground that administration of the funds could not be monitored. The issue of parochial aid will be kept alive as a result of proposals for tuition tax credits and a 1983 United States Supreme Court decision upholding a Minnesota law which allows parents to deduct certain educational expenses from their state tax returns. However, an earlier version of the concept was held to be in violation of New York State's strict constitutional prohibition against aid to religious instruction.[10]

Conclusions

Three variables have to be considered by those who hold the reins of power in New York State—educational equity, political reality, and fiscal availability. Equity must be the primary goal, so that the quality of a child's education will not be determined by accident of geography or disparities in district wealth, socioeconomic background or handicapping conditions. Obviously the educational community must learn to accept political reality. Elected officials can't be expected to commit political suicide by acquiescing to massive losses of school aid for their constituents. Programs that seek the broadest possible consensus enjoy the greatest prospect for approval. This means tradeoffs in which ideas advanced by the senate, assembly and governor are incorporated in the final package. Finally, the availability of fiscal resources must be the backdrop against which all programs are considered. Neither the public nor the private sector can spend money that it does not have.

In the next decades, profound demographic changes will compel rethinking of traditional attitudes about education. Declining enrollment in the schools and an aging population will generate competing demands for state revenue. In the wake of declining scores on standardized tests and critical comments from employers of recent graduates about a lack of marketable skills, critics and crusaders are already seeking higher standards for students, educators and teacher training insitutions. However, calls for excellence and improvement will be meaningless unless policy makers at all levels of government provide adequate resources and accept personal responsibility for their own decisions at the same time that they demand greater efforts from the clients and providers of educational services.[11]

NOTES

1. Michael Timpane, ed., *The Federal Interest in Financing Schooling,* Cambridge, Mass., 1978, pp. xiv-xv; Leonard P. Stavisky, "Federal Funding and Educational Policymaking: A State Perspective," *Public Administration Review,* November/December 1979, pp. 588-589.

2. *New York State Constitution,* Article V, section 4; Article VII, sections 2, 5; Article XI, sections 1-3; *McKinney's Consolidated Laws of New York State,* St. Paul, Minn., 1982, Book 16, *Education Law,* sections 201-202, 301-303, 3601 notes; Michael A. Rebell and Arthur R. Block, *Educational Policy Making and the Courts,* Chicago, 1982, chapters 1 and 6.

3. *Education Law,* passim. The reader should peruse Title I (which deals with the State Education Department); Title II (school district organization); Title IV (teachers and pupils), and Title V (school finance).

4. The State Education Department is the source of numerous statistical reports on education in New York, many of which serve as the basis for data cited in this chapter.

5. Jay D. Scribner, ed., *The Politics of Education,* Chicago, 1977, pp. 2-6, 9-19; Frederick M. Wirt and Michael W. Kirst, *The Political Web of American Schools,* Boston, 1972, pp. 4-11, 61-65; Stephen K. Bailey et al., *Schoolmen and Politics: A Study of State Aid to Education in the Northeast,* Syracuse, 1962, pp. vii, 108; Michael D. Usdan et al., *Education and State Politics,* New York, 1971, pp. v-vii, 3.

6. Bill memoranda filed with the legislative committees provide vital information regarding positions taken by educational organizations. See *New York Teacher,* various issues, for union positions; Edward Sakal, "How Do Board Members View their Policy-Making Role?," *Journal of the New York State School Boards Association,* March, 1980, p. 30; John E. Sackett, "Influencing Political Processes in New York State; The Superintendent's Role," *Council Journal* April, 1982, pp. 1-6; David Wiles et al., "The Changing Role of the New York Educational Conference Board," *Council Journal,* April, 1982, pp. 58-63; Mike M. Milstein and Robert E. Jennings, *Educational Policy-Making and the State Legislature,* New York, 1973, chapter 6.

7. Francis Kemmerer, "The Role of Commissions in School Finance Reform in New York," *Council Journal,* April 1982, pp. 43-46. Serious students should consult the reports issued by the Fleischmann Commission and the Rubin Task Force.

8. Joan Scheuer, "*Levittown* v. *Nyquist:* A Dual Challenge," *Phi Delta Kappan,* February, 1979, pp. 432-436; *Board of Education, Levittown Union Free School District et al.* v. *Ewald B. Nyquist* 94 Misc. 2nd 466 (1978); New York State, Supreme Court, Appellate Division, 2nd Department, *Levittown* v. *Nyquist,* Reply Brief for Defendants-Appellants (1982) and Court of Appeals Opinion (1982); New York State, Division of the Budget, Education Unit, "*Levittown* v. *Nyquist:* The New York State Court of Appeals Decision," Albany, July 12, 1982.

9. New York State Education Department, *Federal Legislation and Education in New York State,* Albany, 1983, pp. 2-3, 6, 10-11, 38-39, 49; Leonard P. Stavisky, "Education and the New Federalism," *State Legislatures,* October, 1982, pp. 16-20.

10. SED, *Federal Legislation,* pp. 12-13; *Education Law,* section 3601 notes; Philip K. Piele ed., *The Yearbook of School Law,* Topeka, 1978, pp. 213-215; John C. Augenblick and C. Kent McGuire, *Tuition Tax Credits,* Denver, 1982, pp. v-vi, 19-25.

11. National Commission on Excellence in Education, *A Nation At Risk: The Imperative for Educational Reform,* Washington, 1983.

Economic Development Policy in the State

by

Sarah F. Liebschutz

Ms. Liebschutz is Professor of Political Science at the State University of New York College at Brockport.

EDITORS' NOTE: *This chapter considers the causes of New York State's new emphasis on business and jobs, explains the opportunities and limits of economic development policy, and presents a case study of a successful application of state policy.*

SARAH F. LIEBSCHUTZ

We live in an unplanned economy in which capital is increasingly mobile. Units of government, in contrast, are locationally specific and therefore vie to capture and retain a level of capital, jobs, and wealth as they deem desirable. While not all units of government have the same level and intensity of preference for economic activity, most prefer more rather than less. These conditions lead to competition among political units, whether they be local governments competing within a metropolitan area or state governments competing with each other.

This chapter is concerned with the linkage between government policy and the economy—between public sector actions and private sector decisions. First, we review the changes since 1960 in the state's economy, followed by a discussion of several factors which establish limits on public sector roles in economic development policy in New York. These include the centrality of private economic decision-making and the control of land use by local governments. Next, we examine the state's goals and current programs for economic development. Finally, a case study of investment in Rochester by a private firm which took advantage of several kinds of public sector incentives is presented.

Counter Trends: Private Sector Decline and Public Sector Growth

In the years immediately following the end of World War II, "the Northeast was the heart of America's industrial might, New York State dominated the Northeast, and New York City dominated New York State. It was as simple as that." [1] By the 1970s, "the colossus of the Northeast was showing unmistakable signs of decay. Advanced decay." [2]

New York's population dropped from 18.2 million to 17.6 million from 1970 to 1980. Its per capita personal income declined from 113 percent of the national average to 109 percent. And New York State's share of the nation's jobs slipped from 11 percent in 1963 to 7.7 percent in 1978. New York, in fact, was the only state to experience a net loss of jobs in the private sector during the decade of the 1970's. While employment in the service sector of the state's economy increased, the loss of more than 370,000 manufacturing jobs could not be overcome. The net result was the decline of 146,000 private sector jobs in the state between 1969 and 1979.

Because New York City accounts for about half of the state's jobs, the condition of the city's economy contributes significantly to the state of economic health of the entire state. Between 1960 and 1980, the city's economy grew slowly (1960–65), then rapidly (1965–69), and then contracted continuously for eight years through 1977. Between 1978 and 1980 New York City's total employment stabilized. During the period of protracted decline, the largest drop in jobs occurred in the manufacturing sector, most notably in the clothing, food, leather and printing industries. The largest gains since 1978 have been in service and clerical jobs. "The net result of the 1970–80 changes is an occupational structure (in New York City) weighted more to office jobs and service worker jobs and less to blue-collar and sales jobs." [3]

This shift away from manufacturing and toward service jobs was not confined to New York City; it was characteristic of changes in the economies of Buffalo, Rochester, Syracuse, Albany, Binghamton, and Utica—the state's major upstate metropolitan areas. The only distinction between the upstate and downstate economies during the 1970s is that the rate of decline in manufacturing employment was gradual for the former and precipitous for the latter.[4]

The reasons for the decline in jobs in New York are many and complex. In part, plant closing and/or relocations occurred as natural outcomes of the free market process—the obsolescence of products or the lure of cheaper land, lower wage rates and lower taxes in the Sunbelt states.[5] In part, however, manufacturers chose to move out of or not locate in New York because of factors specific to the state, including taxes far above the national average.

New York's image as a high taxing, high spending state is easily substantiated. In 1980, the state's overall taxes of $1,495 per person were 58 percent above those of the rest of the United States, giving New York the continuous, dubious distinction since 1970 of first place in state and local tax burden. In 1970, overall taxes for New Yorkers were 61 percent above national averages. By 1980, although personal and corporate tax disparities declined significantly, New York's individual income taxes were still two and one-half times the national average. Local property taxes climbed between 1970 and 1980 from 45 percent to 75 percent above the average for all other states.

Public sector spending is closely related to taxing levels. New York is a high spending state. In 1970, state and local spending per capita in New York was 48 percent above the average for all other states. At $2,203 in 1980, the gap decreased somewhat, to 40 percent. Nonetheless, New York retained its position of fourth highest spender behind Alaska, Wyoming, and the District of Columbia.

Two types of expenditures contribute importantly to New York's high spending/high taxing image—interest on state and local government debt, and assistance to the needy. "Debt levels and obligations are higher in New York, relative to revenue availability, than in most other states."[6] The state's disproportionately large welfare population, more liberal eligibility requirements, and relatively high aid levels also help to account for its high spending reputation.

Economic Development: Opportunities and Limits

"Now the times of plenty, the days of wine and roses are over," declared Governor Hugh Carey in his first State of the State address on January 8, 1975. With that dramatic pronouncement, the new governor signaled his intention to reverse the economic decline of New York by promoting economic development. Before we discuss the specific initiatives undertaken by Governor Carey, we need to briefly consider two broad questions. What is economic development? What can governments do to influence it?

The term economic development incorporates the concept of comparative advantage and the perspective of the long term. Comparative advantage refers to the special attraction for a certain type of economic activity that a state or locality possesses, so that it becomes the center for the production of goods or services that are sold to people from other areas. This exchange of goods and services produced in area "X" for income from outside sources is known as "export" activity and is the foundation for the economic growth of area "X". Economic development, embodying the longterm view, thus, refers to "the transition—sometimes orderly, sometimes chaotic—of the local economy from one export base to another as the area matures in what it can do and as rising per capita income and technological progress change what the national economy wants done."[7]

Governments at local, state and national levels have various tools at their disposal with which to influence economic development. Local governments defer or adjust taxes, provide planning, sanitation, or public safety services, develop roads and install sewers, lend capital at below market rates, zone and assemble land to attract specific investors. State governments adjust tax rates, fund infrastructure projects (roads, sewers, bridges), and make development capital available at below market rates. At the federal level, corporate tax rates are adjusted, the costs of training workers are subsidized, and grants and/or loans for infrastructure development and private economic investment are provided.

What differences do these incentives make in decisions by businesses to invest and to locate? The simple answer is that they make some difference. How much is a matter for conjecture. Roy Bahl, writing about the effects of taxes in New York, points out that "studies of industrial location decision factors almost never show taxes as a primary consideration."[8]

Investment and location decisions, it must be emphasized, reflect assessments by private sector decisionmakers of many factors in addition to tax levels and quality of public services. These include cost and quality of labor, availability of land and capital, state of technology and proximity to markets—factors over which governmental officials have little or no direct control. And even when state and local officials take actions, for example, to decrease the costs of capital or to improve the quality of roads, there is no assurance that private investment will follow. Irrespective of public sector inducements, the private sector remains in the driver's seat.

Within New York, economic policies are further constrained by strong local prerogatives over land use, taxes, and spending. Zoning is the most significant of all land use controls, for it enables the designation of land for industrial, residential, or commercial use and stipulates the density of such use. In New York, the power to zone has been delegated by the state to cities, towns, and villages. County governments perform an advisory role regarding planning and zoning matters. Thus state economic development policies are dependent in a most basic way on the availability of locally zoned suitable land for commercial or industrial use and the willingness of local governments to grant variances to the local zoning ordinance when necessary.

Local governments, including counties and school districts, also play an important fiscal role. Compared to the rest of the nation, "New York is a local government dominated state. The 75.6 percent local share of state and local direct expenditures in New York State in 1975 was well above the median of 62.3 percent among the fifty states. In terms of revenues, the 53.2 percent raised locally was also above the 46.5 percent U.S. median." [9] For New York to succeed in creating a favorable climate for private investment, therefore, changes in taxing and spending practices must occur not only at the state but also at the local level.

New York's goals for economic development are quite straightforward—"the retention of existing jobs and the creation of new ones in the private sector." [10] The relationship of these goals to the multifaceted economy of New York is shown in Figure 10. The economic strategy pyramid in Figure 10 reveals that the current basis of the state's economy is services and that its priorities for growth are technological manufacturing and exports. Retention of jobs is stressed for the state's traditional economic activities—services, agriculture, general manufacturing and tourism—while expansion of jobs is proposed for manufacturing in distressed central cities and development of new jobs is focused on technology and for export industries.

Figure 10

ECONOMIC STRATEGY FOR NEW YORK STATE

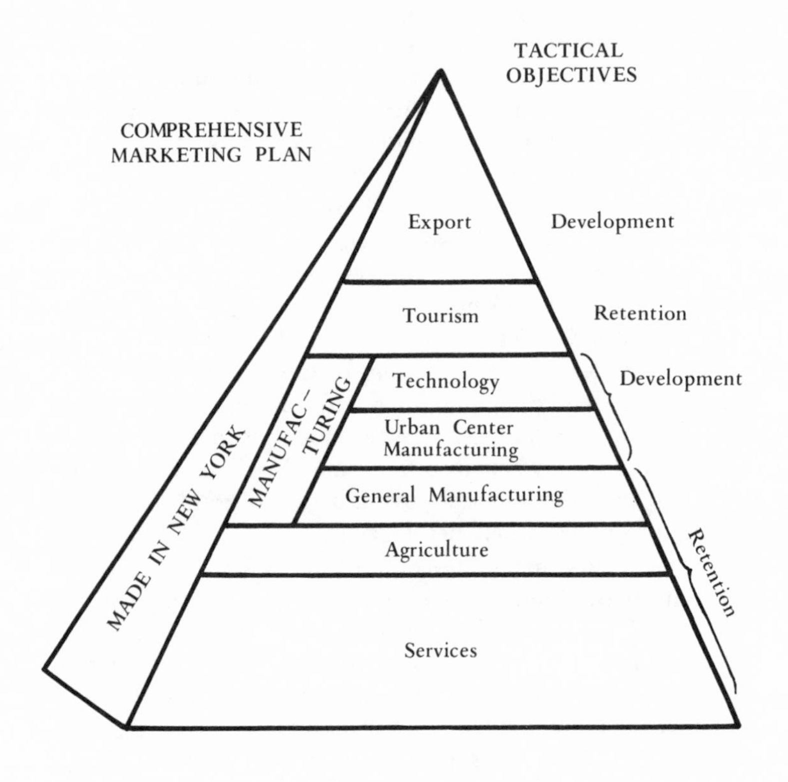

Source: Hugh L. Carey, Building from Strength: A Program for Economic Growth and Opportunity (1982)

The state's programs for attaining these goals and associated objectives rest on the assumption that while job formation is a decentralized, private sector function, governmental incentives can stimulate business to remain, expand or locate in New York. As Governor Carey put in in his 1981 proposal, *The New York State Economy in the 1980s: A Program for Economic Growth:*

> The underlying theme of our entire economic program is entrepreneurship. New York's growth and its ability to adapt to economic and social change

> were not a consequence of monolithic, top-down planning at either state or national levels. They were the result of the energy and inventiveness of millions of individuals. Our future depends on that same spirit. Government cannot create it—but government can create the conditions that allow it to flourish.

A second assumption—the intergovernmental context of economic development—is also emphasized. Governor Cuomo, in his 1983 Budget Message, stressed this understanding in his concept of "joint venture" involving "new partnerships between business, labor, universities and *all levels of government* [emphasis added]."

Initiatives for economic development have taken many forms—from actions to improve the general climate for business in New York to incentives to lower the costs of specific kinds of investment. Since 1975, most attention has been focused on three areas to improve the state's general business climate: taxes, infrastructure, and high technology. The tax on unincorporated businesses was phased out and the maximum tax rate on personal income was reduced from fifteen percent to ten percent between 1975 and 1981. Increased spending for improving state bridges and highways, local roads, and mass transportation in metropolitan areas also occurred during the Carey administration. High technological industrial development was encouraged through state funding for a Center for Industrial Innovation at the Rensselaer Polytechnic Institute in 1982 and for other "centers of excellence." Governor Cuomo embraced these programs for investment in infrastructure and high technology in his 1983 Budget Message. Programs to attract specific investment are aimed at reducing the costs of capital or operations for the investor. Incentives which allow credits against state taxes on business improve the firm's current operating profitability. Incentives which make loans available at below-market rates reduce the cost of capital for new construction or plant modernization.

Such taxing and financing incentives are offered not only by the state, but also by local governments in New York, and by the federal government. As shown in Table 28, current tax incentives to business involve abatements from the local property tax as well as credits against state and federal business taxes. Irrespective of governmental level, these tax incentives are geared primarily toward inducing new construction.

The intergovernmental financing incentives listed in Table 29 are all designed to reduce the cost of capital, again, mainly for new construction or plant modernization. The costs of borrowing funds are reduced because the private investor can take advantage of the tax-exempt nature of the bonds issued by the local industrial development authority or one of the state's public benefit corporations. Public sector participation, in fact, makes these financing arrangements more attractive to both lender and borrower. For the borrower, the interest rate on tax-exempt bonds is, on the average, 30 percent below the prime rate. For the lender—the federal govenment in the case of the CDBG "Float"—the participation of the local government limits the lender's risk.

The Sybron Case

The intergovernmental context in which private investment decisions occur is well illustrated in the case of the Sybron Corporation, a manufacturer of dental equipment and measuring instruments and employer of 5,000 in the Rochester area. In 1976, Sybron faced "the classic problem of a northern industrial concern with old facilities, deciding whether to move an operating division south to a new plant or to stay

Table 28

TAX INCENTIVES FOR PRIVATE INVESTMENT
IN NEW YORK AS OF JULY 1983

LOCAL

1. *Business Investment Exemption*
   Exemption from local property taxes on new construction, alterations, installations or improvements for up to ten years following the investment.
2. *New York City Property Tax Relief*
   Exemption from property tax for new construction or re-construction on predominately vacant land. Tax abatement periods vary according to type of project.
3. *Solar and Wind Energy Tax Exemption*
   Real property tax exemption of fifteen years for construction of approved solar and wind energy systems by individuals or corporations.
4. *In Lieu of Tax Payment Agreement*
   In buildings owned by the local Industrial Development Authority (See Table 2), if less than the total area of a facility is utilized, only that area is included in the tax payment agreement.

STATE

1. *Investment Tax Credit*
   Credit against the state franchise tax on business corporations, or the personal income tax based on the amount of new capital invested in buildings and/or depreciable tangible personal property.

FEDERAL

1. *Historic Preservation of Commercial Structures Tax Incentives*
   Deduction from federal income taxes, and investment tax credit related to rehabilitation of commercial or income producing certified historic structures at least thirty years old.
2. *Economic Recovery Tax Act of 1981*
   Various provisions regarding depreciation (Accelerated Cost Recovery System), tax credits and corporate tax rates.

Table 29

FINANCING INCENTIVES FOR PRIVATE INVESTMENT
IN NEW YORK AS OF JULY 1983

LOCAL

1. *Industrial Development Authority (IDA) Bonds*
   Local industrial development authorities issue negotiable, tax-exempt bonds and notes to acquire land and construct manufacturing, warehousing, research and pollution control facilities. The eligible company locates the buyer of IDA bonds and leases the facility from the IDA for payments equal to the principal and interest on the bonds.

STATE

1. *Industrial Pollution Control Loans*
   Through the sale of special obligation, tax-exempt, revenue bonds, the New York State Environmental Facilities Corporation lends funds to private industry for installation of pollution control facilities.
2. *Job Development Authority (JDA)*
   Long term, low-cost loans for construction, rehabilitation or acquisition of manufacturing facilities which provide additional jobs, through the issuance of special purpose state-guaranteed bonds.
3. *Urban Development Corporation*
   Assistance to private business and industry for modernization, expansion or relocation through the issuance of tax-exempt bonds. Through its lease-finance program, the Urban Development Corporation can purchase a newly developed project from a company at its development cost and lease it back to the company on more favorable terms than private financing.
4. *Business Development Corporation*
   Individually tailored loans for industrial firms when conventional bank sources are not available, for working capital, equipment, plant facilities and debt recasting.

FEDERAL

1. *Urban Development Action Grants (UDAG)*
   Grants awarded on a competitive basis to distressed cities and urban counties to stimulate commercial and industrial development and reclamation of deteriorating neighborhoods. Firm commitments of private sector funding participation in proposed, job-generating, projects must be demonstrated before UDAG funds are awarded. The city then loans the funds to the private developer to be repaid to the city.
2. *Community Development Block Grant (CDBG) Funds*
   (a) Loans and grants out of CDBG funds to qualified individual owners of neighborhood businesses for facade improvement or commercial rehabilitation.
   (b) Short-term loans to assist private developers of eligible block grant activities, using a city's unexpended balance of block grant funds. (CDBG "Float")
3. *Demonstration Loan Program (Section 108 of the Housing and Community Development Act)*
   City issues debentures which are guaranteed by the U.S. Department of Housing and Urban Development (HUD) and sold by the Federal Finance Bank at long-term U.S. Treasury interest rates. The funds are then reloaned to small and medium-size companies for capital expansion and creation of permanent job opportunities for low and moderate-income persons in high unemployment areas.
4. *Small Business Administration (SBA) Loan Program*
   Local Industrial Development Authority (IDA) issues debentures which are guaranteed by the Small Business Administration and are sold at long-term Treasury rates, and then reloaned to SBA-certified companies to finance expansion needs.

at home and rebuild at substantial cost." [11] A relocation would have meant the losses of 2,500 jobs, an annual $40 million payroll, and $5 million in state and local tax revenues.

Sybron's decision to remain in Rochester was the outcome of negotiations over two years with the city of Rochester, the state of New York, and the federal government. These negotiations resulted in:

—the acquisition and clearance by the city government of land for plant expansion;

—a federal Urban Development Action Grant (UDAG) of $5.1 million to Rochester, lent at 3 percent interest to Sybron for plant renovations;

—a $2.2 million subsidy by the New York Urban Development Corporation to lower the interest rate on a private loan to Sybron of $11 million;

—credits estimated at $800,000 for ten years against the state franchise tax on business corporations, awarded by the New York Job Incentive Board[12] for providing jobs to lower income persons;

—abatements estimated at $1 million over ten years against the city property tax; and

—total new investment by Sybron of $21.9 million in plant modernization.

This package of tax and financing incentives reveals the complex and complementary involvement of city, state, and federal governments with business. The largest single component of the package, the UDAG, was federal in origin, but the active role of the city government was critical as were the initiatives of state agencies. And, certainly, the willingness of Sybron to analyze alternatives "at home" as conscientiously as opportunities "abroad" was a key aspect of this case.

Economic Development Policy: A Postscript

Retention of existing jobs and creation of new ones in the private sector continued as high priorities for New York in the latter years of the 1980s. Building on the assumption that "the private sector is the engine which drives New York's economy,"[13] Governor Mario Cuomo's economic development strategy extended tax reduction and financing incentive programs begun by Governor Carey,and also incorporated new initiatives.

A 1985 document, "Rebuilding New York—The Next Phase From Recovery to Resurgence," set forth a multi-year strategy for implementation of Governor Cuomo's goals. The first "Rebuilding New York" initiative proposed by the governor and enacted by the legislature, involved the creation of economic development zones and the reorganization of economic development in the state government.

The economic development zones program was enacted by the state legislature in 1986 to target and to stimulate economic growth in up to sixty-two of the state's most severely distressed areas. The program offers new and expanding businesses within designated zones a combination of tax credits, reduced utility rates, and priority attention for loans, grants, and services from such state agencies as the Urban Development Corporation and the Job Development Authority. In July 1987, ten economically distressed communities were the first chosen for zone designation. Selected in a competition among forty-three counties or parts of counties deemed eligible because of pervasive poverty, high unemployment, and general distress, the ten successful "zone development plans" included areas in the South Bronx, Queens, and Brooklyn, as well as other urban and rural regions of the state. Such plans, tailored to the particular needs of the applicant areas, represented both business and human resource development components. For example, the South Bronx expected to use the development zone taxing and financing incentives to retain small businesses, to induce furniture and apparel industries to relocate, and to provide job training, youth employment, day care, and health services. The net benefits to New York State of the economic developments zones program—that is, the jobs and revenues generated by an enhanced state export base minus the foregone revenues from the incentives offered—of course, remain to be assessed.

New York's economic development policies, according to the "Rebuilding New York" report, have historically evolved on an incremental basis. Integrating the "State's economic development efforts and programs into a single, cohesive whole" was a high priority goal for Governor Cuomo. In 1987, the legislature authorized a "super-cabinet" position, commissioner of economic development, intended to coordinate economic development policy among various state agencies; facilitate and centralize access to state incentives and regulatory processes for the private sector; promote opportunities for economic growth, particularly in manufacturing; and identify international markets for New York products.[14] Not coincidentally, Vincent Tese, appointed by the Governor as the first commissioner of economic development, was also the author of "Rebuilding New York."[15]

The economic state of health of New York toward the end of the 1980s was much improved over that at the start of the decade. Whereas the state's job growth of 5.5 percent between 1975 and 1980 had lagged far behind the national rate of 17.4 percent, it was comparable between 1980 and 1985, at 7.5 percent, with the rest of the nation.[16] In fact, New York, which had fared poorly in most business climate assessments during the 1980s, was ranked twelfth among all states in a 1987 business climate study by the Corporation for Enterprise Development. The state was commended for "its growth potential and desire to set government policies aimed at attracting new business."[17]

Warning signs, however, still persisted, as New York's losses of manufacturing jobs continued unabated, as per capita personnel and property tax burdens still led the nation, and as corporate income taxes ranked tenth highest among the states.[18] Thus, the need for vigilant and aggressive state economic development policies remained intact.

NOTES

The author acknowledges the useful comments of Carl D. Ekstrom on this chapter.

1. Peter D. McClelland and Alan L. Magdovitz, *Crisis in the Making: The Political Economy of New York State since 1945,* New York: Cambridge University Press, 1981, p. 15.

2. *Ibid.*

3. Matthew Drennan, "Economy," in Charles Brecher and Raymond D. Horton, eds., *Setting Municipal Priorities,* 1982, New York: Sage, 1981, pp. 67-68.

4. See McClelland and Magdovitz, op. cit., pp. 41-43.

5. For several explanations of the rise of the Sunbelt, see David C. Perry and Alfred J. Watkins, eds., *The Rise of the Sunbelt Cities,* Beverly Hills: Sage, 1977, Chapter 1-3.

6. Roy Bahl, "Fiscal Retrenchment in a Declining State: The New York Case," *National Tax Journal,* 32, June, 1979, supp. 283.

7. Wilbur R. Thompson, *A Preface to Urban Economics,* Baltimore: Johns Hopkins, 1965, p. 3.

8. Roy Bahl, "Fiscal Retrenchment in a Declining State: The New York Case," *National Tax Journal,* 32, June, 1979, supp. 283.

9. *Ibid.,* p. 283.

10. Hugh Carey, *Targets of Economic Opportunity,* Albany: Office of the Governor, 1979.

11. Thomas Black, Allan Borut, Robert M. Byrne, Michael K. Morina, *UDAG Partnerships: Nine Case Studies,* Washington: Urban Land Institute, 1980, p. 81.

12. This program of tax credits to businesses for creating and retaining jobs by the Job Incentive Board was terminated by New York State as of July 1, 1983.

13. Vincent Tese, "Rebuilding New York—The Next Phase From Recovery to Resurgence," Albany: Office of the Governor, 1985, p. 3.

14. Chapter 839, Laws of 1987.

15. Mr. Tese, a successful lawyer and businessman, had been successively ap-

pointed by Governor Cuomo to several positions in state government—including Commissioner of Banks, Commissioner of Insurance, Commissioner of the Urban Development Corporation, and Commissioner of the High Technology Corporation—before his appointment in 1987 as Commissioner of Economic Development.

16. Public Policy Institute: "Patterns of Migration in New York State: 1980-1985," Albany: Public Policy Institute, 1987.

17. "New York Ranks High in Study," *Democrat-and-Chronicle,* Rochester, 18 March 1987.

18. Center for Governmental Research, "Research Notes," 6 March 1987, Rochester, CGR.

Health Policy in New York

by

Alice Sardell

Alice Sardell is an Associate Professor of urban studies at Queens College, CUNY. Her new book is titled *The U.S. Experiment in Social Medicine: The Community Health Center Program 1965-1986,* and will be published in 1988.

EDITORS' NOTE: *This chapter describes the crisis facing the health care delivery system in New York State, noting the strain that the spread of the disease AIDS places on an already overburdened system.*

Alice Sardell

Health care issues are very much a part of the public policy debate in New York State today. Acquired Immune Deficiency Syndrome (AIDS), high infant mortality rates, the financing of health services for an aging population, the accountability of physicians and hospitals to the public, and the lack of access to health care experienced by some citizens are often discussed in the media. Concerns about these issues are expressed by community and citizen advocacy groups, health professionals, business groups, labor unions, hospitals, and insurance companies, among others. Within New York State government, the governor and his health policy assistants, the Health Commissioner and his staff in the Department of Health, and the Chairpersons and members of the Senate and Assembly Health Committees are most involved in the process of making health policy. When health care issues involve the Medicaid program, the Commissioner of Social Services and the Chairpersons and members of Senate and Assembly Social Services Committees also play a major role. This is a particularly interesting time to examine health policy in New York State because the 1980s has been a decade in which states have assumed a major role in determining how health care services should be provided to their citizens.

Health policy in New York State is made within the context of a federal system of shared responsibility and financing among the national, state, and local levels of government. The health care system itself is a mix of public and private funding and control. The role of government in the financing of health care has increased enormously during the last twenty years at both the federal and state levels. As government has assumed more of the costs of health care services, it has increased its planning and regulatory role in relation to the private sector. New York State has been a leader in this regard.

Many of the current policy concerns in New York State are related to conditions created by the structure of our national health care financing system, particularly the design of the Medicare and Medicaid programs which were enacted in 1965. In addition, the expansion of the state's role in health care policy during the last two decades was a response to the high costs of the Medicaid program.

Paying for Health Care

Health care costs can be paid for by an individual ("out of pocket") or by private or public health insurance programs. In almost all of the industrialized countries of the world there is a public system of health insurance which covers the health care costs of all citizens. In the United States, in contrast, the system of paying for care is fragmented, and about 37 million people have no health insurance.[1] The national government provides tax benefits to employers who purchase health insurance for their employees, but not all employers choose to do this. The Medicare program, which is financed by federal tax funds, pays approximately 45 percent of the health care costs of those over age sixty-five.[2]

The Medicaid program was designed to finance health care for the poor under the age of sixty-five. However, eligibility for Medicaid is linked to eligibility for Aid to Families with Dependent Children (AFDC). Since AFDC eligibility is based on family structure and employment status as well as income, large numbers of those with incomes below the federal poverty level do not qualify for either AFDC or Medicaid. Those left out are likely to be families where one or both parents are employed at low-wage jobs which do not provide health insurance as an employee benefit. In New York State in 1984, 16 percent of the state population under age sixty-five had no health insurance. Most of the uninsured (75 percent) were working adults and children.[3]

Another problem is that Medicare pays for a very limited number of days of long-term care in nursing homes or patients' homes. When senior citizens or disabled persons cannot pay for such services, they can become eligible (by "spending down") for Medicaid coverage. Eligibility levels for the elderly, blind, and disabled (under the SSI program) are more generous than those for parents and children applying for AFDC. For both of these reasons, Medicaid has become a program which pays for the care of the elderly, blind, and disabled rather than for low-income parents and their children. In 1983, the elderly, blind, and disabled were 30 percent of the Medicaid population nationally, but accounted for 75 percent of all expenditures; while AFDC recipients were 70 percent of all Medicaid recipients, but accounted for only 25 percent of Medicaid expenditures.[4]

The high cost of nursing home and hospital care has meant that the Medicaid program is an expensive one. Medicaid is jointly financed by the federal government and the states; the state's share is based on its per capita income. New York, a relatively wealthy state, paid 53 percent of the cost of the program in 1984.[5] While the federal government mandates certain eligibility levels and service requirements for the Medicaid program, states can choose to expand eligibility and provide certain optional services. In the 1960s and 1970s, New York had one of the most generous and costly Medicaid programs in the country. During that time, the state's involvement in the health care system expanded in an effort to reduce costs.

The Expansion of the State Role: Hospital Rate Setting and Health Care Delivery Restructuring

New York's Medicaid program had initially high eligibility levels; in 1966 one quarter of New York City's population was eligible. State policy makers and local government officials (counties shared Medicaid costs with the state on a 50-50 basis) became concerned about Medicaid costs. In the late 1960s, eligibility rules were made more restrictive and the legislature authorized the State Health Commissioner to set rates for Medicaid and Blue Cross payments to hospitals. This expansion of state power was opposed by the hospital industry.[6] During the New York City fiscal crisis in 1975, Medicaid eligibility was again tightened, as was the payment formula for hospital rates. A number of hospitals in New York City closed, and many others in the state experienced fiscal stress. Voluntary (private) hospitals could no longer "shift" the cost of uninsured (non-Medicaid) poor patients to Blue Cross by raising the rates paid for Blue Cross patients. Commercial insurance companies were losing employer business to Blue Cross because the Blue Cross rates were lower. As a response to the concerns of both the hospitals and the commercial insurance industry, the Council of Health Care Financing was established in 1978. This body, mandated to develop a new hospital financing system for New York State, included legislators and representatives of voluntary hospitals, public hospitals, Blue Cross, the commercial insurance industry, and a hospital workers union. It was headed by the Chairman of the Health Committee of the New York State Senate; the Vice-Chair of the Council was the Chairman of the Health Committee in the State Assembly.

The result of negotiations among members of the Council on Health Care Financing, and consultation with representatives of the federal government, was the New York Prospective Hospital Reimbursement Methodology (NYPHRM), an experimental program in effect from 1982 to 1985. It established state rate setting for all hospital payment (including the federal Medicare program) and a bad debt/charity care pool in which a surcharge on all payers was used to reimburse hospitals for the care of uninsured patients.[7]

In late 1987, Governor Cuomo and legislative leaders agreed that in 1988 New York State would begin an "all payers system" of hospital reimbursement in which the state sets rates for all third-party payers (Medicare, Medicaid, Blue Cross, and commercial insurance companies) on a per case rather than the per diem (per day) basis which has been traditionally used in New York.[8] New Yorkers' hospital stays have always been longer than patients in other states, and it is believed that a per case rate will reduce spending by encouraging hospitals to discharge patients as early as possible.

Thus, New York State's response to rapid cost increases in Medicaid spending was to restrict eligibility for the program and to enlarge its regulatory powers by setting hospital rates. The response to hospital deficits, caused in part by these first two actions, was to redistribute monies to financially ailing hospitals, based on their care of the uninsured patient population. In addition, legislation enacted in 1983 provided for the assumption of most of the counties' share of Medicaid costs for long-term care.[9]

A second type of policy response to the cost of the Medicaid program
as to encourage restructuring of the health care delivery system. Begin-
g in the early 1980s, New York State encouraged the expansion of
e health services in local communities as an alternative to nursing
care. At the same time, the Medicaid reimbursement system was
tured to provide incentive to nursing homes not to admit patients
ld be cared for at home. In 1986, 70 percent of all Medicaid money
tionally for home care was spent in New York State.[10] The
Reform Act of 1984 authorized state funds for the development
tion of demonstration projects in which Medicaid recipients
health maintenance organizations (HMOs). The goal of this
s to reduce Medicaid costs by establishing a prepaid delivery
n "alternative" to the fee-for-service system. A prepaid sys-
hoped, would reduce the financial incentives for both un-
atment and hospitalization.[11]

nization of health care services to make them more cost ef-
ore appropriate to patients' needs is a policy recommendation being made in response to many of the health care issues of concern in New York State at the end of the 1980s. This can clearly be seen in the deliberations and actions prompted by the AIDS epidemic in New York State.

AIDS in New York State

AIDS is caused by the presence of Human Immuno Deficiency Virus (HIV) in the body. HIV destroys the immune system, and AIDS patients experience a large number of infections which the normal immune system can successfully fight. HIV can also attack the central nervous system, causing neurological disease and dementia. There is no known cure for AIDS; 58 percent of all of the AIDS cases diagnosed since 1981 have died, most within two years of diagnosis. AIDS has been transmitted through sexual activity, blood transfusion, the sharing of contaminated needles by intravenous (IV) drug users, and to fetuses by infected mothers. Until September 1987, the federal Centers for Disease Control limited its definition of AIDS to the most severe conditions associated with the HIV infection. For that reason, the estimate of the number of AIDS cases up to that time is believed to have been underestimated.

New York State had approximately 11,000 diagnosed cases of AIDS by the spring of 1987, 30 percent of all AIDS cases in the United States.[12] Ninety percent of all cases in the state occur in New York City,[13] where AIDS is the number one cause of death in men ages twenty-five to forty-four and women age twenty-five to twenty-nine. An individual can have HIV in his/her system without having symptoms of AIDS, which can develop later. It was estimated that in 1987, 300,000 to 500,000 people in New York carried the AIDS virus without having symptoms,[14] and that by 1991, 46,000 cases of AIDS will have been diagnosed in New York State.[15] Even if educational efforts are successful in preventing further spread of the disease, the number of new cases will continue to grow.

In 1983, relatively early in the AIDS epidemic, the New York State legislature created an AIDS Institute within the Department of Health. Its purpose is to support research and professional training on AIDS, to develop educational programs for both the general public and specific populations at risk, and to develop services for AIDS patients. Funding for the Institute has increased from $5 million in the 1983-84 fiscal year to $16 million in 1987-88.[16] In 1987, Task Forces on AIDS were established by both the State Senate and the State Assembly to provide policy relevant information to legislators. Both Task Forces have held hearings on AIDS-related issues around the state.

A large number of public policy issues have emerged in relation to the state's responsibilities to prevent the transmission of AIDS and to care for those afflicted with the disease. These include issues of civil liberties and due process in testing for AIDS, how AIDS should be discussed in the schools, discrimination against persons diagnosed as having AIDS—including discrimination by insurance companies—how to prevent the transmission of AIDS by IV drug users, and how AIDS patients shall be treated within the correction system and the foster care system.[17] Only the issue of the financing of care for AIDS patients can be briefly discussed here.

The treatment of AIDS is costly. It is estimated that the cost of caring for an adult AIDS patient is $55,000 a year, while it costs $86,000 for a child. New York State has an AIDS patient population whose treatment is likely to cost the state more than does the treatment of AIDS patients in other states. A much larger proportion of AIDS patients in New York are intravenous drug users and a smaller proportion are homosexual men. Drug users tend to be hospitalized more frequently and are less likely to have private health insurance coverage than are gay men. In addition, New York had 38 percent of all children in the nation with AIDS in 1987. Dr. David Axelrod, the New York State Health Commissioner, has predicted that by 1991 New York will be spending $1 billion a year for hospital care alone.[18]

Nationally, only 1 percent to 3 percent of the costs of paying for care for AIDS patients comes from the Medicare program. When patients do not have private health insurance or sufficient out-of-pocket funds to cover the cost of their care, they can apply for Medicaid. It is estimated that Medicaid pays for approximately 40 percent of health care costs for AIDS patients in New York State. Given the already high levels of spending for Medicaid, state policy on AIDS treatment has focused on alternatives to hospital care which will be less costly and more appropriate. AIDS patients have periods of acute illness when they must be hospitalized, and then periods when they can be treated as an outpatient or at home. In 1986, the AIDS Institute developed the concept of an AIDS Center which would coordinate a wide range of social, financial, legal, and medical services for AIDS patients, and would be reimbursed by the state for doing so. A few hospitals are now designated as AIDS Centers, but the further implementation of this concept is dependent on the availability of community resources such as home health care, hospice care, and housing. The lack of affordable housing for persons with AIDS results in long-term costly hospitalization.[19]

Thus, a central issue in the next several years will be how to develop the services to appropriately and cost-effectively care for persons with AIDS. Financing via an already strained Medicaid program will be a problem. Meeting the health care needs of AIDS patients, as well as the elderly and the uninsured working poor, will require major changes in our system of health care financing. Whether this can be achieved at the state level or will require national action is probably the major question for the future of health care services.

NOTES

1. Irene Fraser, "State Government and Health Care for the Poor: Repairing the Safety Net." Paper presented at the 1987 Annual Meeting of the American Political Science Association, Chicago, Illinois, p. 1.

2. Karen Davis and Diane Rowland, *Medicare Policy, New Directions for Health and Long-Term Care,* Baltimore: The John Hopkins University Press, 1986, p. 33.

3. Subcommittee on Health Insurance, New York State Council on Health Care Financing, "Policy Options to Expand Health Care Coverage for the Uninsured," Draft Preliminary Report, November 1987, p.1.

4. Fraser, p. 8.

5. Edward A. Gargan, "Leaders Reach Medicaid Pact in Albany Talks," *New York Times,* 24 June 1984, p. 24.

6. Kenneth E. Thorpe, "Health Care," in Gerald Benjamin and Charles Brecher, eds., *The Two New Yorks: City and State in a Changing Federal System,* New York: Russell Sage Foundation, forthcoming, pp. 5-6. New York also began to regulate capital expenditures by hospitals in 1965; this was required of all the states by subsequent federal regulation in 1972 and 1974. Peter B. Levine "An Overview of the State Role in the United States Health Scene," in Theodore J. Litman and Leonard S. Robins, eds., *Health Politics and Policy,* New York: John Wiley & Sons, 1984, p. 210.

7. Thorpe, pp. 7-11.

8. Ronald Sullivan, "New Bill Set on Payments to Hospitals," *New York Times,* 19 September 1987, p. 33. The Council on Health Care Financing continues to be a central forum for the development of health care financing policy in New York State. Its Subcommittee on Health Insurance is focusing on the uninsured population in New York State and will propose a series of policy options to deal with this problem.

9. Sarah F. Liebschutz and Irene Lurie, "New York," in R.P. Nathan and F.C. Dolittle, eds., *Reagan and the States,* Princeton, Princeton University Press, 1987, p. 183.

10. Ronald Sullivan, *New York Shifts Care for Elderly to their Homes," New York Times,* 4 May 1987, p. 1.

11. Office of Health Systems Management, New York State Department of Health, *Report to the Legislature on its Implementation of the Medicaid Reform Act of 1984,* 15 January 1987. The New York State Department of Health has also mandated that all health maintenance organizations licensed to operate in New York State must develop and implement a plan to enroll Medicaid recipients along with their privately insured members.

12. New York State Senate Majority Task Force on AIDS, *The AIDS Crisis in New York: A Legislative Perspective and Agenda for Study," June 1987, pp. 19-28 (Hereinafter referred to as AIDS Task Force Report.)*

13. Ronald Sullivan, "Bill of $1 Billion for Treating AIDS Seen in New York," New York Times, 22 May 1987, p.A-1.

14. AIDS Task Force Report, pp. 27-29.

15. Sullivan, p. A-1.

16. AIDS Task Force Report, pp. 35-39.

17. See AIDS Task Force Report.

18. AIDS Task Force Report, pp. 27-29, 113-14, 120.

19. AIDS Task Force Report, p. 112, 117-19, 123, 127.

Welfare in the Cuomo Years: Less Is Less

by

Theresa Funiciello and Sanford F. Schram

Theresa Funiciello is Co-director of Social Agenda, an organization advocating the point of view of people who experience poverty.

Sanford Schram is Associate Professor and Chairperson of Political Science at the State University College of Arts and Science, Potsdam, New York.

The authors thank Tina Seda, Tom Sanzillo, and Cynthia Mann.

EDITORS' NOTE: *This chapter presents a strong case that New York's reputation as a liberal, caring state no longer applies to our welfare policies. Readers should consider the clashing perspectives of those who emphasize the importance of our state's business climate and job growth with the emphasis of this chapter on government's responsibility to the poor.*

New York's "poor relatives" have not fared well in the Cuomo years. The poor just kept getting poorer—especially children.

From 1980 to 1984, while the overall national poverty rate increased from 8.4 percent to 9.7 percent,[1] the percentage of New Yorkers estimated to be living below the poverty level increased from 13.4 percent to over 15 percent.[2] Children, however, fared much worse. The total U.S. child poverty rate increased between 1980 and 1984 from 18.3 percent to 21.4 percent.[3] One of the hardest hit places in the country was New York City, where the already startlingly high poverty rate for children—34.1 percent in 1980—went up to 38.2 percent by 1984. The rest of New York State, where child and adult poverty rates are historically much lower, actually saw a greater per capita rise in child poverty, with a 27 percent increase in just four years—from 12.5 percent to 15.9 percent.[4] New York's child poverty problem was spreading as well as growing.

The vast majority of those children living below the poverty line in fact lived below *75 percent* of the poverty line. Most of these, though not all, lived on welfare and in female-headed families. For those children living in female-headed households, the opportunity to be poor was radically greater than for those in two-parent or male-headed households. And although the public assistance population has decreased slightly, those living in waged poverty have substantially increased.[5] In other words, having a job has not led some out of poverty.

With respect to waged poverty, the restructuring of the U.S. economy has done much to contribute its share of the problem. Yet, what is often overlooked is that the politics of the social welfare system has had its own effects on the worsening conditions of the poor. In New York State, the level of the welfare grant and the administrative tangle of red tape that characterizes the system have resulted in too little income for those who "successfully" negotiate the system and none at all for those who do not.

New York's CQ (Compassion Quotient) and the Welfare Grant

A review of New York's welfare grant exposes a massive rupture between the symbols of compassion and the state's policies toward the poor—a rupture which has played no small part in the frequency and depth of child poverty in the state. The poorest of the poor are far worse off today than they have been since the inception of the so-called flat grant system, which went into effect in 1970 for Aid to Families with Dependent Children (AFDC)—the main cash benefit program for poor families.[6] A major reason for the worsening condition of the poor is the decline in the real value and buying power of the AFDC flat grant (commonly referred to as the "basic allowance").

The flat grant itself was originally initiated to save money. Before 1970, welfare recipients in New York State could receive a series of "special needs grants," such as a furniture allowance every two years, in addition to a recurring monthly grant. The state moved to a flat grant system in 1970 largely as a way to counter organized efforts by welfare rights groups to leverage these special grants for all their recipient members. The state anticipated a savings by consolidating the grant in such a way as to reduce aggregate payments while at the same time eliminating the important organizing tool for welfare rights organizations that the special needs grants had become.[7] The flat grant also facilitated a shift to a more routinized system by automatically providing basically the same benefit to each household (adjusted for family size). In short, it offered standardization and cost savings.[8]

The plummeting of AFDC recipients' buying power since the institution of the flat grant is all the more troubling given the way the state set the original "standard of need" for the flat grant. The development of the standard was precipitated by *Rosado* v. *Wyman* (1970), in which the United States Supreme Court ruled that each state must specify an "*actual* standard of need" as the basis of its AFDC payments. The Court however made allowances for a state "to accommodate budgetary realities" and pay recipients less than the standard of need. The Court stated that while this system "leaves the States free to effect downward adjustments in the level of benefits paid, it accomplishes within that framework the goal, however modest, of forcing a State to accept the political consequence of such a cutback and bringing to light the true extent to which actual assistance falls short of the minimum acceptable."[9] In other words, states were obligated to set a rational standard based on real costs, but they were not obligated to pay it. The difference between what the state paid and what was "needed" constituted the basis for future political discourse. What the Court overlooked is that a state could underestimate need when setting its standard, and then pay recipients the "full amount." In this way, a state could shortchange recipients and save money without paying a political price for the hidden shortfall. This is exactly what New York State did when it used the Bureau of Labor Statistics' Lower Living Standard as the state's standard of need, but only after revising it downward.

Since then, the situation has worsened. At that time, New York's welfare budget was generally divided into two major component parts—a shelter grant and a "basic" grant.[10] (Since 1981, the state has added a home energy allowance.) All items in the basic allowance (other than utilities, about which more later) remain pegged to the cost of living in January 1972, the last time the basic allowance was increased. Excluding utilities, in July 1987 it cost $589 to purchase the same quantity of goods and services that the welfare grant now provides only $243 to cover. As such, welfare recipients in the compassionate "family of New York" today receive an average of $1.96 per person per day to cover about one-half their food (Food Stamps add a modest amount), some of their medical expenses (Medicaid is often erroneously assumed to cover all health care needs), and all of their clothing, furniture, transportation, baby bottles, soap, school supplies, toothpaste, toilet paper, kitchen utensils, and so forth (see Table 30). In other words, an underestimated standard of need has been allowed to erode even further.

While much of the writing on welfare has suggested that benefits are too high in states like New York,[11] such judgments overlook the actual benefits recipients get, the limitations imposed on their usage, and the cost of living. The gross amount of the total monthly New York grant (i.e., the basic allowance, the shelter allowance, and the home energy allowance) reached a maximum of $596 for a family of four in 1987 in New York City.[12] Yet, even this low figure is misleading, as a closer inspection reveals.

There is the high and rising cost of living in New York, particularly in the city. The purchasing power of this state's welfare grant has declined in the past fifteen years more than most, if not all, other states. New York's benefits have only rarely been raised, and when they have, the much ballyhooed increases have not kept pace with inflation.[13]

More importantly, the fact that the New York grant is compartmentalized into different allowances serves to limit recipients' access to all of the grant and to constrain the extent to which they can juggle it. In New York State, as in nine other states, benefits for "shelter" are determined separately from other benefits, and are specifically allocated for housing. This benefit is paid out according to one's actual lease rent up to a specified maximum. If a recipient's lease rent is lower than the maximum (or "shelter ceiling"), the recipient's grant is accordingly lower. On the other hand, if the lease rent is *higher* than the ceiling, the "excess" must be taken from some other portion of the total grant—i.e., from that part which is technically allocated for some other item of need. Relatively high shelter grants may make the total New York grant seem high, but they often merely pay inflated rents for the inadequate housing the poor normally get. In addition, since "shelter" benefits are supposed to be used only for housing, the "basic" grant is left to cover other needs—a job which, as we have already seen, it does not do well.

The problem, however, is more serious and more ironic. To be sure, some income increases have accrued to New York's welfare budget in

Table 30

THE REAL VALUE OF THE BASIC ALLOWANCE EXCLUDING UTILITIES FOR A FOUR-PERSON FAMILY PER MONTH IN NEW YORK STATE

Categories of Goods and Services included in the Basic Allowance (Excluding Utilities)*	Original Basic Allowance set at May 1969 Prices	Current Allowance set at January 1972 Prices	Actual Cost of Items, if Allowance reflected July 1987
Food at Home	$121	$137	$357
Household Furnishings	24	26	54
Public Transportation	7	9	35
Clothing	47	50	85
Personal Care	13	14	39
Education and Miscellaneous	6	7	19
Total (Excluding Utilities)	$218	$243	$589

*Utilities are also included in the basic allowance; but in recent years, grant increases based on energy-related inflation have changed the technical construction of the total welfare grant. These increases have resulted in a somewhat truer-to-real-costs allocation for utilities than for other items in the basic allowance. Originally, utilities were budgeted in the basic allowance at $13 per month, and changed to $15 per month in 1974. This $15 per month is still in the basic allowance, in addition to the other items in the table. However, it would be misleading to show it as "unchanged" since 1974, because in 1981 and 1985 "home energy allowances" were added to the total monthly benefits—in effect increasing the utility portion of the grant by $68.70 for a family of four. The Home Energy Allowance is now listed as a separate grant category alongside the basic and shelter allowances.

Note: Food, furnishings, clothing, and personal care are adjusted according to corresponding items in the Bureau of Labor Statistics' Consumer Price Index (CPI). "Education and Miscellaneous" is no longer used as a category in the CPI, and is adjusted according to the cost of the CPI's "other goods and services" category, as the closest rational approximation. Transportation is adjusted by the rate of change in the actual cost of public transportation in New York City, as per the original "standard of need."

forms other than the "basic" grant. For instance, the shelter allowance has been raised twice during the Cuomo Administration, for a total increase of 51 percent. This sounds like a major benefit increase; and it is. Yet the actual beneficiaries are *not* the poor, whose Food Stamps decrease $1 for every $3 increase they receive in rent allotments. The real beneficiaries are landlords who raise their rents in direct response to each shelter allowance increase. In New York City, for instance, median gross monthly rents had risen by only 6.8 percent during the three-year stretch prior to the first shelter allowance raise implemented in 1984. Experts studying the low-rent patterns had concluded that the ceiling for welfare rents was acting like an informal rent control. They were right: in the very first year subsequent to the shelter grant increase the median gross monthly rent was up 7 percent, and by 1986 had swelled to 19.7 percent.[14]

For the most part, recipients are living in the same quality (usually dilapidated) housing, paying more for it, and eating less. Since more dollars passed through their hands on the way to landlords, fewer "dollars" were available for the purchase of food when their Food Stamps were automatically reduced. For non-welfare poor families who share approximately the same low-rent market, the effects were likely even worse. That is, general housing market increases would not have been met by automatic wage increases on the job.

There has been one portion of the welfare grant in which purchasing power has actually increased: energy. In view of severe oil price inflation, the federal government in 1979 exempted energy-related public assistance grant increases from consideration in the calculation of Food Stamp budgets if states could prove the need for such increases based on actual costs. Since New York had severely underbudgeted utilities in the first place, and given the impact of inflation, the state was able to take advantage of this provision in 1981 and 1985, instituting and increasing a "home energy allowance." (Several other northern states with cold winters and high heating costs did likewise.)

The first and larger of these was enacted during the Carey Administration following a two-year organizing drive for basic grant increases led by welfare recipients themselves. The second was initiated by Governor Cuomo, largely to offset the reduction in Food Stamps precipitated by the first of his two shelter grant increases. Together, these home energy supplements have added a monthly total of $68.70 for a four-person family. As such, energy is the only item of need for which purchasing power bears a resemblance to real costs.

The "basic" grant, the shelter allowance, and now the home energy allowance constitute New York State's "standard of need" for welfare recipients. In 1975, New York State's standard of need for New York City was 110.1 percent of the poverty line for a family of three (the average AFDC family). By 1985, the percentage had dropped to 64.3 percent of the poverty level.[15] Even when Food Stamps were added in, recipients generally still fell below 75 percent of the poverty line.

Viewed from the perspective of purchasing power, the New York State welfare grant looks even worse than the numbers can show. For instance, the shelter allowance has increased 51 percent since the ceilings were first established in 1975. Yet, the housing available to poor people in New York City, where two-thirds of the state's welfare recipients live, has never been more scarce nor in worse condition. It also costs far more than it ever did. That is, recipients must pay more and get less. Purchasing power has therefore decreased even in that part of the grant which has seen the biggest increase over time.

The solution to these problems, however, is not to raise the shelter grant, because of the way the housing market responds to such increases. Instead, an increase in the basic allowance would generalize to an overall increase in purchasing power, because the market for items covered by the basic allowance is not exclusive to the poor. The price of the public transportation system, for instance, is not sensitive to welfare grant levels in any discernible way. Therefore, increasing the allocation for public transportation should not have any effect on its cost. The result would be an increase, then, in the purchasing power of recipients. A substantial increase is particularly critical for the basic allowance, which has declined so much in real value because of inflation. The logic is clear, but it is yet to be followed by New York State.

Churning

Even if recipients get all the income to which they are entitled, they remain among the poorest of the poor. However, securing all they are entitled to can be a major undertaking. In other words, the problem of AFDC in New York State is not just with what is given out but also with what should be given out and is not. For instance, one-quarter of all active public assistance recipients outside of New York City never receive their Food Stamps.[16] In addition, in New York City, over 44,000 people are cut off welfare each month for reasons unrelated to financial eligibility. More than two-thirds of these cases return to the rolls within six months—a clear indication of continued need.[17]

The practice of cutting people off and putting them back on later has been called "churning." For weeks or even months, families churned from the rolls are left with no income whatsoever. This practice has been linked to increased homelessness and hunger.[18]

How does it occur? There are many different ways, but one of the most common is termed "non-compliance" by the welfare department. From their point of view, non-compliance occurs when a client is cut off welfare for failing to meet some obligation. One frequent case of non-compliance is "letter recertifications"—especially in New York City, where the mail tends to be erratic. In such instances, questionnaires are mailed to the homes of recipients with a specified return date. Thousands of people are erroneously cut off every time recertification letters go out. It is difficult to imagine that willful disregard by the recipient is the reason why the "mailout" is not returned to the welfare department, since the result most often is termination of one's entire income. In fact, it has been shown that in many cases, the original "mailout" was never received by the families, or its return was not recorded properly by the department, or the recipient could not read English and treated it like junk mail.

One such "mailout" generally results in thousands of terminations from the welfare rolls in New York City alone. The local welfare offices argue that such terminations are "correct" in that irrespective of *cause,* the recipients did not get the letter back to them. This is taken de facto as non-compliance.

When confronted with the facts about churning, the State Department of Social Services (DSS) responded in 1984 by performing an internal audit of case closings and reopenings.[19] The Department reported that the problem of churning was not confined to the city but was a statewide practice. Although DSS did not dispute the two-thirds figure representing cases returned to the rolls within six months, they maintained that "only" 54 percent of the cutoffs could be categorized inappropriate. (The Department decided that only those cases returned to the rolls within sixty days, not six months, should be considered inappropriate closings.)[20] Of this 54 percent, about one-half were the result of technical glitches; but DSS characterized the other one-half as absolute welfare worker errors. For example, some recipients who had clearly notified their workers of a change of address were cut off for "whereabouts unknown." This occurred because the information on change of address which was in the worker's case file was never entered into the computer, resulting in a "mailout" to the wrong address. When recipients in these cases "did not comply," they were terminated from the rolls. These and similar terminations were classified "worker errors."

Despite a commitment to reduce the frequency of these "administrative closings" (as they prefer to call them), no progress has been made. Instead the practice has increased. According to Anna Lou Dehavenon, an anthropologist working primarily in this field, over 400,000 people, at least one-half of whom are children, are churned from the welfare rolls in New York City alone each year.[21] In *Below the Safety Net: A Study of Soup Kitchens,* Doug Lasden et al. reported that 64 percent of those interviewed at soup kitchens were eligible for welfare but not getting it.[22] In some cases, applicants had been incorrectly rejected at intake; in others, recipients had been cut off for "administrative reasons." In an era of retreat from social responsibility, the callous administration of welfare—even to the extent of denying essential legal entitlements to poor people—becomes acceptable.

It is most likely that "churning" is due largely to the State's attempts to reduce its error rate in overpayments to recipients and payments to ineligibles, in order to avoid penalties in lost funds which the federal government has threatened to impose under its Quality Control procedures. The federal government only counts errors in granting aid, not in its denial. This built-in bias, in effect, encourages states to deny aid to many who are eligible. At present, there is a moratorium on the imposition of federal penalties, and in fact such penalties have never been implemented in the history of welfare.[23] However, error rates are considered politically potent and every effort is made to keep overpayments and payments to ineligibles low. Meanwhile, for active and potential recipients, keeping and getting much needed, if inadequate, benefits is increasingly difficult.

Conclusion

In an era of deindustrialization, changes in the U.S. economy are taking place in ways which are ominous for many Americans. Yet, the ways in which welfare policy gets made and executed increasingly demonstrate the precarious nature of the so-called safety net. Ironically, in New York State, the welfare system may appear to be doing more; but the fact remains that the poor are getting less. In the face of persistent poverty and growing homelessness, the welfare system is preoccupied with its own internal and contradictory logic. Policy makers increase the welfare grant only to see it reduce the buying power of recipients. The welfare bureaucracy "churns" cases, denying aid to eligible families.

None of this would matter if it were not for one simple fact: Poverty is the number one killer of children in the country. New York State's welfare system in particular seems to be more and more preoccupied with its own internal concerns at the expense of confronting this horrible reality.

NOTES

1. *Counterbudget: A Secure New York is Secure for all New Yorkers,* Albany, N.Y.: Statewide Emergency Network for Social and Economic Security (SENSES), December 1986, p. 1.

2. Diane L. Baillargeon, *Dependency: Economic and Social Data for New York City,* New York: New York City Human Resources Administration, Office of Policy and Economic Research, June 1986, p. 12.

3. U.S. Bureau of the Census, *Current Population Reports: Characteristics of the Population Below the Poverty Level,* Series P-60, Washington, D.C.: U.S. Government Printing Office, 1982 and 1984, no. 133, p. 46, and no. 152, p. 28.

4. Baillargeon, *Dependency,* p. 12.

5. *Ibid.,* p. 17.

6. For AFDC, benefit levels are set by states and reimbursed 50 percent by the federal government. In New York State, the remaining 50 percent is shared equally between the state and county government, except in New York City, where the city and the state split the remaining 50 percent. The other major cash benefit program for non-aged persons is Home Relief (HR), which also uses the same flat grant system with comparable benefits adjusted for family size. The HR program does not exist at the federal level and is split 50-50 between the state and the local governments. It is, however, primarily for childless adults.

7. See Frances Fox Piven and Richard A. Cloward, *Poor People's Movements,* New York: Pantheon Books, 1977; Nick Kotz and Mary Lynn Kotz, *A Passion for Equality,* New York: W.W. Norton and Company, 1977; and Guida West, *The National Welfare Rights Movement,* New York: Praeger Publishers, 1981.

8. See William Simon, "Legality, Bureaucracy and Class in the Welfare System," *Yale Law Journal,* 92 (1983), pp. 1198-1286.

9. *Rosado* v. *Wyman* 397 U.S. 412-414 (1970).

10. New York is one of ten states which separates shelter payments from the "basic" grant. See *Characteristics of State Plans for Aid to Families with Dependent Children,* Washington, D.C.: United States Department of Health and Human Services, Family Support Administration, Office of Family Assistance, 1987, pp. 402-3.

11. Most of the recent writings by conservatives on the topic of social welfare have suggested that states like New York have benefits which are so high as to encourage welfare dependency. See Martin Anderson, *Welfare: The Political Economy of Welfare Reform in the United States,* Stanford, Calif.: Hoover Institution, 1978; Charles Murray, *Losing Ground: Social Policy 1950-1980,* New York: Basic Books, 1984; and Lawrence Mead *Beyond Entitlement: The Social Obligations of Citizenship,* New York: The Free Press, 1986.

12. *Characteristics of State Plans for Aid to Families with Dependent Children* (1987), pp. 402-3.

13. The real value of the maximum AFDC benefit for a family of four in 1986 dollars has declined in New York State from $921.03 in 1969 to $566.00 in 1986. See *Characteristics of State Plans for Aid to Families with Dependent Children* (1969-1986). Benefits were adjusted according to the consumer price index as it is reported in the *Survey of Current Business,* Washington, D.C.: U.S. Department of Commerce, Bureau of Economic Analysis, monthly, p. s-5.

14. *Shelter Allowance Policy Options,* Policy Brief, New York: New York City Human Resources Administration, June 1987, Table 2.

15. Baillargeon, *Dependency,* p. 62.

16. The estimate comes from the New York State Department of Social Services, Bureau of Data Management as reported in *1984-1985 New York State Statistical Yearbook,* Albany, N.Y.: Nelson A. Rockefeller Institute of Government, 1985, pp. 86, 95.

17. Timothy Casey, *The In-Human Resources Administration's Churning Campaign,* New York: Downtown Welfare Advocate Center, May 1983.

18. Timothy J. Casey, "Public Assistance Policy and Homelessness," Prepared

statement for testimony before the New York State Joint Legislative Hearings on "Homeless Families: Causes and Solutions," June 12, 1987.

19. Casey, *The In-Human Resources Administration's Churning Campaign.*

20. See *Administrative Closings in New York City Public Assistance Cases,* Albany, N.Y.; New York State Department of Social Services, April 1984.

21. Anna Lou Dehavenon, *Toward a Policy for the Amelioration and Prevention of Family Homelessness and Dissolution,* New York: East Harlem Interfaith Welfare Committee, May 1987.

22. Doug Lasden, et al., *Below the Safety Net: A Study of Soup Kitchen Users in New York City,* New York: Legal Action Center for the Homeless and New York University, April 1987.

23. See U.S. Congress, House of Representatives, Committee on Ways and Means, *Background Material and Data on Programs within the Jurisdiction of the Committee on Ways and Means,* Washington, D.C.: U.S. Government Printing Office, 1987, pp. 683-99. For analysis of Quality Control, see Evelyn Brodkin and Michael Lipsky, "Quality Control in AFDC as an Administrative Strategy," *Social Service Review,* March 1983, pp.1-34; and Michael Lipsky, "Bureaucratic Disentitlement in Social Welfare Programs," *Social Service Review,* 1984, pp. 3-27.

Primer on Civil Service: The State of Personnel in New York

by

Karen S. Burstein

Karen S. Burstein is Auditor General for the City of New York.

EDITORS' NOTE: *Ms. Burstein formerly headed Civil Service in New York. Her article carefully outlines the way the state conducts its personnel policy, and it identifies problems as well as strengths in the system.*

Government policy and programs are not self-executing. A bill, passed by the legislature and signed by the governor, can mandate the treatment of the developmentally disabled, the issuance of motor vehicle licenses, the counselling of Vietnam-era veterans, the monitoring of water quality, or the preservation of public safety. However, such a mandate is only translated into action when the tasks necessary to its accomplishment are defined, jobs comprising those tasks created, and people chosen and deployed to do them.

These are functions common to all enterprises. Private firms must also define the tasks essential to achieve their goals and then fill positions encompassing those tasks by selecting appropriate and capable employees; but these companies have considerably more flexibility in the fashioning and operation of a personnel structure than does government. Like such firms, New York State is bound by civil rights law not to discriminate among people on the basis of sex, race, or religion. As well, it must observe the terms of collective bargaining agreements with its labor unions. In contrast with the private sector, though, its freedom of decision is further circumscribed by the strictures of the country's second oldest civil service system. Moreover, unlike the oldest, the federal government's, which was substantially overhauled under President Carter, New York's system has demonstrated a remarkable continuity since 1883, when young Assembly member Theodore Roosevelt helped shepherd to passage its first statutory formulation. In 1909, all civil service provisions, like those concerning other agencies and functions, were organized into a chapter of the Consolidated Laws of the State of New York. While individual amendments and additions have been made over the years, the 1909 version was recodified (completely resystematized) only once, in 1958. The major reason for this continuity is the language of Article V Section 6 of the New York State Constitution, which since 1894 has directed that

> appointments and promotions in the civil service of the state, and all of the civil divisions thereof, including cities and villages, shall be made according to merit and fitness to be ascertained, as far as practicable, by examination which, as far as practicable, shall be competitive; . . .

Because of this constitutional injunction, civil service in New York is frequently called the "merit system," to contrast it with the "spoils system" which it superseded. The latter described the practice of filling government posts on the basis of whether individuals belong to the political party in power. (William Marcy, United States Senator from New

York in 1831, is credited with the first defense of such patronage hiring on the grounds that "to the victor belong the spoils.") The distinguishing characteristic of a merit system is the selection of employees based on their performance on objective examinations in which the talents of each candidate are measured fairly and consistently against those of every other.

Still, neither the framers of the constitutional language nor the legislators who crafted the Civil Service Law expected unvarying reliance on exams. Rather, whether there will be such reliance depends on the constitutionally created concept of "practicability." To flesh out this concept, the Law establishes four categories, called "jurisdictional classifications," to which all non-elected positions in the executive branch of local and state government can be assigned—competitive (where ranking devices are used); non-competitive (where applicants are judged not against each other but against a set of formal qualifications); labor (which involves unskilled work); and exempt (where the employer must have maximum freedom to hire and fire because of the appointee's policy influence, sensitive program responsibilities, or confidential relationship to the boss).

To ensure that the existence of alternatives to the competitive class does not become an invitation to circumvent merit principles of personnel selection, the Constitution and the Civil Service Law establish a number of conceptual and structural barriers to the exercise by a local or state agency of the unfettered power to choose, move, promote, demote, and discharge staff. First, the statute presumes that every job is capable of being tested for. Second, the burden of overcoming that presumption rests with the agency, which must convincingly demonstrate "impracticability" to the New York State Civil Service Commission, a bi-partisan group each of whose three members is appointed by the governor and confirmed by the New York State Senate to a term of six years. (In the case of local government, such demonstration must first be made to a municipal commission or personnel officer after a public hearing.) Then, the State Commission's decision to place a state post outside the competitive class, by adding it to a list of published exceptions contained in the *Appendix to the Rules of the Civil Service Commission,* must be approved by the governor. (The Commission, not the governor, has ultimate authority to accept or deny a *local* rule.) Finally, the rule can be challenged in court on the grounds that the Commission acted in an arbitrary or capricious way or abused its discretion.

To fill any group of jobs that remains in the competitive class, a test must be given. Thereafter, a list of the successful test-takers, ranked in score order, will be issued. From that list, agencies may choose one of the top three willing candidates for each position that is open.

This procedure is known as the "Rule of Three." Such lists last a minimum of one year and a maximum of four, and are considered "viable" so long as there are at least three names on them. If there is no list (because no test has been administered) or the list has been "exhausted" (fewer than three candidates willing to accept jobs exist), an agency may fill the slot with anybody who meets the qualifications established for the position. That individual is called a "provisional" appointee, and can stay in the slot until a viable list is produced. Theoretically, provisionals may not serve for more than nine months; in practice, that period is regularly exceeded because of legal challenges to exams, resistance by agencies to exam administration, and resource constraints. However, within a few months of the establishment of a viable list, the provisional appointment will end. The individual, if among the top three scoring candidates on the test, may be made permanent. If not selected for a permanent appointment or if unsuccessful on the exam, he or she must cease working in the job. In that instance, should the agency not like anyone else on the list, its only alternative will be to keep the post vacant.

It is true that the above set of injunctions can have a perverse effect in a particular case, as when newcomers displace most of a unit comprising very long-term productive provisionals because the latter did not score as well as the former on a test. This displacement inevitably causes short-run difficulties in program operation. On the other hand, timely administration of the exam, as the law requires, would have obviated the problem from the beginning. In any event, whatever the occasional cost, the fact that provisionals do not mature into permanency merely by the passage of time confers a major system benefit by assuring that objective assessment devices instead of political and personal preference are relied on to pick those who do the people's business.

Another major protection against the reemergence of spoils-system distortions is tenure. Either by statute or union contract, people in the competitive, non-competitive, and labor classes, after service of varying lengths of time (from six months to five years), hold their jobs for life and can be fired only after an extensive hearing in which the agency shows cause to support its contention that the employee is incompetent or venal. Of course, because of budget exigencies, positions can be cut and people laid off. But, if they are competitive or tenured non-competitive civil servants, they receive what are called "preferred list" rights—that is, they go on a roster which must be used to fill their own old job or comparable ones before agencies can hire other people.

The last barrier to erosion of the merit system is the fact that agencies where the jobs exist do not themselves generally classify those jobs, produce the tests, issue the lists, and determine tenure rights. Instead, primary responsibility for those functions is borne by the Department of

Civil Service, which shares a common leader with, but is operationally independent of, the Commission; one of the latter's three members is chosen by and serves at the pleasure of the governor both as the Commission's President and the Department's Commissioner.

The Department annually writes and administers nearly 5,000 state and local exams. About 210,000 men and women take those exams each year, and some 40,000 are actually appointed to more than 7,000 separately titled position classes (groups of the same jobs) in state service. Every time one of those new entrants is hired or a current participant in the system is promoted, transferred, demoted, fired, retires, or resigns, the Department processes a piece of paper called a personnel transaction, entering the data into a computer system shared with the State Comptroller. The Department yearly handles 300,000 such transactions. On a cyclical basis, it also certifies, as the law requires, that every state worker properly holds his or her post, so that the Comptroller can cut payroll checks. In addition, the Department maintains career tenure histories on all civil servants. When layoffs occur, it makes thousands of rulings on the relative rights of individuals to displace (bump) others.

Final Department determinations may be appealed by agencies and employees to the Civil Service Commission. Besides settling questions of jurisdictional classification, then, the Commission can overrule a finding on the proper grade level of a job, change minimum requirements for entry to an exam, rescore test papers, or overturn a preferred list decision. (The Commission also oversees all local civil service administration.)

No description of Civil Service activities is complete unless it includes those Department and Commission responsibilities which are independent of or ancillary to core merit system protection obligations. For example, the Department employs the nurses who staff emergency stations in state buildings throughout New York, administers the health insurance program for most state and local government workers, promulgates a plan for affirmative action, and monitors agency compliance efforts. The Commission interprets leave and attendance rules for unrepresented workers, runs the State's Suggestion Program, and grants waiver of the Retirement Law limits on how much rehired pensioners can earn.

Moreover, even an exhaustive catalogue of Department and Commission roles will not fully explicate New York's human resources management structure, for they are only two of the entities charged with formulating and implementing state policy and practice in this area. In truth, no understanding of New York's personnel system is possible without a discussion of the sea change wrought by adoption in 1967 of Article 14 of the Civil Service Law. The Taylor Law, as Article 14 is known, was intended to assure an orderly process for containing public sector labor disputes. By allowing workers to organize for collective negotiations, though, it significantly shifted the pre-1967 balance of personnel power. First, management could no longer act unilaterally to determine questions of wages and benefits. Second, once these matters became mandatory subjects for bargaining, the governor, as the state's Chief Executive Officer, required a sophisticated staff capability to make timely responses to labor demands and set out management's counterproposals. The Civil Service Department was (and remains) ill-equipped to fill that need because its administrative head, though a political appointee of the governor, also functions as the tenured guardian of a neutral merit system intended precisely to insulate personnel decisions from daily fiscal and program pressures and the changing policy concerns of the state's elected leadership. Instead, as an outgrowth of the Taylor Law process, the Governor's Office of Employee Relations (GOER) was established to formulate management's philosophy and articulate its interests. GOER's power and voice have grown with labor's.

Third, as the unions became more sophisticated, and as their economic power made them formidable legislative lobbyists, the bargaining season began to expand. While contracts run for three years, the policy they set—in areas as diverse as classification, training, and health insurance—is implemented in the period between contracts, often on a project basis by joint committees on each of which GOER sits as lead management representative. Frequently, such committees make interim policy adjustments or commission new studies to produce data for future negotiations.

Finally, what is agreed on in the bargaining is extended, by executive fiat (with subsequent legislative ratification), to those employees (called managerial/confidential or m/c's) who are barred, by the Taylor Law, from membership in an employee organization (labor union). Again, since it is a management decision—not a neutral civil service act—the extension of the agreement to such m/c's has increasingly occurred under the aegis of GOER.

The presence of so many primary actors in the field of personnel administration and oversight does constitute a significant check on agency discretion and potential breach of the procedures and rules for fair and equal employment opportunity. Moreover, having such rules set centrally encourages statewide consistency in the treatment of the government labor force, and vindicates the concept of the state as a single employer rather than an aggregation of idiosyncratically organized agency fiefdoms. At the same time, though, the existence of so many centralized control organizations has negative implications for system coherence and rationality. In the case of labor and management, there will inevitably and understandably be points of contest. However, under the current dispensation, management suffers from internal disputes as a product, in large measure, of pressure put on the personnel structure by collective negotiations—such as the training of workers, and the area of health insurance—which are critical to the quality of working life but ancillary to merit system questions of when and what kind of an exam should be given.

Simply put, New York State's personnel structure is not a single, seamless entity but rather a set of systems which sometimes work in concert and sometimes in conflict. Courts have determined that when the Civil Service Law is different from a provision of an extant contract between the state and one of its unions, the contract provision has primacy. But when there is no explicit contract requirement or statutory direction, and GOER and the Civil Service Department/Commission clash, a resolution is not always immediately easily achievable.

For example, although the state provides that employees must charge time off for unforeseen emergencies to their five days of personal leave credits, the Civil Service Commission has the power to waive this rule. GOER sought such a waiver on behalf of workers who did not report to their state offices when a water main in Binghamton broke. Invoking a past precedent that, by contract and policy, the five-day personal leave balance contemplates such catastrophes, the Commission denied the request. GOER than agreed with union leaders that their members should be able to restore leave balances for the day, effectively "renegotiating" the contract midstream. Thereafter, GOER returned to the Commission urging reconsideration for the unrepresented m/c's. The Commission underlined the rectitude of its original decision and insisted that GOER's power in this instance was at least ambiguous. However, it finally yielded, because it felt that the two branches of the same executive should not diverge in position, m/c's and organized labor should be treated alike, and the Commission imprimatur would assure that the benefit was legally conferred on both.

The above case, though narrow in ambit, is nonetheless emblematic of the problems attendant upon the present personnel dispensation. At best, management's failure to speak with a single voice is embarrassing. At worst, it can lead to distortions in policy, duplication of efforts, and waste of resources. For instance, GOER employs a group of individuals largely to oversee Civil Service's administration of the contract that GOER initially negotiated with the unions.

Again, GOER controls training, to which, because it is a visible and exciting area, more and more dollars have flowed. The Civil Service Department, on the other hand, has the power to determine, by examination, who will enter and progress in the system. However, since it is not a direct participant in the collective bargaining process, where critical decisions about resource allocations are made, the Department has not been able to secure the necessary money for the politically unrewarding, if essential, work of crafting and giving exams. In consequence, New York rarely connects training to tests which means that it cannot deliver real career development planning. Equally important, the state is unable to invest in expensive and sophisticated selection devices and thus overrelies on written multiple choice tests. These not only have a differentially negative impact on black and hispanic candidates but they cannot assess some qualities—such as communication skills—essential to the best performance of particular jobs.

Notwithstanding the above, New York human resources management system, its civil service, has signal strengths. Over the last decade, it has shown increasing capacity to offer women and minorities non-discriminatory entry and promotion opportunities, to purge its selection instruments of racial and sexual bias, to increase mobility among clerical workers, to focus on improving the skills of incumbent employees, and to mitigate the pain of layoff by carefully anticipating and planning workforce contractions. Given the continuing growth in and vibrancy of labor involvement with the system, it seems inevitable that over time its disparate management parts must merge. After all, it is not an abstract government which takes care of people in wheelchairs or hands out motor vehicle licenses or tests the quality of water or patrols our streets. Men and women do these jobs; and it is the state's personnel system which is responsible for choosing and nurturing them. The pressure to ensure that the structure is rationally organized to provide such sustenance will grow with the growing sophistication of the government work force. For citizens, this bodes well. The higher the quality of our public servants, the better served the public will be.

The Political Economy of the Property Tax

by

Edward Howe and Donald Reeb

Dr. Reeb is Associate Professor in the Department of Economics and Director of the Center for Financial Management, Rockefeller College, State University of New York at Albany.
Dr. Howe is Associate Professor at Siena College in New York.

EDITORS' NOTE: *More than half of local government's own source revenue in New York State comes from the property tax. In 1980, receipts amounted to nearly $9 billion, more than the state income tax ($7 billion) or the sales tax ($6.3 billion). This chapter provides an introduction to the rationale and administration of the property tax, its strengths and weaknesses as a source of government revenue, and the prospects for reform.*

Each of the local governments in New York State—counties, cities, towns, villages, and school districts—may tax real property. The process begins with the adoption of a budget setting forth proposed expenditures and an estimate of revenue. Localities initially estimate state and federal aid, non-property tax revenues (mainly sales and utility taxes), and departmental income (fees, licenses, and so on). Generally, any additional revenue needed will have to be made up by property tax revenue. This needed amount, divided by the taxable value of real property in a locality, determines the tax rate. The tax rate, which traditionally has been the same for all types of real property in a given jurisdiction, is applied *ad valorem* (according to the assessed value of property) in order to determine the owner's tax payment. The tax rate for property is usually stated in mills per dollar. A *tax rate* of 50 mills per dollar equals $5 per $100 of assessed value. If a house is *assessed* at $25,000 for tax purposes, the property tax payment owed, in the example, is $1,250. Thus, the two crucial variables which explain differences in tax bills both within the same classification of property (for example, residential) and among property classes (for example, residential and commercial) are the tax rate and the assessed value of property.

The local real property tax is the single largest source of revenue in New York State. Total local property taxes and assessments are estimated at $10 billion for fiscal year 1982. For fiscal year 1980, the latest year audited, total local property taxes and assessments amounted to $8.9 billion, compared to the two largest sources of total state revenues—the personal income tax ($7.0 billion) and the sales tax ($6.3 billion).

In 1980 this $8.9 billion accounted for 54.2 percent of the revenue raised by all local governments. In terms of level of government, there was wide variation in reliance upon the property tax. If New York City is excluded, school districts derived 86.6 percent of their locally derived revenues [local taxes and local non-taxes] from the property tax, followed by towns (70.6 percent), counties (58.2 percent), villages (54.3 percent), and cities (38.2 percent). New York City (including its school district) derived 42.5 percent of its local revenue from property taxes. This reliance upon the property tax has decreased over the last twenty years relative to other income. In 1960, all localities in New York State collected $2.2 billion in property tax revenues which was 66.3 percent of their local revenues. The decreased relative dependence on the property tax is largely explained by the increasing use of the sales tax which was made available to all local governments by state law in 1967. When revenue from all sources, including state and federal grants, are used as the base, property taxes are 48.3 percent of revenues in 1960 and 20.2 percent in 1980 for New York State's local governments.

The experience of localities with the property tax in New York State has been similar to that of all localities in the U.S. Property tax revenues accounted for 50.5 percent of all revenues collected by local governments in the U.S. in 1980, compared to 70.6 percent in 1960.[1]

In sum, while receipts from the property tax for all localities combined have continued to increase, its importance relative to all general revenue, especially state and federal grants to localities, has declined significantly in New York State and elsewhere.

Property Tax Administration

The administration of the property tax is essentially the responsibility of local assessors, supplemented by state assistance. The duties of the local assessors include: (1) the identification of all land and buildings in their assessment districts; (2) the valuation of land and improvements; (3) the preparation of a final assessment roll for property tax purposes; and (4) the review of assessed valuations for the correction of inequities.[2] The process of assessment is done in "assessing units" consisting usually of cities, towns, and villages. Villages have the option of using town assessment rolls rather than undertaking the task of preparing their final assessment roll.

Three different methods are available for placing value on buildings and improvements. The comparison sales method is used for residential buildings, where the assessed value placed on one house depends on recent sales prices of similarly sized and located homes. The capitalization of income method is used principally for commercial and apartment buildings and involves determining the market value on the basis of estimated net rental income. The replacement cost method, used primarily for industrial and utility improvements, estimates the current replacement cost of the improvements.[3] In all cases, estimating the market value of land involves the combined effect of such factors as existing use, lot size, location, and so on, which is then added to the market value of buildings or other improvements to determine the total value of real property. The result of these calculations is an estimate of full or market value, i.e., the price which would be willingly paid by a buyer.

The advantages of using a full value standard are: (1) it allows for uncomplicated comparison of assessments among the same type of properties in a given jurisdiction and, (2) it allows the total tax burden to be distributed equitably among different taxing jurisdictions in a county or school district.

Actual assessment practices in New York have long ignored the use of the full value standard. A basic reason for assessing property at less than full market value (i.e., fractional assessment) has been the mostly upward climb in property values due to inflation. In addition, local governments [assessing units] vary greatly with respect to the assessing expertise of local officials, the size of parcels to be assessed, differing types of property, political favoritism towards some property owners, and views of assessors about what objectives the property tax system should try to accomplish. Many assessors lack tax maps, i.e., comprehensive lists of all property, while many others simply do not have the time to reassess property on an annual basis because of the sheer magnitude of the task confronting them.[4]

As a result, the State Board of Equalization and Assessment implemented in 1974 a modern, highly sophisticated, computerized assessment system as a service for localities—the New York State Real Property Information System. This system relies on a statistical model together with the manual collection of specific information about parcels—size, location, types of buildings, recent improvements—based on tax maps compiled for all counties. The statistical model estimates the value of the parcel. Field surveys are conducted to check on the full value estimates. However, local officials are still responsible for making the final determination of assessments.[5] As of April, 1983, about one-half of all the parcels in the state still need to be revalued. Fifty-five of sixty-two counties have received final state approval with respect to their tax maps, the first step in undertaking revaluation of assessed property.[6]

The average relationship between the assessed values and the full value of taxable property in a locality is called the equalization rate. Equalization rates are widely different from each other, even in adjoining towns. Equalization rates are important in (1) apportioning county and school district levies among the cities and towns, (2) computing constitutional tax and debt limits, and (3) allocating state aid payments, especially aid to school districts and general revenue sharing. The State Board of Equalization and Assessment determines the equalization rate in each locality from a sample of parcels sold or appraised in each of the cities and towns (including villages) in the state.

Assessment Appeal

After the local assessor makes public a tentative assessment roll, each property owner has a right to look at the value placed on his or her property and to compare this with other assessments. A property owner who thinks an assessment is inaccurate may file an appeal, or grievance, with the local assessment review board. Four grounds for complaint exist:

1. over-valuation—the property has been assessed in excess of full value;
2. inequality—the property has been assessed at a higher proportion of full value than similar properties;
3. illegal assessment—the property has not been assessed in accordance with law; and
4. the property was not granted a partial exemption to which it was entitled.

The local assessment review board may decide to reject a complaint or to raise or lower an assessment. In preparing the final assessment roll the assessor must follow the direction of the board.[7]

If a property owner is still dissatisfied after a decision by the board, a petition may be filed with the Small Claims Court (730 of the Real Property Tax Law). The Small Claims Court will review the current final assessment of an owner-occupied one, two, or three-family residential structure, if a prior grievance had been filed with the local assessment review board. However, the "total anticipated reduction in taxes" may not exceed $750 in any one year, assuming the Small Claims Court favors the plaintiff (property owners).

All property owners who disagree with the decision of the local board may file a complaint with the Supreme Court. In practice, most complaints are filed by non-residential property owners. Property tax hearings currently represent a substantial part of the work of a number of lawyers and local courts.

The Courts and the 1981 Property Tax Law

Provisions for judicial review and remedies for an alleged illegal, erroneous, or unequal property tax assessment date back to 1880. For the most part, the process of appealing an assessment was a long, difficult, and costly process. Part of the difficulty appeared to be removed in the wake of the Court of Appeals decision in *Ed Guth Realty, Inc. versus Gingold,* 34 New York, Second 440 (1974). The court ruled that a property owner, seeking a reduction in an assessment, could use the state equalization rate (expressing the average relationship between assessed values and the full value of taxable property in a locality) as supporting evidence of inequity. The Court of Appeals then ruled, in *Hellerstein versus Town of Islip,* 37 New York, Second 1 (1975), that Section 306 of the Real Property Tax Law meant what it said—all property had to be assessed at full value, not some fraction thereof.

The potential existed for challenging and overturning the entire assessment roll in each jurisdiction, not just the assessment of each parcel.

Faced with the need to implement the Hellerstein ruling and fearing a shift in property tax burdens, the State Legislation acted. It voted, in 1981, over-riding a veto by Governor Hugh L. Carey, to repeal the 1788 law requiring full value assessment of all property (Chapter 1057 of the Laws of 1981).

The new legislation creates two systems of property taxation—one for Nassau County and New York City and another for the rest of the state.[8] Property in Nassau County and New York City must be classified into one of four types: (1) one, two, and three-family residences; (2) all other residential property; (3) utilities; and (4) all other property. The law further mandates that the share of total property tax collections provided by these classes as of 1981 remain the same in the future. Individual assessment increases for one, two, and three-family residences are limited to 6 percent on an annual basis and to 20 percent over a five-year period. But for the rest of the state, localities may exercise a local option and create two property classes, (1) one, two, and three-family residences, and (2) all other property, but only if a revaluation of all property is undertaken. The share of total property taxes provided by these classes of property would be governed by the shares paid in the year prior to revaluation. Individual assessment increases or decreases are limited to 20 percent per year for five years, if revaluation has been completed.

The mandatory provisions affecting Nassau County and New York City are intended to continue the practice of favoring homeowners, whose homes are often under-assessed, at the expense of businesses. In other areas of the state, a homeowner bias is not universal, though it often occurs.

Property Tax Exemptions

The assessed value of real property in New York State was $129,615,800 in fiscal year 1979–1980. Some one-third of this amount $42,873,900 was either wholly or partially exempt from taxation. This exempt property was worth an estimated $100 billion on a full value basis.

Cities, among all local government entities, appear to be especially affected by the amount of tax-exempt property. Approximately 40 percent of the assessed value of property in the 62 cities of the state was exempt from taxation in 1979–1980. The City of Watervliet headed the list with 77 percent of its property value exempt, followed by the City of Albany (70 percent). Among the "Big Five" cities, Syracuse recorded 46 percent of its property value exempt. This was followed by Buffalo and New York City (each with 41 percent), Rochester (31 percent), and Yonkers (27 percent).[9] The accuracy of these percentages is questionable since exempt real property tends to be ignored by the assessors.

The State Board of Equalization and Assessment has estimated, in the case of wholly exempt property, that 86 percent is used for special benefit purposes by governmental and private groups, while less than 1 percent is used for economic benefit purposes. The remainder is used for unknown reasons. [10]

The State Board has pointed out several administrative difficulties with exemptions. One problem has been the steady proliferation of them over time. There are currently about two hundred and twenty exemptions contained in the real property tax laws and other statutes, many of them complex. Local assessors often have difficulty in both deciding what particular exemption statute applies to a particular piece of property and in coping with the political pressure to provide exemptions for questionable parcels. Additionally, some exemptions are stated in the law as fixed dollar amounts, such as those for senior citizens. Since assessment practices and local tax rates vary, a fixed dollar exemption could result in differing benefits being obtained on an individual basis in neighboring jurisdictions.

The proportion of all assessed real property in New York State classified as "exempt from taxation" has risen from 11 percent in 1900 to 33 percent as of 1980.[11] Although often characterized as an erosion of the tax base, it is better understood as a tax shift. The taxable and partially exempt portions of the tax base will generally have to shoulder a greater share of the property tax burden as more exemptions are granted.

One way to offset the impact of the growing value of exemptions on local taxpayers is to make greater use of the concept of *payment in lieu of taxes.*[12] Currently, certain public authorities, such as a local public housing authority, make payments in lieu of property tax, either as required by law or voluntarily through negotiations with municipal officials. There is no guarantee that the amount will actually cover the cost of services provided.

The State Legislature did make a notable attempt in 1971 to aid localities through a so-called "service charge" law. Localities would have been permitted to charge exempt property owners for police and fire protection, sanitation and water supply services, and for street and highway construction, maintenance, and lighting. The law was never implemented, because of the difficulty of finding a method to compute specific charges and was repealed in 1981.[13]

Constitutional Tax and Debt Limits

The continuing proliferation of tax exemptions and the resulting need to raise more revenue has forced a reexamination of constitutionally fixed property tax limits. These taxing limits, stated as a percentage of taxable real property, date back to 1884, and are embodied in Article VIII, Section 10 of the State Constitution. They apply to counties, cities, city school districts (both dependent and independent), and villages. There are no constitutional tax limits for towns and for school districts outside of cities. The tax limit is generally set at a maximum of 2.0 percent of the latest five-year full value average of taxable property. New York City, the lone exception, has a maximum tax rate of 2.5 percent.

The problem of constitutional tax limits is most acute for the people of the Big Five cities and their fiscally dependent school districts.[14] Over the period 1975–1982, New York City, on the average, came within 96.2 percent of its tax limit. The City of Yonkers, over the same period, has been the most affected, coming within 99.1 percent of its tax limit, on the average.[15] It was followed by Rochester (90.5 percent), Syracuse (86.7 percent), and Buffalo (76.6 percent). About one-third of all cities in the state, 19 out of 62 cities, exhausted in excess of 70 percent of their tax limit, for one or more years during the 1975–1982 period.

In recognition of the constitutional fiscal constraints facing large cities and their dependent school districts, particularly in light of the *Hurd versus City of Buffalo* court decision (1974), the state legislature has acted to provide various forms of special state aid. This assistance has taken the form of municipal "over-burden" aid, and other changes in formulas used to compute state aid for education payments.

The Outlook: Relief or Reform?

The property tax system possesses certain strengths: (1) the source of taxation is readily available and immobile, (2) it is easy to enforce, (3) there are relatively low costs of administration,[16] (4) it is responsive to changes in property values, (5) it is durable, (6) there is a vast body of knowledge about its characteristics, and (7) the tax is likely to be, implicitly, progressive over most of the income range when it is well administered. The disadvantages of the property tax system are: (1) it is considered regressive, especially at lower current income levels (though there is some dispute about this)[17] and (2) its administration is often of poor quality and subject to political manipulation.[18]

Actual or proposed changes in the property tax system in New York State have been generally aimed at the aforementioned weaknesses. The intent has often been to provide property tax relief—any action designed to reduce actual property tax payments below what they would have been in the absence of such change.[19] Although indirect and difficult to quantify, perhaps the largest source of relief has been the recent growth in federal and state aid payments and local non-property tax revenue. In New York property tax revenue increased by 306.8 percent from 1960–1980, federal aid to localities rose 2,673.8 percent, state aid went up by 576.2 percent, and local non-property tax revenue (mostly the sales tax) climbed by 645.7 percent.

More specific forms of relief have been targeted at specific types of property, such as preferential assessment of farmland. Tax exemptions, constitutional or statutory, provide further relief to property owned by various organizations or individuals, such as religious institutions, new businesses, veterans, and senior citizens. Senior citizens in New York State can currently benefit from three relief programs.[20] New York State currently has circuit breaker relief for both the elderly and non-elderly, subject to eligibility limits. Originally enacted in 1978, it gives relief to homeowners and renters by providing a credit against the state personal income tax, whereby the amount of relief decreases as the level of income rises.[21]

As discussed above, the 1981 Real Property Tax Law contained a provision for classification of different types of property. The intent was to ensure preferential tax treatment for homeowners in Nassau County and New York City by segregating real property into various classes and freezing the share of taxes paid by these classes. Without such action being taken, it was feared that residential property owners would experience a significant increase in taxes stemming from court-mandated adoption of full value assessment.

Property tax reform—any fundamental change in the existing administration of the system—would involve, at a minimum, assessment and exemption reforms. Although the 1981 Real Property Tax Law makes state-wide adoption of full value assessment less likely, the implementation of such a standard would result in uncomplicated comparisons of assessments and a simple distribution of the tax burden among different types of property. A thorough revision of statutory tax exemptions would prevent further shifts in tax burden to taxable property and arrest further pressures on constitutional tax and debt limits.

More radical reforms have been suggested. Some public finance experts argue that exemptions granted on the basis of need should be abolished and replaced with state aid payments. Another has been the adoption of a state-wide property tax to fund education and possibly other services. Still another suggestion is property tax base sharing in metropolitan areas, as in Minneapolis. A further suggestion, dating back to Henry

George, is site (land) value taxation. The current property tax on both land and improvements would be replaced by a tax on the value of land only. The major problem of the land tax is to find a court-approved system of land value assessment and to implement such a system without widespread disruption of the governmental process.

NOTES

1. U.S. Bureau of the Census, *Government Finances in 1979-1980,* Table 27, p. 95; *Governmental Finances in 1960,* Table 22, p. 37.

2. New York State Department of State, *Local Government Handbook,* Albany, 1982, p. 169.

3. New York State Board of Equalization and Assessment, *Reassessment and Your Property Tax,* Albany, 1980, pp. 4-5.

4. League of Women Voters of New York State, *Toward An Evaluation of the Property Tax System in New York State,* Albany, 1979, pp. 88-89.

5. New York State Board of Equalization and Assessment, *The New New York State Board of Equalization and Assessment and Your Property Taxes,* Albany, 1981, pp. 19-23.

6. Peter A. Wissel, New York State Board of Equalization and Assessment.

7. New York State Board of Equalization and Assessment, *The Facts About Property Assessment,* Albany, 1981.

8. "Highlights of New York State Law on Property Tax Assessment," *New York Times,* December 4, 1981, p. B6.

9. New York State Board of Equalization and Assessment, *Property Tax Exemptions in New York State,* paper presented at the 47th International Conference on Assessment Administration, October 1981, pp. 7-9.

10. New York State Board of Equalization and Assessment, *Property Tax Exemptions in New York State,* p. 10.

11. Temporary Commission on State and Local Finances, *Volume 2, The Real Property Tax,* p. 37.

12. New York State Board of Equalization and Assessment, *Property Tax Exemption,* p. 4.

13. New York State Board of Equalization and Assessment, *Property Tax Exemptions,* p. 3.

14. New York State Board of Equalization and Assessment, *Taxation at the Constitutional Limit: A Status Report on Real Property Taxes in New York State, 1975-1982,* Albany, 1983, p. 11.

15. *Ibid.,* p. 26.

16. League of Women Voters, *op. cit.,* p. 13.

17. *Ibid.*, p. 9.

18. Temporary State Commission on State and Local Finances, *Volume 2, The Real Property Tax,* pp. 58–59.

19. Steven D. Gold, *Property Tax Relief,* Lexington, Massachusetts: Lexington Books, 1979, p. 1.

20. New York State Board of Equalization and Assessment, *New York State Real Property Tax Circuit Breaker Relief,* Albany, 1979, p. 3.

21. League of Women Voters, *op. cit.,* p. 106.

Hard Times Come to Campus

by

Henry Steck

Henry Steck is Professor of Political Science at the State University College at Cortland, New York.
He has taught at Vassar College and was Visiting Professor of Political Science at the University of British Columbia.

EDITORS' NOTE: *One of the greatest achievements of the expansive Rockefeller years was the creation of the State University of New York system alongside the City University of New York and the many private colleges and universities of the Empire State. As hard times have come to New York, hard times have necessarily come to higher education. The future of SUNY and the other systems is evaluated in this chapter.*

HENRY STECK

As New York's new Governor, Mario Cuomo, pieced together his first budget in an atmosphere of near financial crisis in early 1983, the State's colleges and universities awaited the impending budget debate with an unusual mixture of anxiety and hope. With a massive $1.8 billion budget deficit facing the state, it was certain that severe austerities would be imposed on education spending. But there was cause for some optimism as well. On private college campuses, Cuomo was remembered as a private school graduate and the president of the St. John's alumni association. On the public college campuses, he was seen as a liberal with a commitment to an active role for government and to public education. He had, moreover, the powerful teachers' unions to thank for the support that, against all predictions, had helped put him in the Executive Mansion. Cuomo would not—could not—turn his back on his friends. Sacrifice, yes, everyone knew that, but surely it would not be "all that bad".

Yet when the budget was unveiled, it was "that bad" and worse, especially for public higher education. Indeed, the ax fell hardest, it seemed, on the State University of New York (SUNY).[1] So deep were the cuts planned for SUNY's 32 campuses that Albany headlines soon announced "SUNY Trustees Warn Cuts May Force Some Closings." For the City University (CUNY), the news was almost as bad. Even New York's private schools had reason for uneasiness: despite a modest increase in aid, the budget ignored their more pressing difficulties. It was a bad budget for higher education.

To some, the budget was a fiscal Pearl Harbor. More detached observers saw it as conclusive evidence that the politics of scarcity had displaced the politics of growth. A strange jargon that spoke of cutback management, retrenchment, downsizing, productivity, and privatization signaled the new approach to public policy. "How to make do with less" replaced "what more can we do" as the task facing educational planners. Not even a liberal Governor could ignore a $1.8 billion deficit.

In the tense weeks that followed, thousands of careers, scores of academic programs, countless student budgets, and all the intangible qualities of academic life were placed at risk. By the eve of Passover and the start of Easter, crisis-induced lobbying, desperate bargaining, and emergency planning had spared SUNY/CUNY the worst. Whether they would experience the joy of resurrection was problematic. "Restoration" of proposed cuts did not—could not—mean business as usual.

The 1983 budget battle crystalized policy choices: that much was certain. Was New York to continue supporting higher education at the same levels it had over the previous twenty years? Was the state drawing back on its commitment to public higher education? Was it failing to meet the needs of private colleges and universities? Was a new balance in the making that would readjust state support between the State University, the City University, and the private sector? Were students and their families to bear a larger share of college costs, as a result of higher tuition and dorm fees, just as federal student aid was shrinking? These questions were troubling enough. But the events of February–March raised as many questions about the decisional process as it did about the substance of policy. During Hugh Carey's eight years in office (1974–1982), the fate of higher education policy seemed to depend on the vagaries of *sub rosa* decremental budgeting by the division of the budget. Would this now continue under the new governor or would public debate come into play? How open was the process? Had a choice been made long before February 1, 1983 to redefine New York's commitment to higher education generally and to public higher education in particular?

Beyond questions of policy and process, moreover, lay troubling questions of politics. A healthy rivalry had always existed between the public and private sectors, but as times grew hard the tensions that simmered beneath the surface began to break into the open. A new kind of education politics appeared in the making as claimants who once cooperated in enlarging public support, now competed for scarce resources in a contracting educational market. At the heart of the policy, process, and politics lay SUNY's massive budget. We can gain some insight into this complex subject, then, by looking at the course of SUNY's budget curve during the 1970s.

The Political Environment of Higher Education Policy

Although mass public higher education has been traditional in the American west, its role in the east was historically minor. In New York, where some of the oldest, most prestigious universities in the nation are found, higher education was the preserve of privately supported institutions. Except for the municipal colleges of New York City, the private schools catered chiefly to the very bright, the well-to-do, or those seeking a church-sponsored college. In the post-war years, however, pressure grew for expanding educational opportunities and for making college accessible to those from limited economic backgrounds. With the creation of a state university in 1948, New York took a tentative step toward building a comprehensive accessible system of public higher education. It was not until the 1960s that the State delivered on this early promise. During the ebullient Rockefeller take-off years, SUNY grew by non-incremental leaps and bounds while a system of support, known as Bundy Aid, poured millions into the private sector. At the same time, the state created a need-based tuition assistance program (TAP) for students. There seemed to be no end to resources.

By 1983, higher education in New York State sported a sizeable price tag. Overall public support for all forms of higher education exceeded $2 billion, third in the nation behind California and Texas, and enrollments reached one million. If, compared to other states, New York's generosity did not always score well—eighteenth in terms of per capita appropriations and thirtieth when measured by appropriations per $1,000 of personal incomes—its support was strong. Even in the period of austerity, 1981-1983, New York was ranked sixteenth in terms of percent increase in appropriations. Generating nearly $7 billion of both public and private funds, then, higher education in the Empire State was clearly a big business.

Not surprisingly, it is also the object of big politics. Outsiders might assume that higher education policy is the result of quiet, reasoned, and slightly stuffy discussion. In reality, it is a tough, gritty, and contentious arena of politics, complete with its own unique swirl of bureaucratic interests (centered in the Division of the Budget), institutional needs of a public and private sector, organized interest groups, and mobilized social constituencies. At the center of higher education politics in New York and enmeshed in a complex decisional network lies the rising level of SUNY's budgetary needs and the growing tension between New York's public and private system of education.

The State University of New York

Only thirty-five years after its inauspicious founding, SUNY has grown from a scatter of teachers' and specialized colleges into one of the world's largest education systems with an enrollment approaching 200,000 and a budget approaching $1.4 billion. SUNY is unavoidably a significant factor in Albany's political calculations. To the Division of the Budget, with its eye on the bottom line, SUNY no doubt appears to be a never-sated empire whose claims for resources require constant disciplining. To the governor, SUNY, which is both part of the executive and, politically at least, independent of it, must be handled with special care. To the state legislature, however, SUNY provides both educational opportunities for an expanding number of constituents and an attractive form of local assistance for hardpressed communities. With a SUNY unit in virtually every county, SUNY has found shelter under the protective wing of the legislature.

Figure 11. Present Structure of Postsecondary Education in New York State*

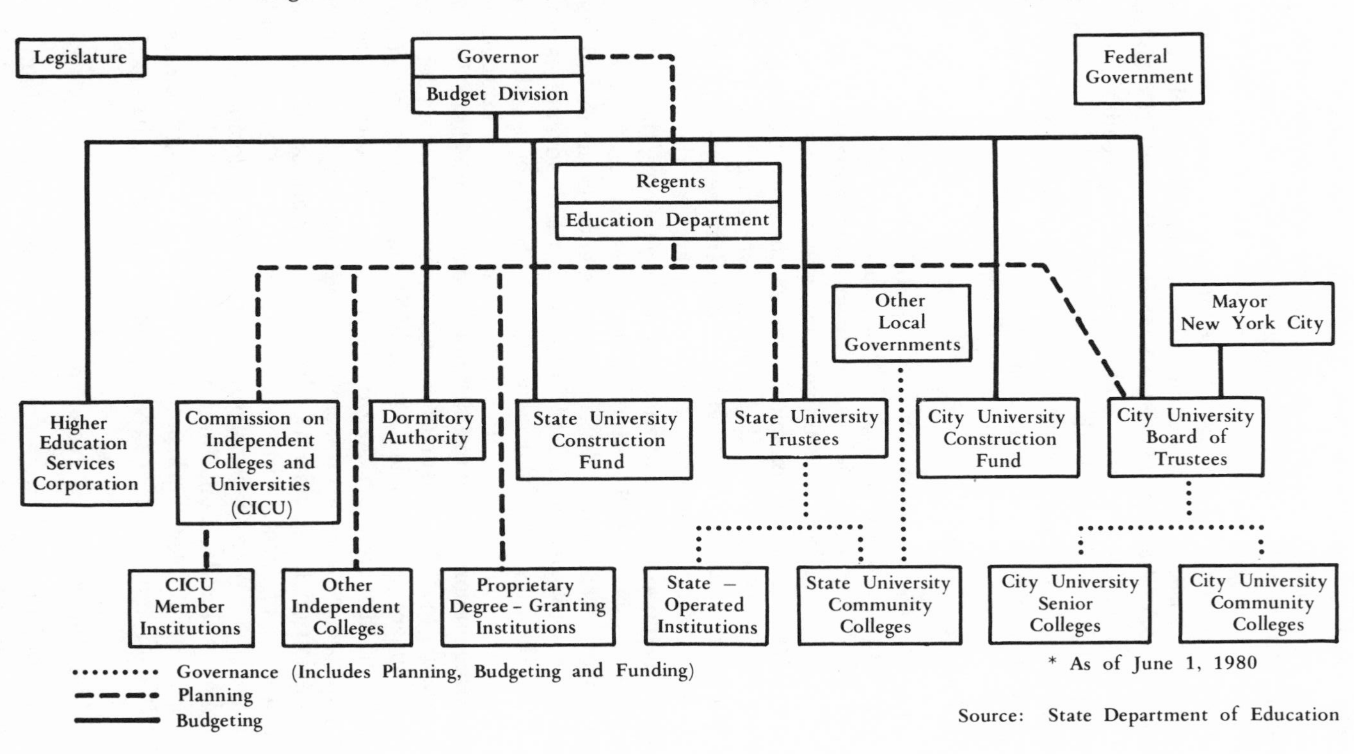

* As of June 1, 1980

Source: State Department of Education

This support is not exclusively the result of political altruism. It was created and nurtured by an amorphous but skillfully led SUNY-based coalition consisting of SUNY's student association, its faculty and staff organized through the faculty union, a lobby of officials composed informally of the trustees, the chancellor, and campus presidents; civic and business leaders from communities surrounding SUNY units; parents of SUNY students; and SUNY alumni. With SUNY budgets the increasingly visible focus of budget politics, the coalition makes its presence felt—each year with more polish and know-how—as SAVE SUNY lobbyists annually swarm over the legislative chambers. By the early 1980s, SUNY had come of age politically as well as academically.

The Private Sector

Long-established, ivy covered, and justly proud of its historic role, the private sector consisting of about 115 institutions, continues to exceed SUNY in overall levels of enrollments (excluding two-year schools), in diversity of colleges and universities, and in many cases, academic prestige. Despite its preeminence, however, the private sector has grown steadily nervous about the threat it perceives from SUNY. As SUNY expanded in enrollments, programs, and campuses, as inflation drove costs and tuitions upward in a dizzying spiral, as the baby-boom ran its course, and as student financial aid became scarce, the private sector began to display a well-justified concern for its health and, as some small institutions went under, its very existence. Some institutions had to scramble to survive and SUNY's competitive advantages only intensified the pressure. Even before the 1970s, of course, the state had provided assistance for private schools. Bundy Aid, for example, soared from $25.5 million in 1969 to $92.4 million eleven years later. In addition, the formula for TAP meant that the average TAP award for a private school student was double that of a SUNY Student. Such aid was insufficient, however, and the private sector was inexorably drawn into the political arena as a measure of self-defense. Its lobbying arm, the Commission on Independent Colleges and Universities (CICU), gained a reputation in Albany circles as as potent a lobby as any fielded by SUNY-CUNY. With the legislature overwhelmingly composed of private school alumni and alumnae and with its trustees and alumni occupying key positions in New York political, professional, and business circles, CICU could draw on impressive resources in arguing its case.

The City University of New York

The City University swept onto this already crowded Albany political stage in the late 1970s. Despite its distinguished, even mythical, past,

CUNY had not been well treated by the resource-scarce 1970s. Traumatic social change, turbulent enrollment shifts, and rapid institutional expansion left CUNY in a battered state. The fiscal crisis of 1974–1975 administered the final coup de grace. Clearly, the city could no longer afford to keep up with other municipalities in funding a comprehensive university.[3] To relieve the city of the burden, the state agreed to assume full financial responsibility for CUNY in 1979 and for its nearly 100,000 students, ten colleges, and $350 million-plus budget. For skeptical upstaters, this "takeover" was regarded as an expedient back-door bailout of the City and its profligate big-city ways. But whatever the reality, the state could not turn its back on this member of New York's higher education community.

Neither SUNY nor the private sector could have greeted this new partner-competitor without deeply ambivalent feelings. Here was a new factor in the political equation and a new drain on scarce resources. While CUNY might be regarded as the new kid on the block, it had an enormously significant card to play: the role of New York City in state politics. Through whatever channel—the mayor, the unions, the massive bloc of city assemblymen, the financial community—the city was in a position to look after its own. Junior partner, perhaps, but CUNY was no 98-lb. political weakling.

In sum, Albany decision-makers face the task of resolving complex policy choices regarding higher education, e.g., balancing access against quality in SUNY, or public with private overall, in a highly politicized environment. Legislators are able to deflect pressure by satisfying all comers in classic logrolling style or by passing unpalatable decisions on to the Governor. Executive decision-makers are less able to sidestep the dilemmas confronting them. The Constitutional requirement for a balanced budget, for example, is simply one action-forcing choice-limiting constraint. For DOB, whose concern was budget first, and for a Governor intent on avoiding fiscal or political default, the easiest course was to take aim on the fattest target of them all: SUNY's billion dollar budget.

No More Wine and Roses

The 1960s were a prosperous time for higher education in New York. The State responded to the needs of an expanding pool of college-bound New Yorkers with increased appropriations that went to both the public and private sector. Expansion of educational opportunities went hand-in-hand with balanced support for both sectors. During the 1960s SUNY was well into its take-off period and by all measures—enrollments, faculty-student ratios, allocation of resources to instruction, quality of instruction and research, new campus construction, prestige—it was on the brink of becoming a major university with a record of excellence and access. Nor were SUNY's successes purchased at the expense of its private sector counterparts. The Bundy Aid formula was enriched four times between 1969 and 1979 and the level of aid more than doubled from 1969-1974 alone. Average TAP support for private school students more than quadrupled from 1973-1978.[4]

Even in the best of times, this growth curve would have leveled off, as is the case with most new agencies or programs. But the 1970s were not the best of times. When Hugh Carey began his administration with the words "the days of wine and roses are over", he left no doubt that the Rockefeller days were a thing of the past. Throughout the state, the lights began to go off.

Nowhere were campuses darker than in the public sector. The new austerity struck SUNY and CUNY especially hard. CUNY's troubles—it was the only City agency to close its door in 1976—can be attributed to the unique impact of the fiscal crisis, but no such explanation accounts for the steady erosion of support for SUNY that resulted from successive state budgets. While the Governor continued to speak publicly of the State's commitment to SUNY, the DOB was pursuing a decremental strategy whose accumulated consequences were soon to undermine SUNY's quality while narrowing its philosophy of access. "Budget clerks," one SUNY college president put it angrily in a private moment, "they make all the decisions."

Simple figures suggest the extent of the reduced priority. From 1974 to 1983, over 3,000 positions were cut from the SUNY staff, resulting in a sharp increase in student-faculty ratios, the prime measure of instructional quality (see Figure 12). In constant dollars, state expenditures per student fell by 18% or half of what would have kept spending equal to the inflation rate.[5] The withering of support is also revealed in the decline of budget support per student credit hour (see Figure 13). Contrary to all predictions, enrollments stabilized and even began to rise again, but as funding levels sank, resources were diverted from academic programs to meet fixed operating costs.[6] Increasingly, the gap between the University's definition of its needs and DOB's definition of those same needs grew wider until in 1983 it reached $80 million. Over the eight-year period, as SUNY's Chancellor pointed out, the University had suffered the equivalent in "hidden closing" of five of its four-year colleges or one of its university centers and one hospital center.[7]

At the same time, the basic philosophy that the University should be as accessible as possible to all without regard to economic or other barriers was compromised by a slow but erratic shift of more of the burden of SUNY funding from direct State appropriations to students

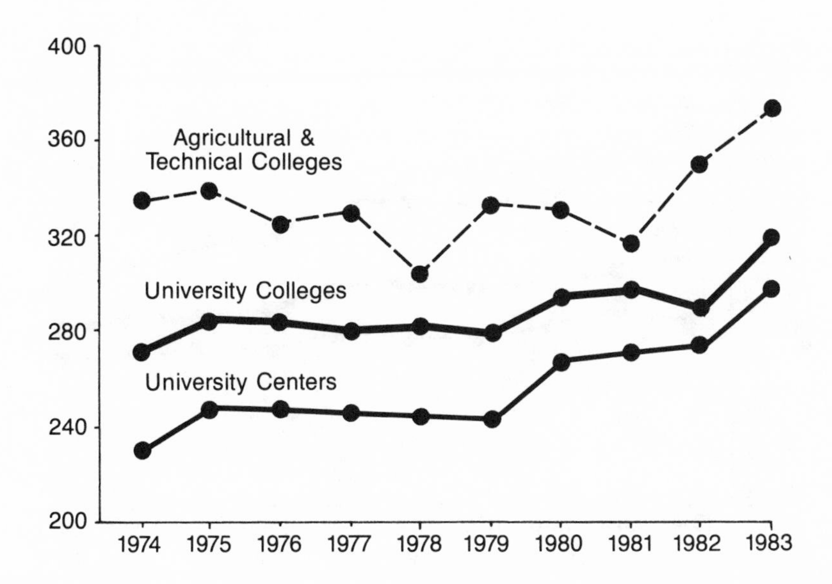

Figure 12

Source: State University of New York.

and other users. From 1975 to 1984, tuition rose by 10% and dorm fees by 115% as the State's share of SUNY shrank from 75% to a proposed 65%. The notion that public higher education was a public service and a public good similar to free elementary and secondary education was replaced by the Proposition 13 principle that the cost of public goods and services be shifted from the general taxpayer onto the particular user. This philosophical change also entailed the assumption that public higher education was to be regarded as a private benefit.

Looking at these parallel trends, SUNY officials were compelled to ask whether the State was intent on reducing the size, redefining the mission, and weakening the quality of the University. State officials were always quick to deny that any fundamental change was being called for and they called on SUNY for greater productivity and efficiency. Nonetheless, it was undeniable that state priorities were changing

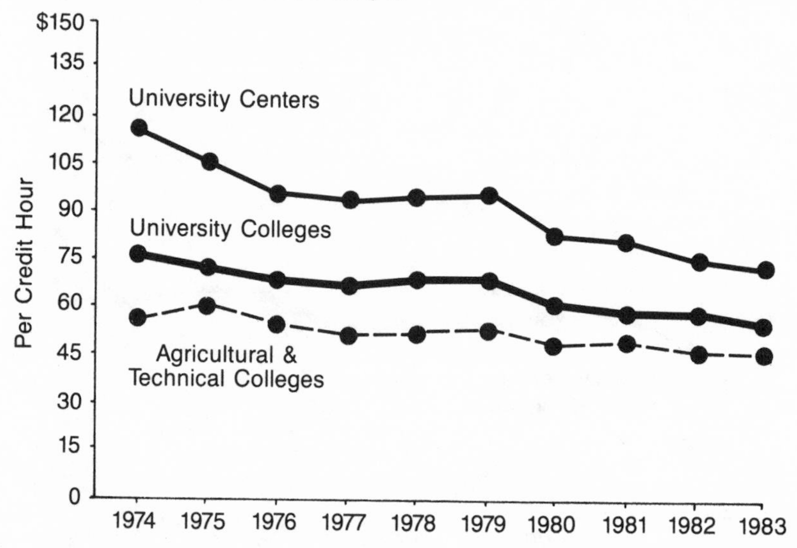

Figure 13

Source: State University of New York.

in reality whatever the subjective perceptions of budget officials. From 1975–1976 through 1982–1983, SUNY's share of the general fund of the state budget dropped from 5.4% to 4.7%, a short-fall equivalent to $150 million.[8] The inescapable conclusion to be drawn from nearly a decade of decremental budgeting, whether direct or indirect, was that the university would have to do with less and that students and others would have to pay more for less.

Equity on the Public-Private Front

The fiscal politics of higher education involve yet another dimension. It might be argued that times being what they are the taxpayers of the state could not be expected to continue to support SUNY and CUNY at the levels they had grown to. This argument would carry some force were it not that support for the private sector by comparison remained so steady that in the eyes of some the pattern of higher education policy began to reveal a subtle shift in the direction of the private sector. In absolute terms, of course, there is no equality: support for the public sector is roughly ten times that for the private. In considering the question of equity, therefore, the emphasis must be on "relative." The matter of fair shares is a complex one that is approached in part by tracing the changing proportions of budgetary support.

Aid to private institutions involves a fundamental policy choice, and since the 1960s the State has been unwavering in its decision that the public interest is served by a healthy private sector parallel to the State University. New York currently provides more support—whether through straight subsidy or student aid—to the private sector than any other state. But a commitment to the diversity, integrity, traditions, and value of private higher education could not obscure the tilt toward the private sector that emerged in the 1970s: State operations spending has outstripped spending on SUNY, SUNY is receiving a lesser share of the state budget, and state spending on the private sector has run ahead of expenditures on SUNY.

That the needs of the private sector are as great as SUNY-CUNY's in a period of cost inflation, economic recession, and demographic downturns has not prevented a rising, and increasingly angry, debate between the two sectors. Public colleges may bear the brunt of the cutbacks resulting from federal and state cuts,[9] but that has not stilled complaints that SUNY is a subsidized competitor enjoying unfair advantages in the educational marketplace. Nor has the apparent immunity of Bundy Aid from the budgeteer's ax dissuaded CICU spokesmen from protesting bitterly about a state "policy that closes its eyes to the needs of the independent sector." [10]

The growing bitterness that has characterized the inter-sectoral debate in the last several years suggests in part that SUNY, CUNY, and the private institutions are competing with one another for a fixed sum of funds. Policy-makers shrink from this generalization. Logrolling, not zero-sum distribution, is the preferred strategy and legislators routinely urge both sides to cooperate in the interests of a common good. That view, however, ignores the fact that other areas of policy, aside from fiscal support, are involved. The question of tuition, as one example, is very much a contested issue. Whereas SUNY would prefer to keep tuition as low as possible in order to maximize access for students, private school spokesmen have argued for a SUNY tuition policy that would link SUNY tuition to the actual cost of education. Another is the construction of a new engineering school by SUNY. These issues have been resolved, at least for the moment. The engineering school will be built, and the 1983–1984 budget quietly formalized the decision on tuition that had been implicit in a decade of budgetary decisions.

Rather than setting tuition so as to minimize the cost to the student, future tuition would be set in a way that would "help preserve balance among the State's sectors of higher education by requiring public institution tuition to increase with costs in a fashion more consistent with practice in the independent sector." [11] As dollars grow scarce in a Hobbesian world, it is likely not only that state policy will continue to downsize and privatize the public institutions, but also to strengthen the private institutions by greater levels of direct and indirect aid of various kinds.

The Political Economy of Public Higher Education

For the past several years, observers of SUNY's travails have pointed out that SUNY is not alone among public universities in suffering from the national trend toward a reduced public sector. Compared to some other states, some have argued, SUNY has gotten off rather lightly. Moreover, there are good reasons for a period of belt-tightening. Skepticism about the efficiency of an over-built system, the inevitable levelling off of budgets after a rapid growth period, declining enrollment projections into the 1990s, and the State's continuing fiscal problems are routinely cataloged as the explanation for the erosion in support for public higher education.

There can be no question that these elements enter into the political and fiscal equation. But they do not fully explain the differential decline in SUNY funding compared to overall levels of state expenditures nor do they explain the pattern, revealed in recent budgets, of shifting priorities in the direction of the private sector. Without discounting the shift to more conservative politics generally, it appears that the Executive has put into motion a coherent fiscal policy that has as its purpose the restructuring of New York's higher education policy. As the Stephens Report concluded:

> In 1975, the State University of New York was a public higher education system committed to providing access to a quality education. In 1982 SUNY is a higher education system being forced to chose between access and quality education.

What has made this change possible in a political sense? To an extent the tactics used, which may not be fully apparent even to the decision-makers, has eased the political path. The policy shift has been executed through the dense encoded language of the Budget and the detailed budget bulletins that routinely flow from DOB to state agencies. It has been made in small steps free from focused public discussion.

But running across this and other considerations is a fairly hard-nosed calculation. For thousands of New York families, a college degree is still a necessary certificate for entry into the middle-class labor market, whatever the quality of the education represented by the degree itself. From this perspective, a SUNY and CUNY degree, however diminished in quality, remains a good bargain. Consumer demand for it remains strong. As the cost of a college education continues to rise, students will continue—no matter what—to seek entry into SUNY schools. As economists put it, demand will continue to appear relatively inelastic as long as the price (though increasing) remains well below that of competitors. It makes good business sense, therefore, for DOB to lower overall state costs, first, by raising the price to the customer at a rate that holds the price of SUNY/CUNY below that of, say, a $8,000 a year competitor, and, secondly, by decreasing the cost of production (i.e., the cost to the producer) by lowering quality. It is a solution that pleases few of the participants: the SUNY/CUNY coalitions grow dissatisfied as both access (tuition costs) and quality (e.g., faculty-student ratios) are sacrificed; the private sector is not appeased because SUNY continues to undercut it in a shrinking marketplace. But it is a compromise that adjusts the public-private balance somewhat, reduces state expenditures, and keeps public higher education in business.

It is, finally, a policy that also avoids informed public debate on the key questions facing both the public and the policy-makers: What should be the proper balance between public and private education? Is public education to be regarded as a public good or a subsidized private benefit? What share of educational costs should students and their families bear? How big, how good, and how diverse should a public university be? What should be the balance between access as a social value and quality as an intellectual value? As New Yorkers face the late 1980s and the uncertain 1990s, it is unlikely that these questions will disappear from the public agenda or that the politics they generate will grow less heated.

Postscript: The Politics of Austerity in a Time of Prosperity

For readers of the October 12, 1987 *New Yorker,* the charming "Talk of the Town" description of Mario Cuomo's visit to the Soviet Union was just a further example of the governor's flirtation with presidential politics.[13] But one passage in particular no doubt caught the attention of faculty and administrators on the campuses of CUNY and SUNY. "I'm glad to say," the governor observed, "that we have about two thousand students studying Russian at New York's state and city universities, and eighteen of them are actually over here now. I'm going to ask both SUNY and CUNY to increase their studies of glastnost and perestroika."

Glastnost, indeed, college deans must have said to themselves, but who is going to foot the bill?

From one perspective, Cuomo's Moscow visit was a symbol of the changes that swept New York State since 1983. In four years, Cuomo himself was transformed from an unknown hometown boy into the dominant political force in the state and a major national figure. In those years also, the state's fiscal climate had changed for the better. The bleak days of 1983, when the state faced a $1.8 billion deficit, were nearly forgotten. When the legislature convened in January 1987, two months after Cuomo's historic landslide reelection, the state was in the final year of a massive three-year tax cut program, and politicians competed with each other in debating how much of the state's surplus should be returned to the taxpayers. By July it had adopted the largest tax cut in the State's history and had turned the $1.67 billion Federal tax windfall back to the taxpayers. Without question, then, the fiscal crisis of 1983 was over.

Despite the improved financial climate, the politics of austerity had not ended for the state's universities. It was all well and good for the governor to make pronouncements about what SUNY and CUNY should do—contribute to the state's economic revival, assist disadvantaged and minority students, become a world-class research institution—but when it came to budgeting, the Division of the Budget's "expenditure equation" that governed the state's fiscal strategy defined SUNY/CUNY's budgetary and academic options as well. That equation provided that "new or expanded needs cannot be met without redirecting resources and improving efficiency."[14] In plain English, this meant, as Mario Cuomo repeatedly told his campus critics, if you want more money for the universities, tell me where to take the money from.

Cuomo made fiscal responsibility, stimulation of the private sector, and tax-cutting the heart of his budgeting philosophy, and this gave his administration a conservative tone that muted the social liberalism embodied in his idea of the "family" of New York. His liberalism was not based on a redistributivist philosophy that a policy of accessible, quality, low-cost public higher education seemed to entail. For the Cuomo Administration, as for the Carey Administration, budgeting was a zero-sum affair.

Throughout the Cuomo years, higher education budgets were kept tight as Cuomo strove to impose an expenditure cap on state spending. Each successive budget contained enough budget wizardry to raise the possibility of severe cuts, layoffs, austerity, and set-backs to the missions of CUNY and SUNY.[15] Although the legislature repeatedly came to the rescue of the universities, and fought recurrent pitched battles with the executive branch over higher education budgets, it could do little more than modify the budget at the margin. It could not provide what the universities claimed they needed most: a substantial infusion of fresh support.

"Restoration" as much as "improvement" or "innovation" were the constant themes of SUNY's budget requests. But Cuomo's fiscal strategy permitted little recovery and little advance. Standard indicators reflected bad news. Between the periods 1975-76 and 1987-88, for example, staffing fell by 10 percent while enrollment remained steady.[16] Faculty staffing fell 9.3 percent below the levels indicated by standard staffing models, and it was a struggle simply to meet inflationary costs of doing business.[17] At a time (1986) when, in response to the recommendations of the Independent Commission Report, SUNY did undertake an ambitious five-year $80 million "graduate research initiative," it faced proposed executive budgets that threatened significant personnel cuts.[18] Although the cuts were avoided in the final appropriations, a result of legislative-executive compromise and heavy lobbying, the experience did little to lift the fiscal cloud from the university.

Still, the Sisyphean energy of SUNY seemed inexhaustible. As the governor and the legislature prepared for the 1988-89 budgetary battles, the university proposed a costly five-year undergraduate initiative that was slated to cost $17 million in the first year alone. Within days of its publication, the stock market fell and, as the office of the new Assembly Speaker, Mel Miller, was quick to point out, Black Monday was just something that the university would have to take into account.[19] In short policy makers were committed to a vigorous, contributing public-private sector of higher education; but the budget implications and dilemmas arising from that commitment were no more resolved than they had been in 1983.

NOTES

1. The State University of New York is a multi-institutional complex. In this case study all references to SUNY will refer only to the state-operated portions and will exclude the two-year community colleges. The state-operated units include: university centers, university colleges, health science centers, some specialized colleges, and agricultural-technical colleges.

2. No single figure adequately conveys enrollment. One must distinguish between headcount enrollments and other forms of enrollment. For many years, the State used the concept of "full-time equivalent", a way of standarizing enrollments that takes both full-time and part-time students into account. More

recently, the Division of the Budget imposed a new standardizing measure known as "equated students" and this measure deflates enrollments. When enrollment figures are used for budgeting, it matters which formula is used. Thus, in 1981, the actual headcount was 198,150; the full-time equivalent enrollment was 169,318; and the full-time equated was 159,255. The Regents refer to "degree-credit enrollment" and show a 1979 enrollment for independent institutions of 392,704. All figures include full-time, part-time and graduate students. For SUNY figures, see SUNY, *Formal Budget Hearing* (1979). For Regents figures, see, State Education Department, *Regents Statewide Plan for the Development of Postsecondary Education (1980), p. 5.*

3. Educational Priorities Panel, *Budgeting and Resource Allocation at the City University of New York, New York, 1980,* p. 6.

4. State Education Department, *New York State Bundy Aid Program 1969–1981 (1981). New York State Statistical Yearbook* (1979–1980 Edition).

5. Willis H. Stephens, et. al. (Ranking Minority Member, Assembly Ways and Means Committee and Staff), *SUNY: 1975–1982. A Budgetary Battle of Access Versus Quality* 1982, p. 2. (Hereinafter, Stephens Report)

6. State University of New York, *Data Resource Book,* 1982–1983 (1982)

7. Testimony of Dr. Clifton R. Wharton, Jr., Chancellor, State University of New York, Before a Joint Hearing of the Assembly Ways and Means Committee, Senate Finance Committee.

8. Stephens Report, p. 2.

9. *Chronicle of Higher Education* May 25, 1983, p. 1. Rochelle L. Stanfield, "Public, Not Private, Colleges Bearing The Brunt of Federal Aid Cutbacks", *National Journal,* December 4, 1982, p. 2072.

10. Testimony by James C. Finaly, S.J., Chairman of the Commission on Independent Colleges and Universities, Before the Higher Education Committee, New York State Assembly, May 6, 1983.

11. "Expansion of SUNY Inappropriate, Wasteful", Statement of Presidents of 40 Independent Colleges and Universities, January 30, 1983. *1983–1984 Executive Budget* for the statement on tuition policy.

12. Stephens Report, p. 5. It should be noted that, as the Stephens Report also makes clear, that a shift within SUNY is also taking place from "the traditional providers of a SUNY education to the highly specialized, high cost, and high revenue generating health science" centers and programs.

13. *New Yorker,* October 12, 1987, p. 36.

14. Memo from R. Wayne Diesel, director of the Budget, to Department and Agency Heads, August 27, 1987.

15. It must be understood that budgetary levels were rarely cut in absolute terms. But the normal increases because of inflation, salary, additional students, and the like, often fell short of what was needed. Budgeting formulae or the requirement that the universities raise additional revenues often had the effects of cuts. Thus, in the 1987-88 proposed Executive budget, SUNY is required to "save" $17 million of its appropriation; according to university officials, this would force a reduction equivalent to 450 positions. Additionally, insufficient funding was proposed to cover utility costs or inflationary increases.

16. State University of New York, *1987-1988 Budget Request,* p. 13, and *1988-*

1989 Budget Request, pp. 15 and 100. Between the periods 1983-84 and 1987-88 there was roughly a 3 percent improvement.

17. *1988-1989 Budget Request,* p. 17.

18. According to the *Chronicle of Higher Education* (November 4, 1987), New York appropriated $2,936,954 for higher education in 1987-88. But the overall New York State budget for higher education is so complex that it is misleading to try to describe it with a single figure. Support is provided not only for the state-operated campuses of SUNY and CUNY, but also for several statutory colleges, which are part of various private institutions, e.g., Cornell. Unrestricted subsidies are also provided for over 100 private colleges and universities: in fiscal year 1988, this "Bundy Aid" was approximately $112.4 million. Community colleges receive state aid, but the bulk of their support derives from county governments: SUNY and CUNY community colleges received $295 million in state aid. In addition, substantial student aid is provided under several programs: in 1985-86, $380.5 million of TAP/STAP aid was expended. Budgets for CUNY and SUNY are made up of income as well as appropriations, so that an increase in the total budget figure may not fully convey—e.g., may understate— the magnitude of increase of state dollars. In 1987-88, the SUNY budget contained $1.5 billion in *appropriations* and $1.0 billion in tuition payments and other income. CUNY received $535 million in state appropriations. See also, 1987-1988 *Executive Budget* and 1988-1989 *SUNY Budget Request.*

19. "SUNY Expected to Seek $150 Million for Undergraduate Effort," *New York Times,* October 26, 1987.

The Future of New York: Excerpts from Project 2000

by

Glenn Yago, Charlene S. Seifert, Diane M. Fischer, and Sen-Yuan Wu

The authors are members of the Economic Research Bureau at the State University of New York at Stony Brook.

EDITORS' NOTE: *This chapter appeared in longer form in the Project 2000 series published by the Nelson A. Rockefeller Institute of Government in 1986. The authors describe several recent economic trends in New York State—noting that the immediate past has not been kind to New York—and they advocate ways to improve the state's economic prospects.*

We are not accustomed to thinking of New York State as a developing country, much less as a competitive enterprise that is badly in need of turnaround management and a winning strategy for economic growth. But the main theme of this chapter is that we must create opportunities for innovation and growth. Demographic, international, and technological circumstances are challenging state policy makers and businesses responsible for optimizing economic opportunity, employment, and productivity. New York has long been a successful competitor and a wellspring of innovation and growth. But as this chapter indicates, the halcyon days may be over.

Since the 1970s, New York's growth rates of real income, employment, and population have declined relative to the nation's. An increasing share of the population lives in poverty and long-term unemployment, while highly skilled workers and technology firms are emigrating. Although the service sector is vigorous, it has yet to compensate for the sharp decline in manufacturing. Service-sector job growth is expected to ebb in the future, and its income-generating capacity is being questioned. New York receives far less than its share of business start-ups, and yet suffers more than its share of plant closings. Public investment is needed, but the tax base is loaded and growing slowly.

What factors are responsible for these trends? Some are purely cyclical, such as the last two recessions and the recently overvalued dollar. But there are disturbing signs that the conditions underlying New York's original economic success have been seriously eroded by fundamental structural changes.

This chapter suggests that New York needs a new economic development strategy to handle this challenge. Implementation requires additional analysis and planning, but the following are suggested as possible guidelines:

- New York's traditional approach, like those of other states, was an unwieldy package of tax subsidies, low cost financing, and other programs awarded to specific projects. Evidence of state benefits from these past passive programs is unclear. Similar subsidies are offered by competing states, yielding endless bidding wars and little value to the states or the nation.
- The issue is not whether New York should be deeply involved in economic development, since state and local government are the source of over one-half of all net investment in areas such as education, infrastructure, and power generation. The state can have a powerful impact on economic development and the competitive

strength of the private sector by better managing its own delivery of services. To gain a maximum impact for needed new targeted programs, the state should continue its initiative in coordinating its existing agencies, staffs, and programs that affect economic development.

- New York must continue to move beyond the passive subsidies and tax breaks of the past to develop value-based strategies for economic development. We must invest in ourselves for others to invest here—in literacy and skills, technologies, and plants for equipment. We require new community spirit among labor, management, and government with less "zero-sum" bargaining and more "positive-sum" cooperation. We cannot avoid declines of particular industries, but we can remake them to compete in new markets.

Recent initiatives from the executive and legislature reflect an emerging consensus for a new economic development strategy for the state, addressing many of the initiatives suggested in this chapter. These initiatives reflect an understanding of the structural problems of the state's economy and the need for major program initiatives, accompanied by better and more rational coordination of the economic development efforts.

Some of New York's structural problems have accumulated gradually, such as labor and capital costs, energy, housing, and taxes. Others are more recent, such as the impact of the federal budget and increased global competition. Some problems are industrially and regionally specific—industries like textiles, steel, and paper are undergoing shakeouts everywhere, but such shakeouts are concentrated in distressed regions.

Whatever the causes, the overall impact is clear. New York now faces an unparalleled challenge to its ability to compete for new investment, jobs, and income. The consequences of failing to cut the costs of doing business or to address structural problems are the costs of not doing business: growing poverty and economic decline.

While state government must operate within an environment of shifting structural changes in our economy, it must continue to aggressively respond to those challenges that threaten the state's economic well-being. Our future should not be imperiled by these problems or by poor private and public management. Without effective value-based strategies for capital, labor markets, and public-sector agencies, the downward structural trends outlined in this chapter will continue and will take the state down with them.

Regional Disparities in New York State

Patterns of structural change are repeated throughout the state, but its regions respond differently to the shifts. A picture of the state's economy cannot be painted with one brush, nor should policies be insensitive to these vast regional differences.

Leading other New York State regions in total manufacturing, New York City (particularly its outer boroughs) had a net loss of 106,270 jobs since 1975, accounting for a 20 percent decrease from the city's 1975 manufacturing base. Buffalo's net loss of manufacturing jobs (34,948) represented a 25 percent reduction. Relatively large gains occurred in Long Island, the Mid-Hudson region, and New York suburbs (35,978, 9,423, and 8,014, respectively), representing 25 percent, 17 percent, and 10 percent increases for those regions.

The boom areas in technology appear to be the New York suburbs, the Southern Tier around Binghamton, and Nassau-Suffolk. New York City, Syracuse, and the Mid-Hudson region fared the worst. Although overall job gain in technology-intensive industries peaked in 1979, subsequent years saw slower growth as high technology industries were booming nationally. Examining those industries that have been the fastest growing, the New York suburbs, Buffalo, and Rochester had the most growth.

With respect to output and employment, New York State will continue to lag behind the nation. Upstate is expected to outperform downstate in the next decade, in terms of output, employment, and productivity growth. Upstate's relatively poor economic performance during the last decade resulted from the sharp employment and output losses in Buffalo, combined with weak to moderate growth in the Albany-Schenectady-Troy and Syracuse-Utica-Rome regions.

New York City employment will increase slowly until 2000. The western suburbs will maintain employment growth, but may be constrained by the difficulty of drawing on the unskilled and semi-skilled labor pool from New York City. Long Island's economy (Nassau-Suffolk) will remain strong, but its rate of employment growth will decline 37.5 percent from the 1975 to 1984 period. Upstate employment gains will be below the national average but close to the level of national GNP growth (2.7 percent). All the upstate regions except Albany-Schenectady-Troy and Binghamton-Elmira should experience significant improvements in employment, yet the depressed outlook for Elmira clouds the future of that area. The lower Hudson Valley should show the highest level of growth in the next decade.

New York City's problems will continue to exceed those of the rest of the state. Sixty percent of the state's poor live in the city. The largest concentration of poor outside that region is on Long Island (144,000), even though that subregion's rate of poverty is relatively low (5.6 percent). Patterns of structural economic change are largely responsible for the variation in poverty rates. Poverty rates remain highest in those areas where the economic base has eroded. Buffalo, Syracuse, Utica-Rome, and Elmira have a high concentration of declining and trade sensitive industries.

Industries: Declining and Increasingly Vulnerable to Competition

The outlook for industry includes deindustrialization in older manufacturing, decreased international competitiveness, and unstable development in high technology. New York preceded the other forty-nine states in a long-term trend of manufacturing decline, and by 1968, as the industrial mix became more specialized, the state began to lose employment rapidly. Sixty-eight percent of the job loss between 1968 and 1985 occurred in the first seven years of that period.

A number of factors point to the shrinkage of New York's manufacturing base. During 1975 to 1984:

- Manufacturing declined as a share of New York employment from 20.8 percent to 17.6 percent.
- All categories of manufacturing employment declined, including production, professional and technical, and clerical.
- As New York's manufacturing declined both absolutely and relatively, so did its share of U.S. employment and employment growth.

Declining International Competitiveness

Trade imbalances in durable and nondurable consumer gods, as well as capital goods, have widened the gap between imports and exports (as a percent of U.S. spending) at a faster rate, especially since 1981. After allowing for business cycle changes and exchange rate fluctuations, trade performance decline is still attributable to structural changes in industries that impinge upon their competitiveness. Fifty percent of all basic capital equipment purchases and 75 percent of technology equipment purchases are imports. Our modest increases in capital spending over the past cyclical recovery helped capitalize and reindustrialize foreign industries.

The state's average trade-sensitive industry (one with a high or increasing level of import penetration) has declined by 18.4 percent since 1975, and by more than 32 percent between 1968 and 1984. Employment losses ranged from 2 percent to 63 percent in the same period. New York's trade-sensitive industries comprised 64 percent of dollar-related job loss in the state, compared with 58 percent nationwide.

In examining the New York Metropolitan Region, the Port Authority has found a close linkage between trade-related jobs in manufacturing, either as exports or end-state manufacturing of imports, to service-sector jobs. For each manufacturing job, twice as many service-related jobs are created.

New York's position in the global economy is unresolved and problematic. Many manufacturers have been hard hit by foreign imports, yet many trade, transportation, financial, and service jobs have been created by the increased activity of foreign firms in New York. Focusing on imports will not save New York firms in an era of increased global manufacturing interdependence.

Technology is Uneven and Insecure

High technology and its applications in industry will help increase productivity, competitiveness, and employment. Although New York remains a strong technology-based industrial sector, its relative performance has been eclipsed by other regions in recent years. In 1960, New York manufactured 33 percent of the nation's computer equipment and 56 percent of scientific instruments. By 1980, the state's relative share of those markets fell to 12.6 percent and 14.6 percent, respectively.

Overall, technology performance in New York has been uneven. Since 1968, 100,800 jobs (or 16.4 percent of technology-intensive industrial employment) were lost, and technology industries were responsible for 7.8 percent of manufacturing job loss since 1975. In those technology-intensive industries that have experienced increased employment nationwide, New York lost employment and competitiveness.

Newer industries with higher growth rates have done better than other technology-intensive industries with more established product lines. This pattern's consistency is, in our view, ominous. It seems that employment in the state increases in firms during the early stages of their research and development. As those technologies mature, however, those companies are more likely to pursue their expansion out of state. It appears that New York is subsidizing early industrial growth in new technologies, but then exporting those firms and jobs when the development stage evolves toward greater production.

Capital Markets Are Tight

The most influential element in New York's future may be capital markets, yet they elude most quantifiable descriptions. New York City, being the world's financial center, adds to this paradox, since national and international trends greatly influence New York firms' access to capital. Because so much capital flows through the state, barriers to capital markets need to be examined. The supply, availability, cost, and allocation of capital affect the number and location of business births and the number and quality of jobs they create.

Meeting the Economic Challenges

Unique among the fifty states, New York must compete on a world scale: its competitors are not only other cities, states, or regions, but other countries and continents. To reverse the past fifteen years of decline, New York's resurgence will depend upon advantages that sustain diversification, balance, and competition. If attuned to private-sector needs, state actions will enhance New York's prospects for prosperity.

From Franklin Roosevelt's New Deal to Ronald Reagan's New Federalism, traditional approaches toward state economic development have included fiscal incentives (tax, interest, subsidization, financial market stabilization) to facilitate business cycle adjustments, as well as direct subsidies and credits allowing individuals and firms to adapt to business cycle transitions. These approaches promised relatively rapid integration into a private sector oriented largely toward a domestic market. Regulatory adjustments, aggregate demand management, social safety net programs, extension of political rights, education and training, and business stimulation were measures that worked for New York as long as the United States dominated world markets, enjoyed regular increases in productivity, and maintained technological superiority.

Facing new strategic requirements to develop an internationally competitive state, New York confronts the limits of its traditional policies. The evidence is that universal tax incentives are ineffective and costly. Expensive direct subsidies and credit by states displace, rather than create, new investment and jobs. Privatization is limited by the cost and scale of public goods and services. Despite reports, we have not sold the Brooklyn Bridge nor found a corporate raider interested in acquiring a subway. Restricting or increasing the flow of funds through existing corporate markets and government agencies will not position the state in the new technologically driven world economy.

Until recently, states have been reluctant to conduct experiments in economic policy. They have relied instead upon the federal government's traditional regulatory and taxation policies to accommodate market cycles, options which no longer exist.

States have tried to attract branch plants of large manufacturing firms through infrastructure development, tax breaks, preferential financing techniques, and regulatory relief. At best, states have achieved short-run and temporary advantages, since bidding by other states neutralizes their ameliorative effects. Some interventions and regulatory relief measures, intended to promote economic growth, actually inhibit aggregate demand and reduce industrial activity. A comparative assessment of state measures reveals the following:

- Direct subsidies, tax incentives and expenditures, and industrial at-

traction programs have no effect, but are perhaps needed to compete with other states.
- Post-secondary education support and job training (as it currently exists) do not raise wage levels or increase job opportunities for dislocated or hard-core unemployed workers.
- Right-to-work laws, restrictions on unemployment insurance, and regulatory relief depress wages, income, and aggregate demand, and increase federal and state social costs.

The greatest barriers to economic growth are those affecting capital and labor markets. Since capital investment influences the extent to which businesses start, grow, decline, or thrive, and, therefore, how well the investment creates jobs, New York must enhance its capital markets in order to decrease the number of declining industries, encourage the expansion of existing firms, attract new businesses, and foster new ventures.

Recommended: Invest for Value

States are actually this country's social and economic laboratory: unemployment compensation, home mortgage finance, technological support in agriculture and transportation, aid to small business, tax revolts, and government reorganization were developed at the state level. National debates have obscured trends in state and regional economies, where an array of policies has been developed. Although federal legislation for urban enterprise zones and industries has floundered, most states currently have enterprise zones programs in place, with a number of small, publicly funded investment banks targeting capital toward both traditional and new technologies and industries.

New York's previous economic advantage hinged upon its superiority in technology and productivity. For 2000 and beyond, the state's contribution to economic value will be essential. New York can compete by enhancing the skills of its people and the competitiveness of its firms both domestically and internationally.

Past state economic policies largely ignored the distribution of economic activity and evaluation of performance by industrial sector, regions, or population group. Strategic targeting and coordination of state resources is needed to enhance the value of production and trade, appreciate the value of capital stock, facilitate technology transfer, and increase human resources necessary for equitable and balanced growth.

Economic development in New York State must harness and coordinate the state's physical, capital, human, and information resources—not create new agencies or funding. New York no longer lives in a world where its technological superiority and productivity are automatic, or where its international preeminence can be assumed. Economic growth fueled by unsustainable levels of deficit financing will not solve the problems of our distressed regions, industries, and social groups. Single-minded attention to economic aggregates and the business cycle cannot explain the paradox of rising poverty at a time of cyclical recovery or the varying fortunes of our state's regions. Nor can those measures help dislocated workers hit by trade and technological change, impoverished rural communities, or the long-term unemployed.

We need policies that address the structural forces shaping our future—the costs of doing business in terms of capital and labor—in order to shape our future toward balanced economic growth, participation, and equity.

A Brief Guide for Further Research

by

Peter W. Colby

EDITORS' NOTE: *Many readers of this volume will want to learn more about the politics and governance of our state. This short bibliographic essay provides information of how to get started on further research.*

PETER W. COLBY

Constructing a *brief* bibliography on New York State politics, government, and public policy is no easy task, for there is an enormous amount of quality material easily accessible to students and other readers. Thus, there will be no attempt here to be comprehensive. Instead, this essay will try to point to a few of the most valuable resources one may use to begin to research a specific topic.

General Information

The Encyclopedia of New York (Beth Blentz and Thomas Gergel, eds. Somerset, 1982) is an excellent general reference covering many topics—including a chronology of important dates in history, brief biographies of famous New Yorkers, information on major cities, and a directory of state services.

Those interested in a thorough, well-written history are directed to *A History of New York State* (David M. Ellis, James A. Frost, Harold C. Syrett, and Harry J. Carman, Cornell University Press, 1967). The book particularly is notable for a highly-detailed forty-page bibliographic essay organized by historical period and subject.

The best comprehensive source for current data concerning the Empire State is the *New York Statistical Yearbook* (Rockefeller Institute of Government, Albany). Among the many tables are data on government finance and operations, elections, population, the state economy, and policy concerns such as health, housing, transportation, and the like. The Rockefeller Institute also publishes a variety of reports, conference proceedings, working papers, and reprints on public policy in New York.

Textbooks

Besides this volume, a number of general books on politics and government are available, including Warren Moscow, *Politics in the Empire State* (Knopf, 1948); Lyndon Caldwell, *The Government and Administration of New York* (Crowell, 1954); Ralph Straetz and F.J. Munger, *New York Politics* (New York University Press, 1960); Robert H. Connery and Gerald Benjamin, *Governing New York State: The Rockefeller Years* (Academy of Political Science, 1974); Joseph Zimmerman, *Government and Politics in New York State* (New York University Press, 1981); and Lee M. Miringoff and Barbara L. Carvalho, *The Cuomo Factor: Assessing the Political Appeal of New York's Governor* (Marist Institute for Public Opinion, 1986).

More limited in scope but still of general interest are Howard Scarrow,

Parties, Elections, and Representation in the State of New York (New York University Press, 1983) and Robert P. Kerker, ed., *The Executive Budget in New York State: A Half-Century Perspective* (New York State Division of the Budget, 1981). Though now over a decade old, Alan Hevesi's *Legislative Politics in New York State: A Comparative Analysis* (Praeger, 1975) remains the best book-length treatment of the state legislature. Of course all three of these authors update their books' major themes here in *New York State Today.*

New York State, A Citizen's Handbook (League of Women Voters of New York State, 1979) outlines the basic structure of state government, delineates powers and responsibilities, and describes administrative and fiscal relationships, generally from a formal, legal perspective.

Another book of interest is Gerald Benjamin and T. Norman Hurd, eds., *Making Experience Count: Managing Modern New York in the Carey Era* (Rockefeller Institute, 1985), which covers the 1975-82 governorship of Hugh Carey.

State Documents

State documents are the official and unofficial publications produced by the three branches and many agencies of New York government. They are often a bit difficult to discover and obtain, despite the regular checklists and compilations produced by the New York State Library. *Official Publications of New York State: A Bibliographic Guide to Their Use* (Dorothy Butch, New York State Library, Albany, 1981) provides an annotated list, organized by subject matter, of important documents and information sources available at the New York State Library. In addition to helping one locate specific documents, it is very useful in determining the kinds of reports produced by the state. Many colleges and public libraries do have some state documents in their collections. If you must have a personal copy of a current document, your State Senator or Representative can often be helpful.

The *Manual for the Use of the Legislature of the State of New York* (New York State Department of State) provides a current guide to the people and entities which compose state and local government, along with certain statistical data, particularly election results in some detail.

Another highly useful reference to government operations is the *Local Government Handbook* (New York State Department of State, 1982), which describes the history, structure, functions, and current challenges facing New York's counties, cities, towns, villages, schools, and special districts.

People

Biographies, autobiographies, and memoirs also are an excellent source for students of New York public affairs. Two of the real classics are William Riordan, *Plunkitt of Tammany Hall* (Dutton, 1963) and Robert Caro's book about Robert Moses, *The Power Broker* (Knopf, 1974). A number of books cover the fascinating times of Governor Nelson Rockefeller, including Robert H. Connery and Gerald Benjamin, *Rockefeller of New York: Executive Power in the State House* (Cornell University Press, 1979); Joseph Persico, *The Imperial Rockefeller* (Simon and Schuster, 1982); and James E. Underwood and WIlliam J. Daniels, *Governor Rockefeller in New York* (Greenwood Press, 1982).

An interesting recent trend is the publication of memoirs by currently active politicians. Certainly Governor Mario Cuomo's diaries and the various reminiscences of Mayor Ed Koch are of interest.

New York City

Good books on New York City politics also abound. Though dated, Wallace Sayre and Herbert Kaufman, *Governing New York City* (Russell Sage, 1960) remains an indispensable foundation for understanding the city's public life. Many volumes provide a more current treatment, most with a focus on the events leading to and following from the fiscal crisis of the mid-1970s, among them Ken Auletta, *The Streets Were Paved With Gold* (Random House, 1979); and Robert Bailey, *The Crisis Regime* (State University of new York Press, 1984). An excellent recent work dealing with the substance of public policy in the city is Charles Brecher and Raymond D. Horton, eds., *Setting Municipal Priorities: American Cities and the New York Experience* (New York University Press, 1984).

Current Events and Public Policy

Three journals provide quality coverage of current public policy issues. *Empire State Report* is a slick monthly magazine devoted to current statewide policy concerns. A supplementary publication, *ESR Weekly,* focuses more closely on the people and the politics involved in state government. The other two journals, *New York Affairs* (published quarterly by the Urban Research Center at New York University) and *City Almanac* (published monthly by the New School for Social Research's Center for New York City Affairs), concentrate more narrowly on the New York City metropolitan area.

Two popular magazines which regularly produce insightful articles on state and city government are the *New Yorker* and *New York.* Each is conveniently indexed in both the *Reader's Guide to Periodical Literature* (under New York, politics and government and New York, New York, politics and government) and the *Magazine Index* (under New York [State]: politics and government and New York [City] politics and government).

The New York Times Index is the best single source reference to the day-to-day events of state politics and policies. The index consists of abstracts entered under subject matter headings in chronological order. Each entry contains a precise reference to the whole article (date, page, column) and notes whether it is short (s), medium (m), or long (l) to assist users in determining which articles to locate and read.

Index

INDEX

INDEX

INDEX

INDEX

INDEX